Creating Games with cocos2d for iPhone 2

Master cocos2d through building nine complete games for the iPhone

Paul Nygard

[PACKT] open source ✳
PUBLISHING
community experience distilled

BIRMINGHAM - MUMBAI

Creating Games with cocos2d for iPhone 2

First published: December 2012

Production Reference: 1171212

Published by Packt Publishing Ltd.
Livery Place
35 Livery Street
Birmingham B3 2PB, UK.

ISBN 978-1-84951-900-7

www.packtpub.com

Cover Image by Abhishek Pandey (abhishek.pandey1210@gmail.com)

Credits

Author
Paul Nygard

Reviewers
Dave Hersey
Marcio Valenzuela P

Acquisition Editor
Usha Iyer

Lead Technical Editor
Llewellyn F. Rozario

Technical Editors
Sharvari Baet
Komal Chheda
Kirti Pujari
Brandt D'Mello

Project Coordinator
Abhishek Kori

Proofreaders
Bob Phillips
Bernadette Watkins

Indexer
Monica Ajmera Mehta

Production Coordinator
Shantanu Zagade

Cover Work
Shantanu Zagade

About the Author

Paul Nygard has been a computer and technology enthusiast since he was introduced to his first computer at the age of six. He has spent most of his professional life building reporting and analytical systems for a large company. After teaching himself Objective-C in 2010, he has focused most of his attention on iOS programming. Paul created a personal development label, Troll Cave Games (`http://www.trollcavegames.com`), to release his mobile gaming efforts. Paul also works as a consultant and developer-for-hire for visionaries in need of a coder. In his leisure time, Paul is passionate about games, books, and music.

I would like to thank my family for their support and for allowing me to hide in my troll cave and pursue my passions. This book is for you!

I would also like to thank Ricardo Quesada and Steve Oldmeadow, for all their hard work on cocos2d and cocosDenshion. They have helped to mold a new generation of developers by giving us all a wonderful world to play in. And to the cocos2d community: I have never seen such a large group of developers so eager to help each other along. Thanks for the support, advice, and humor over the years.

About the Reviewers

Dave Hersey has over 35 years of experience in Apple software development, dating back to the Apple II personal computer in 1977. After a successful career of more than 6 years at Apple Computer, Inc., Dave started Paracoders, Inc. in 2000 focusing on custom Mac OS X-based application and driver development. In 2008, Dave's business expanded into iOS (iPhone) mobile applications, followed by Android applications soon after. Some bigger-named clients include Paramount Home Entertainment, Lionsgate Entertainment, Seagate, Creative Labs, and Kraft. Most recently, Dave's business expansion has included additional mobile and server-side platforms as well as support services. This has led to rebranding his company as "Torchlight Apps" (`http://www.torchlightapps.com`).

Dave is also a moderator and active participant on the `cocos2d-iphone.org` forums under the username `clarus` when he's not busy with his wife raising three children, three dogs, three parakeets, four ducks, and seven ducklings at last count.

Marcio Valenzuela P is a biochemist who has studied programming as a hobby for over 12 years. He is perseverant, auto-didactic, and is always looking into the latest technologies. Marcio started by picking up ASP back in the early 1990s as Chief Web Developer for a consulting company that developed web applications for private companies. He also delved into PHP applications with a MySQL database backend. Then in 2008 he started his path down iOS and has had experience developing applications and games for the platform. His experience is mostly in business applications where there exists a cloud-based web service to interact with and more recently in games created in cocos2d.

Marcio is cofounder of `Activasolutions.com` and currently runs a small iOS project called `Santiapps.com`, which programs for companies wishing to enter the iOS platform. Marcio is a forum moderator at `RayWenderlich.com`.

I would like to acknowledge the time I have taken from raising my son to dedicate to this book. I just hope someday Santiago follows in the programming tradition as it fosters critical skills such as problem solving and innovation which is something we share.

www.PacktPub.com

Support files, eBooks, discount offers, and more

You might want to visit www.PacktPub.com for support files and downloads related to your book.

Did you know that Packt offers eBook versions of every book published, with PDF and ePub files available? You can upgrade to the eBook version at www.PacktPub.com and as a print book customer, you are entitled to a discount on the eBook copy. Get in touch with us at service@packtpub.com for more details.

At www.PacktPub.com, you can also read a collection of free technical articles, sign up for a range of free newsletters, and receive exclusive discounts and offers on Packt books and eBooks.

http://PacktLib.PacktPub.com

Do you need instant solutions to your IT questions? PacktLib is Packt's online digital book library. Here, you can access, read, and search across Packt's entire library of books.

Why Subscribe?

- Fully searchable across every book published by Packt
- Copy and paste, print and bookmark content
- On demand and accessible via web browser

Free Access for Packt account holders

If you have an account with Packt at www.PacktPub.com, you can use this to access PacktLib today and view nine entirely free books. Simply use your login credentials for immediate access.

Table of Contents

Preface

Cocos2d for iPhone is a robust framework for developing 2D games for any iOS device. It is powerful, flexible, and best of all it is free to use for your own projects. Thousands of apps, including many top selling games, have been written using cocos2d.

Creating Games with cocos2d for iPhone 2 will take you on a tour of nine very different games, guiding you through the designing process and code needed to build each game. All of the games were specifically selected to highlight different approaches to solving the challenges inherent in designing a game.

The games covered in this book are all classic game styles. By focusing on games you probably already know, you can see how everything works "under the hood" with cocos2d.

What this book covers

Chapter 1, Thanks for the Memory Game, covers the design and building of a memory tile game. It covers basic concepts such as grid layouts, using cocos2d actions, and using CocosDenshion for sound effects.

Chapter 2, Match 3 and Recursive Methods, walks through the design and building of a match-3 game. This chapter covers two different approaches to checking for matches, as well as an extensive section on predictive matching and how to generate artificial randomness.

Chapter 3, Thumping Moles for Fun, provides the basic concepts of how to design a mole thumping game. This game uses Z-ordering to "trick the eye", and uses cocos2d actions extensively to give a very polished game with very little coding needed.

Chapter 4, Give a Snake a Snack..., follows the design and building of a snake game. Some of the topics covered in this chapter include overriding methods, making sprites follow each other, and implementing increasing difficulty levels.

Chapter 5, Brick Breaking Balls with Box2D, covers the building of a brick-breaking game using the Box2D physics engine. In this chapter, you will find a basic primer on how to use Box2D, using plists to store level data, and implementing power-ups.

Chapter 6, Cycles of Light, takes us to an iPad only multiplayer game. This game allows two players to compete head-to-head on the same iPad, or by using GameKit's Bluetooth connectivity to play against each other on two iPads. This chapter also walks through how we can use a single pixel to draw almost everything in the game.

Chapter 7, Playing Pool, Old School, revisits the Box2D physics engine to build a top-down pool game. The focus on this chapter is to implement a simple "rules engine" into the game, as well as how to easily build multiple control methods into the same game.

Chapter 8, Shoot, Scroll, Shoot Again, walks through the building of a top-down scrolling shooter. This chapter walks you through how to use readily available outside tools and resources, including Sneaky Joystick and the Tiled tile map editor. It also covers two different forms of enemy AI, including A* Pathfinding.

Chapter 9, Running and Running and Running..., brings us to the most ambitious game of all, the endless runner. The primary topics covered are how to create random terrain that characters can walk on, parallax scrolling backgrounds, and implementing a lot of different types of enemies.

What you need for this book

The book and code bundle contain the complete source code you will need to run all nine games. You will only need a few items to run the games:

- An Intel-based Macintosh running OS X Lion (or later)
- Xcode version 4.5 (or higher)
- To run any games on a real device (iPhone, iPad, or iPod Touch), you will need to be enrolled in the Apple's iOS Developer program. You will be able to run the games in the iOS Simulator without enrolling, but the tilt controls in *Chapter 8, Shoot, Scroll, Shoot Again* and the Bluetooth multiplayer mode in *Chapter 6, Cycles of Light* will only work on a real iOS device.

Who this book is for

This book is written for people who have basic experience with cocos2d, but want some guidance on how to approach real-world design issues. Although the book does revisit some basic concepts, we hit the ground running, so having a basic understanding of cocos2d is recommended. At least some knowledge of Objective-C is also strongly recommended.

Conventions

In this book, you will find a number of styles of text that distinguish between different kinds of information. Here are some examples of these styles, and an explanation of their meaning.

Code words in text are shown as follows: "We can include other contexts through the use of the `include` directive."

A block of code is set as follows:

```
-(void) makeTransition:(ccTime)dt
{
  [[CCDirector sharedDirector] replaceScene:
    [CCTransitionFade transitionWithDuration:1.0
      scene:[MTMenuScene scene] withColor:ccWHITE]];
}
```

When we wish to draw your attention to a particular part of a code block, the relevant lines or items are set in bold:

```
-(void) makeTransition:(ccTime)dt
{
  [[CCDirector sharedDirector] replaceScene:
    [CCTransitionFade transitionWithDuration:1.0
      scene:[MTMenuScene scene] withColor:ccWHITE]];
}
```

New terms and **important words** are shown in bold. Words that you see on the screen, in menus or dialog boxes for example, appear in the text like this: "clicking the **Next** button moves you to the next screen".

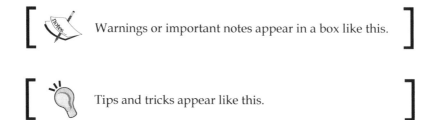

Warnings or important notes appear in a box like this.

Tips and tricks appear like this.

Reader feedback

Feedback from our readers is always welcome. Let us know what you think about this book—what you liked or may have disliked. Reader feedback is important for us to develop titles that you really get the most out of.

To send us general feedback, simply send an e-mail to feedback@packtpub.com, and mention the book title through the subject of your message.

If there is a topic that you have expertise in and you are interested in either writing or contributing to a book, see our author guide on www.packtpub.com/authors.

Customer support

Now that you are the proud owner of a Packt book, we have a number of things to help you to get the most from your purchase.

Downloading the example code

You can download the example code files for all Packt books you have purchased from your account at http://www.packtpub.com. If you purchased this book elsewhere, you can visit http://www.packtpub.com/support and register to have the files e-mailed directly to you.

Downloading the color images of this book

We also provide you a PDF file that has color images of the screenshots/diagrams used in this book. The color images will help you better understand the changes in the output.

You can download this file from http://www.packtpub.com/sites/default/files/downloads/9007OS_ColoredImages.pdf

Errata

Although we have taken every care to ensure the accuracy of our content, mistakes do happen. If you find a mistake in one of our books—maybe a mistake in the text or the code—we would be grateful if you would report this to us. By doing so, you can save other readers from frustration and help us improve subsequent versions of this book. If you find any errata, please report them by visiting http://www.packtpub. com/support, selecting your book, clicking on the **errata submission form** link, and entering the details of your errata. Once your errata are verified, your submission will be accepted and the errata will be uploaded to our website, or added to any list of existing errata, under the Errata section of that title.

Piracy

Piracy of copyright material on the Internet is an ongoing problem across all media. At Packt, we take the protection of our copyright and licenses very seriously. If you come across any illegal copies of our works, in any form, on the Internet, please provide us with the location address or website name immediately so that we can pursue a remedy.

Please contact us at copyright@packtpub.com with a link to the suspected pirated material.

We appreciate your help in protecting our authors, and our ability to bring you valuable content.

Questions

You can contact us at questions@packtpub.com if you are having a problem with any aspect of the book, and we will do our best to address it.

1

Thanks for the Memory Game

As children, we learn many useful skills by playing games. We learn coordination, strategy, and memory skills. These are all skills we take with us throughout our lives. The perfect place to start is a traditional childhood game.

In this chapter, we cover the following topics:

- Scenes versus layers
- Sprites and sprite sheets
- Loading sequential files
- Random playfield generation
- Touch handlers
- Using actions
- Basic matching strategies
- Scoring
- Tracking lives
- Game over conditions
- SimpleSoundEngine

The project is...

We will begin with classic **memory game**. Not just any memory game – *the* memory game that is the source of joy and frustration of children everywhere. In case you've never been exposed to this game (really?), the gameplay is simple. The playing field is a set of tiles with pretty pictures on the front, and a generic back image. You turn over two tiles to see if you made a match. If not, you turn them back over. Pick another pair of tiles and see if they match. Repeat this till all the tiles are matched. Let's take a look at the finished game:

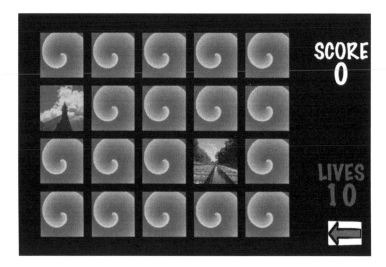

Our memory game needs to be flexible enough to allow different skill levels in the game. We will create different skill levels by varying the number of memory tiles on the board. If there are four tiles (two each of two designs), that's pretty easy. Creating a 4 x 5 grid of tiles is a lot more challenging (20 tiles, 10 designs). We will build a single project that will handle these variations dynamically.

Our game will be a little different from the traditional version in two ways: it is single player only, and we will add a way to lose the game, to make it more exciting. We'll go into detail on that aspect later.

We will detail several foundational design approaches in this chapter that will be used throughout the book. To avoid repetitive code, later chapters will omit some of the boilerplate detail that we cover here.

Let's build a menu

We'll start building the project from the default cocos2d v2.x - cocos2d iOS template. Once the project is created, we first remove the HelloWorldLayer.h/.m files. HelloWorld is a good starting point for learning the code structure, but we don't really want (or need) this boilerplate class for anything (don't forget to remove the #import "HelloWorldLayer.h" at the top of the IntroLayer.m class). For now we'll leave the reference in the bottom of the IntroLayer.m's makeTransition class.

One of the most commonly used classes in the cocos2d framework is probably the CCLayer. A CCLayer is the object that is (usually) represented on the screen, and acts as our "canvas" for our game. We use the CCLayer object as a basis, and then create subclasses of it to add our own game code.

There is another often-used class, the CCScene class. A CCScene class can be thought of as a "container" for CCLayer objects. A CCScene object is rarely used for much more than adding CCLayers as children. A good comparison is like the creation of cartoons before the age of computers. Each scene was assembled from a stack of transparent plastic sheets, each with a different part of the scene on it: each main character would have their own layer, another for the background, another for each different element of the scene. Those plastic sheets are the equivalent of a CCLayer objects, and the CCScene class is where these are stacked up to display on screen.

We will start with a basic CCLayer subclass, MTMenuLayer. We create a title, and a basic menu. We need to pay attention to how we call the MTPlayfieldScene class (our main game screen) from the menu.

Filename: MTMenuLayer.m

```
-(void) startGameEasy {
    [[CCDirector sharedDirector] replaceScene:
     [MTPlayfieldScene sceneWithRows:2 andColumns:2]];
}

-(void) startGameMedium {
    [[CCDirector sharedDirector] replaceScene:
     [MTPlayfieldScene sceneWithRows:3 andColumns:4]];
}

-(void) startGameHard {
    [[CCDirector sharedDirector] replaceScene:
     [MTPlayfieldScene sceneWithRows:4 andColumns:5]];
}
```

You will notice that the startGameXXX methods are calling a custom constructor for the scene, rather than the normal [MyLayer scene] that is commonly used. We will explain the sceneWithRows:andColumns: method shortly.

This book will not include the complete code within the text. Portions that aren't interesting for the discussion will be omitted.

Downloading the example code

You can download the example code files for all Packt books you have purchased from your account at http://www.packtpub.com. If you purchased this book elsewhere, you can visit http://www.packtpub.com/support and register to have the files e-mailed directly to you.

Where is the scene?

Oh, you noticed? The boilerplate cocos2d template includes a class method +(id) scene inside the layer (in HelloWorldLayer). While this approach works, it can lead to confusion as we build more complex scenes with multiple layers. Using the template-based approach may seem odd when you call a method that takes a CCScene object as a parameter, yet you pass it a value like [MySpecialLayer scene]. So are you referencing a CCScene or CCLayer object? It makes a lot more logical sense to us that you would, in this example, pass a value like [MySpecialScene scene]. It is less confusing to pass a scene object when a CCScene is requested. A CCScene object is a higher-level container that was designed to contain CCLayer objects, so why not keep it as its own class? Let's go ahead and examine our approach:

Filename: MTMenuScene.h

```
#import <Foundation/Foundation.h>
#import "cocos2d.h"
#import "MTMenuLayer.h"

@interface MTMenuScene : CCScene {
}

+(id)scene;

@end
```

Filename: MTMenuScene.m

```
#import "MTMenuScene.h"

@implementation MTMenuScene

+(id)scene {
    return( [ [ [ self alloc ] init ] autorelease ] );
}

-(id) init
{
  if( (self=[super init])) {
        MTMenuLayer *layer = [MTMenuLayer node];
        [self addChild: layer];
  }
  return self;
}


@end
```

Here we have followed the convention that the scene method returns an autoreleased object. We do not explicitly call alloc on it (when we instantiate the class), so we don't "own" the object.

Now we can go back to the IntroLayer.m file, and change the makeTransition method to point to our new menu scene:

```
-(void) makeTransition:(ccTime)dt
{
  [[CCDirector sharedDirector] replaceScene:
     [CCTransitionFade transitionWithDuration:1.0
        scene:[MTMenuScene scene] withColor:ccWHITE]];
}
```

We also need to make sure we are importing the MTMenuScene.h file in the AppDelegate.m file. Now that our menu is complete, we can concentrate on the game itself.

It is important to note that this design of using CCScene as a separate class in the structure is not universally adopted. Many people choose to follow the same approach as the templates. Both ways will work, but we are of the "camp" that strongly believes these should kept separate, as we have done here. Both ways are perfectly valid coding practice, and you are free to structure your code in other way.

Building the playfield

Next, we will add a CCScene class to drive our main game screen, here named MTPlayfieldScene. Much of this looks the same as the MTMenuScene class we defined earlier, except here we define a method sceneWithRows:andColumns: instead of the simpler scene method we used in the previous code.

Filename: MTPlayfieldScene.m

```
+(id)  sceneWithRows:(NSInteger)numRows
        andColumns:(NSInteger)numCols {
  return [[[self alloc] sceneWithRows:numRows
                              andColumns:numCols]
                                autorelease];
}


-(id)  sceneWithRows:(NSInteger)numRows
        andColumns:(NSInteger)numCols {

  if( (self=[super init])) {
      // Create an instance of the MTPlayfieldLayer
      MTPlayfieldLayer *layer = [MTPlayfieldLayer
                                  layerWithRows:numRows
                                  andColumns:numCols];
      [self addChild: layer];
  }
  return self;
}
```

Here we have the custom sceneWithRows:andColumns: method we referenced in the MTMenuLayer earlier. The class method handles the alloc and init methods, and identifies it as an autoreleased object, so we don't have to worry about releasing it later. The sceneWithRows:andColumns: method passes the rows and columns variables directly to the MTPlayfieldLayer class' custom init method, layerWithRows:andColumns:. This lets us pass the requested values through the scene to the layer, where we can use the values later.

We need sprites

Before we proceed with building the playing field, we need some graphics to use in our game. Our design calls for square images for the tiles, and one image to use for the common back of the tiles. Because we want them to be able to scale to different sizes (for our different skill levels), we need images large enough to look good at the simplest skill level, which is a two by two grid. Unless your goal is the "chunky pixel" look, you never want to scale images up. Based on the screen size, we want our tiles to be 150 points wide and 150 points high. Since we want to use better graphics on iPhone (and iPod Touch) Retina Display devices, our -hd version of the graphics will need to be 300 pixels by 300 pixels.

Points are the easiest way to use cocos2d effectively. On an older iOS Device, one point equals one pixel on the screen. On Retina Display devices, one point equals *two* pixels, which occupy the same physical space on the screen as the one pixel on the non-Retina screens. From a practical perspective, this means that once you provide the -hd graphics, cocos2d will treat your Retina and non-Retina layouts identically, with no extra layout code. You *can* do things in pixels if you really want to, but we wouldn't recommend making a habit of it.

For this game, we will be using a variety of photos. There was some amount of manipulation needed to arrive at the proper aspect ratio and size. This is a great place to make use of Automator that is part of Mac OS X. There is an Automator script in the source code for this chapter inside a folder called Helpers. When you run it, it will prompt for a folder of images. Once selected, it will create a folder on your desktop called ch1_tiles, and it will contain sequentially numbered images (that is tile1.png, tile2.png, and so on), with each image being exactly 300 pixels by 300 pixels.

Two other images will be needed to build the game: backButton.png will be used for navigation and tileback.png will be used as the image for the back of the tiles when they are face down.

Building a sprite sheet

Sprite sheets are one of the foundations of any effective cocos2d game. Compiling all of your sprites into sprite sheets lets cocos2d load fewer files as well as giving you the ability to use a batch node. We won't delve into the "under the hood" details of the CCSpriteBatchNode class here except at a high level. When you load a sprite sheet into a batch node, it acts as a "parent" for all the sprites on it. When you use a batch node, the calls to draw the sprites on the screen are batched together, which gives a performance boost. This batch drawing allows the system to draw 100 sprites with about the same efficiency (and speed) as drawing one sprite. The bottom line is batch nodes allow you to draw a lot more on-screen without slowing your game down.

There are two files needed for a sprite sheet: the texture (image file) and the plist file. We don't even want to think about attempting to hand-build the sprite sheet. Fortunately, there are a number of very good tools that were built for this. The most established sprite sheet tools in the cocos2d community are TexturePacker (http://www.texturepacker.com) and Zwoptex (http://zwopple.com/zwoptex), although there are a number of newer apps that are also available. Which tool you use is a matter of personal preference. Regardless of the tool, you will need to create both the standard and -hd versions of the images. (Most current tools have built-in options to aid in this process.)

No matter which tool is used, the desired result is four files: memorysheet.png, memorysheet.plist, memorysheet-hd.png, and memorysheet-hd.plist. The -hd files include the 300 x 300 images for the iPhone Retina Display, and the others include the 150 x 150 pixel images for non-Retina iPhone Displays. We also include the backButton.png and tileback.png files in appropriate sizing in both sprite sheets as well. Let's take a look at the final sprite sheet we will use for this game:

On to the playfield

Now we're ready to get to the playfield layer itself. We know we need to keep track of the size of the game screen, how big each tile should be, how big the game board should be, and how much spacing we need between the tiles when they are laid out in a grid.

Creating the playfield header

In the header, we also have the declaration for the class method initWithRows:andColumns: that we called in the MTPlayfieldScene class.

Filename: MTPlayfieldLayer.h

```
#import <Foundation/Foundation.h>
#import "cocos2d.h"
#import "MTMemoryTile.h"
#import "SimpleAudioEngine.h"
#import "MTMenuScene.h"

@interface MTPlayfieldLayer : CCLayer {
    CGSize size; // The window size from CCDirector

    CCSpriteBatchNode *memorysheet;

    CGSize tileSize; // Size (in points) of the tiles

    NSMutableArray *tilesAvailable;
    NSMutableArray *tilesInPlay;
    NSMutableArray *tilesSelected;

    CCSprite *backButton;

    NSInteger maxTiles;

    float boardWidth; // Max width of the game board
    float boardHeight; // Max height of the game board

    NSInteger boardRows; // Total rows in the grid
    NSInteger boardColumns; // Total columns in the grid

    NSInteger boardOffsetX; // Offset from the left
    NSInteger boardOffsetY; // Offset from the bottom
```

```
        NSInteger padWidth; // Space between tiles
        NSInteger padHeight; // Space between tiles

        NSInteger playerScore; // Current score value
        CCLabelTTF *playerScoreDisplay; // Score label

        NSInteger livesRemaining; // Lives value
        CCLabelTTF *livesRemainingDisplay; // Lives label
        BOOL isGameOver;
    }

+(id) layerWithRows:(NSInteger)numRows
        andColumns:(NSInteger)numCols;
```

@end

One item to point out in the header is the `CGSize size` variable. This is a convenience variable we use to avoid repetitive typing. The name `size` is an abbreviation for `winSize`, which is a value that the `CCDirector` class will provide for you that identifies the size of the screen, in points. You can read the value from the `CCDirector` every time you use it, but doing so will make your code lines a bit longer. Our approach will work fine, as long as we do not support both portrait and landscape modes in the same layer. If we do allow both orientations, then the value we have cached in the `size` variable will be incorrect. Since our app only allows `LandscapeLeft` and `LandscapeRight` orientations, the size is identical in both orientations, so the `size` will be stable for our game.

Creating the playfield layer

In the `MTPlayfieldLayer.m` file, we implement our custom `layerWithRows:andColumns:` and `initWithRows:andColumns:` methods as follows:

Filename: `MTPlayfieldLayer.m`

```
+(id) layerWithRows:(NSInteger)numRows
        andColumns:(NSInteger)numCols {
  return [[[self alloc] initWithRows:numRows
                    andColumns:numCols] autorelease];
}

-(id) initWithRows:(NSInteger)numRows
        andColumns:(NSInteger)numCols {
```

```objc
if (self == [super init]) {

    self.isTouchEnabled = YES;

    // Get the window size from the CCDirector
    size = [[CCDirector sharedDirector] winSize];

    // Preload the sound effects
    [self preloadEffects];

    // make sure we've loaded the spritesheets
    [[CCSpriteFrameCache sharedSpriteFrameCache]
     addSpriteFramesWithFile:@"memorysheet.plist"];
    memorysheet = [CCSpriteBatchNode
            batchNodeWithFile:@"memorysheet.png"];

    // Add the batch node to the layer
    [self addChild:memorysheet];

    // Add the back Button to the bottom right corner
    backButton = [CCSprite spriteWithSpriteFrameName:
                @"backbutton.png"];
    [backButton setAnchorPoint:ccp(1,0)];
    [backButton setPosition:ccp(size.width - 10, 10)];
    [memorysheet addChild:backButton];

    // Maximum size of the actual playing field
    boardWidth = 400;
    boardHeight = 320;

    // Set the board rows and columns
    boardRows = numRows;
    boardColumns = numCols;

    // If the total number of card positions is
    // not even, remove one row
    // This against an impossible board
    if ( (boardRows * boardColumns) % 2 ) {
        boardRows--;
    }

    // Set the number of images to choose from
    // We need 2 of each, so we halve the total tiles
    maxTiles = (boardRows * boardColumns) / 2;
```

```
        // Set up the padding between the tiles
        padWidth = 10;
        padHeight = 10;

        // We set the desired tile size
        float tileWidth = ((boardWidth -
                            (boardColumns * padWidth))
                            / boardColumns) - padWidth;
        float tileHeight = ((boardHeight -
                            (boardRows * padHeight))
                            / boardRows) - padHeight;

        // We force the tiles to be square
        if (tileWidth > tileHeight) {
            tileWidth = tileHeight;
        } else {
            tileHeight = tileWidth;
        }

        // Store the tileSize so we can use it later
        tileSize = CGSizeMake(tileWidth, tileHeight);

        // Set the offset from the edge
        boardOffsetX = (boardWidth - ((tileSize.width +
                        padWidth) * boardColumns)) / 2;
        boardOffsetY = (boardHeight - ((tileSize.height+
                        padHeight) * boardRows)) / 2;

        // Set the score to zero
        playerScore = 0;

        // Initialize the arrays

        // Populate the tilesAvailable array
        [self acquireMemoryTiles];

        // Generate the actual playfield on-screen
        [self generateTileGrid];

        // Calculate the number of lives left
        [self calculateLivesRemaining];

        // We create the score and lives display here
        [self generateScoreAndLivesDisplay];
    }
    return self;
}
```

The class method `layerWithRows:andColumns:` is the method we saw in the `MTPlayfieldScene` class earlier. The class method calls the `alloc` and `initWithRows: andColumns:` methods, and then wraps it all in an `autorelease` call since it is a convenience method. The instance method `initWithRows:AndColumns:` (called by the class method) sets up a few of the variables we established in the header, including the assignment of our passed `numRows` and `numColumns` parameters into the instance variables `boardRows` and `boardColumns`.

Memory games are traditionally played with a square or rectangular layout. They also need an even number of tiles in the game, since there will be two of each type of tile. Because we are allowing flexible parameters for the number of rows and the number of columns, there are certain combinations that will not work. Requesting five rows and five columns means we will have 25 tiles on the board, which is impossible to win. To protect our game from these invalid values, we multiply the `boardRows` times the `boardColumns`. If the result is not even (using the % 2 check), then we remove one `boardRow` from the game. From the prior example, if we requested a five by five board (resulting in 25 tiles), the code would alter it to a four by five grid, which has 20 tiles.

We also set the `tileSize` value here, based on an even spacing of the tiles, along with the extra pad space we will be using between the tiles. Because we need square tiles, there is also the additional check to force the tiles to be square if the source images are not. This will distort the images, but it won't disrupt the game mechanics. Additionally, the `boardOffsetX` and `boardOffsetY` variables simply ensure the board will be nicely centered in the available board space.

The flow of the game

We will need several arrays in the game to help track the tiles. The first, `tilesAvailable`, will be used in the loading and building of the playfield. The second, `tilesInPlay`, will contain all of the tiles that have not yet been matched. The third, `tilesSelected`, will be used for the match detection methods. Since we are handling a relatively small number of tiles, using this multiple array structure will work fine for our purposes without any performance concerns. Let's add the code for the arrays now:

Filename: `MTPlayfieldLayer.h` (already in variable declarations)

```
NSMutableArray *tilesAvailable;
NSMutableArray *tilesInPlay;
NSMutableArray *tilesSelected;
```

Filename: `MTPlayfieldLayer.m` (`initWithRows`, add after "Initialize the arrays")

```
        tilesAvailable = [[NSMutableArray alloc]
                            initWithCapacity:maxTiles];
        tilesInPlay = [[NSMutableArray alloc]
                        initWithCapacity:maxTiles];
        tilesSelected = [[NSMutableArray alloc]
                            initWithCapacity:2]; MTPlayfieldLayer.m:
- (void) dealloc
{
    // Release of the arrays
    [tilesAvailable release];
    [tilesInPlay release];
    [tilesSelected release];

    [super dealloc];
}
```

Here we established the three `NSMutableArray` arrays in the header as variables, instantiated them in the `initWithRows:andColumns:` method, and added them to a new `dealloc` method. The `dealloc` method releases the three arrays. The `[super dealloc]` call is always required, and it should be the last line of the `dealloc` method. This call to `super dealloc` tells the parent class of the current class to do whatever it needs to clean up. This is important to call because our current class doesn't have to worry about the details of any clean up that is done by the parent `CCLayer` class.

A stack of tiles

Now we need to define the class for the tiles themselves. We have a few variables we need to track for the tiles and we will use the `MTMemoryTile` class to handle some of the touch detection and tile animation.

The memory tile class

For this, we will be subclassing `CCSprite`. This will allow us to still treat it like a `CCSprite`, but we will enhance it with other methods and properties specific to the tile.

Filename: `MTMemoryTile.h`

```
#import <Foundation/Foundation.h>
#import "cocos2d.h"
#import "SimpleAudioEngine.h"

// MemoryTile is a subclass of CCSprite
```

```objc
@interface MTMemoryTile : CCSprite {
    NSInteger _tileRow;
    NSInteger _tileColumn;

    NSString *_faceSpriteName;

    BOOL isFaceUp;
}

@property (nonatomic, assign) NSInteger tileRow;
@property (nonatomic, assign) NSInteger tileColumn;
@property (nonatomic, assign) BOOL isFaceUp;
@property (nonatomic, retain) NSString *faceSpriteName;

// Exposed methods to interact with the tile
-(void) showFace;
-(void) showBack;
-(void) flipTile;
-(BOOL) containsTouchLocation:(CGPoint)pos;

@end
```

Here we are declaring the variables with an underscore prefix, but we set the corresponding property without the underscore prefix. This is usually done to avoid accidentally setting the variable value directly, which would bypass the getter and setter methods for the property. This split-naming is finalized in the @synthesize statements in the .m file, where the property will be set to the variable. These statements will be of the basic format:

```objc
@synthesize propertyName = _variableName;
```

We're planning ahead with this class, including the headers for three methods that we will use for the tile animation: flipTile, showFace, and showBack. This class will be responsible for handling its own animation.

All animation in our game will be done using cocos2d actions. Actions are essentially transformations of some sort that can be "run" on most types of cocos2d objects (for example, CCLayer, CCSprite, and so on). There are quite a number of different actions defined in the framework. Some of the most commonly used are actions such as CCMoveTo (to move an object), CCScaleTo (to change the scale of the object), and CCCallFunc (to call another method). Actions are a "fire and forget" feature. Once you schedule an action, unless you explicitly change the action (such as calling stopAllActions), the actions will continue until complete. This is further extended by "wrapping" several actions together in a CCSequence action, which allows you to chain several actions together, to be run in the order specified.

We will use CCSequence "chaining" extensively throughout the book. Actions can be run on most cocos2d objects, but they are most commonly called (via the runAction: method) on the CCSprite and CCLayer objects.

Filename: MTMemoryTile.m

```
@implementation MTMemoryTile

@synthesize tileRow = _tileRow;
@synthesize tileColumn = _tileColumn;
@synthesize faceSpriteName = _faceSpriteName;
@synthesize isFaceUp;

-(void) dealloc {
    // We set this to nil to let the string go away
    self.faceSpriteName = nil;

    [super dealloc];
}

-(void) showFace {
    // Instantly swap the texture used for this tile
    // to the faceSpriteName
    [self setDisplayFrame:[[CCSpriteFrameCache
                            sharedSpriteFrameCache]
                spriteFrameByName:self.faceSpriteName]];

    self.isFaceUp = YES;
}

-(void) showBack {
    // Instantly swap the texture to the back image
    [self setDisplayFrame:[[CCSpriteFrameCache
                            sharedSpriteFrameCache]
                spriteFrameByName:@"tileback.png"]];

    self.isFaceUp = NO;
}

-(void) changeTile {
    // This is called in the middle of the flipTile
    // method to change the tile image while the tile is
    // "on edge", so the player doesn't see the switch
    if (isFaceUp) {
        [self showBack];
    } else {
        [self showFace];
```

```
        }
    }

    -(void) flipTile {
        // This method uses the CCOrbitCamera to spin the
        // view of this sprite so we simulate a tile flip

        // Duration is how long the total flip will last
        float duration = 0.25f;

        CCOrbitCamera *rotateToEdge = [CCOrbitCamera
                    actionWithDuration:duration/2 radius:1
                    deltaRadius:0 angleZ:0 deltaAngleZ:90
                    angleX:0 deltaAngleX:0];
        CCOrbitCamera *rotateFlat = [CCOrbitCamera
                    actionWithDuration:duration/2 radius:1
                    deltaRadius:0 angleZ:270 deltaAngleZ:90
                    angleX:0 deltaAngleX:0];
        [self runAction:[CCSequence actions: rotateToEdge,
                        [CCCallFunc actionWithTarget:self
                        selector:@selector(changeTile)],
                        rotateFlat, nil]];

        // Play the sound effect for flipping
        [[SimpleAudioEngine sharedEngine] playEffect:
                                    SND_TILE_FLIP];
    }

    - (BOOL)containsTouchLocation:(CGPoint)pos
    {
        // This is called from the CCLayer to let the object
        // answer if it was touched or not
      return CGRectContainsPoint(self.boundingBox, pos);
    }
    @end
```

We will not be using a touch handler inside this class, since we will need to handle the matching logic in the main layer anyway. Instead, we expose the containsTouchLocation method, so the layer can "ask" the individual tiles if they were touched. This uses the tile's boundingBox, which is baked-in functionality in cocos2d. A boundingBox is a CGRect representing the smallest rectangle surrounding the sprite image itself.

We also see the `showFace` and `showBack` methods. These methods will set a new display frame for the tile. In order to retain the name of the sprite frame that is used for the face of this tile, we use the `faceSpriteName` variable to hold the sprite frame name (which is also the original image filename). We don't need to keep a variable for the tile back, since all tiles will be using the same image, so we can safely hardcode that name.

The `flipTile` method makes use of the `CCOrbitCamera` to deform the tile by rotating the "camera" around the sprite image. This is a bit of visual trickery and isn't a perfect flip (some extra deformation occurs nearer the edges of the screen), but it gives a fairly decent animation without a lot of heavy coding or prerendered animations. Here we use a `CCSequence` action to queue three actions. The first action, `rotateToEdge`, will rotate the tile on its axis until it is edge-wise to the screen. The second calls out to the `changeFace` method, which will do an instant swap between the front and back of the tile. The third action, `rotateFlat`, completes the rotation back to the original "flat" orientation. The same `flipTile` method can be used for flipping to the front and flipping to the back, because the `isFaceUp` Boolean being used allows the `changeTile` method to know whether front or back should be visible. Let's look at following screenshot, which shows the tile flips, in mid-flip:

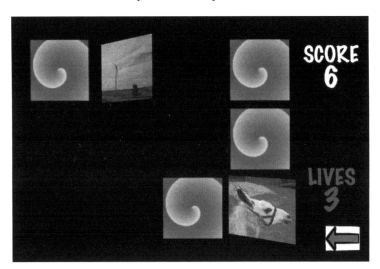

Loading tiles

Now we have our tile class, we're ready to load some tiles into the
`tilesAvailable` array:

Filename: `MTPlayfieldLayer.m`

```objc
-(void) acquireMemoryTiles {
    // This method will create and load the MemoryTiles
    // into the tilesAvailable array

    // We assume the tiles all use standard names
    for (int cnt = 1; cnt <= maxTiles; cnt++) {
        // Load the tile into the array
        // We loop so we add each tile in the array twice
        // This gives us a matched pair of each tile
        for (NSInteger tileNo = 1; tileNo <= 2; tileNo++) {
            // Generate the tile image name
            NSString *imageName = [NSString
                    stringWithFormat:@"tile%i.png", cnt];

            //Create a new MemoryTile with this image
            MTMemoryTile *newTile = [MTMemoryTile
                    spriteWithSpriteFrameName:imageName];

            // We capture the image name for the card face
            [newTile setFaceSpriteName:imageName];

            // We want the tiles to start face down
            [newTile showBack];

            // Add the MemoryTile to the array
            [tilesAvailable addObject:newTile];
        }
    }
}
```

Here we loop through all the unique tiles we need (up to the value of `maxTiles`, which is set to half of the available spaces on the board). Inside that loop, we set up another *for* loop that counts to 2. We do this because we need two copies of each tile to assemble our board. Since we have established that our tiles are named as `tile#.png`, we create an `NSString` with the incremental name, and create an `MTMemoryTile` object with a standard `CCSprite` constructor. As we said earlier, we want to keep a copy of the image name for the `showFace` method, so we set the `faceSpriteName` variable to that value. It wouldn't be much of a game if we had all the tiles face up, so we call `showBack`, so the tiles are face down before they are used on screen. Finally, we add the tile we just created to the `tilesAvailable` array. Once this method completes, the `tilesAvailable` array will be the only retain we have on the tiles.

Drawing tiles

Now we need to draw a randomly selected tile in every position to make a nice grid. First we need to figure out where each tile should be positioned. If we were using a fixed number of tiles, we could use absolute positioning. To account for the dynamic number of tiles, we add a "helper" method to determine positioning as follows:

Filename: `MTPlayfieldLayer.m`

```
-(CGPoint) tilePosforRow:(NSInteger)rowNum
              andColumn:(NSInteger)colNum {
    // Generate the coordinates for each tile
    float newX = boardOffsetX +
            (tileSize.width + padWidth) * (colNum - .5);
    float newY = boardOffsetY +
            (tileSize.height + padHeight) * (rowNum - .5);

    return ccp(newX, newY);
}
```

To calculate the x position, we determine the total footprint of a single tile and the associated padding. We multiply this times the column number minus one half. We add this result to the board offset we calculated earlier. Why do we subtract one half? This is because our positions are based on the complete size of the tile and the padding. What we need is the center point of the tile, because that is our `anchorPoint` (that is the point on which the tile will pivot or rotate.). We need this anchor point left at the center (the default `anchorPoint` for a `CCSprite` object, as it happens), because when we flip the tiles, the flip will be based on this `anchorPoint`, so we want them to flip around the middle of the tile. Now that we have our tile positioning established, we can go ahead and start building the tiles on the screen.

Filename: `MTPlayfieldLayer.m`

```objc
-(void) generateTileGrid {
    // This method takes the tilesAvailable array,
    // and deals the tiles out to the board randomly
    // Tiles used will be moved to the tilesInPlay array

    // Loop through all the positions on the board
    for (NSInteger newRow = 1; newRow <= boardRows; newRow++) {
        for (NSInteger newCol = 1; newCol <= boardColumns;
            newCol++) {

            // We randomize each card slot
            NSInteger rndPick = (NSInteger)arc4random() %
                                ([tilesAvailable count]);

            // Grab the MemoryTile from the array
            MTMemoryTile *newTile = [tilesAvailable
                            objectAtIndex:rndPick];

            // Let the card "know" where it is
            [newTile setTileRow:newRow];
            [newTile setTileColumn:newCol];

            // Scale the tile to size
            float tileScaleX = tileSize.width /
                        newTile.contentSize.width;

            // We scale by X only (tiles are square)
            [newTile setScale:tileScaleX];

            // Set the positioning for the tile
            [newTile setPosition:[self tilePosforRow:newRow
                                        andColumn:newCol]];

            // Add the tile as a child of our batch node
            [self addChild:newTile];

            // Since we don't want to re-use this tile,
            // we remove it from the array
            [tilesAvailable removeObjectAtIndex:rndPick];

            // We retain the MemoryTile for later access
            [tilesInPlay addObject:newTile];
        }
    }
}
```

Here we use two nested *for* loops to iterate through all rows and all columns. We use `arc4random()` to select a random tile from the `tilesAvailable` array and build a new `MTMemoryTile` object that references the tile selected. After setting the `MTMemoryTile` object's variables for which row and column it represents, we set the scale factor for the tile. Since our images are bigger than needed for most game types, we divide the desired `tileSize` by the actual `contentSize` of the image. When applied, this will correctly scale our image to the desired display size. We only use the x (width) value, since we already enforced in the `initWithRows:andColumns:` method that the images will always be square.

We use the `tilePosforRow` method to determine where it should be on the layer, and we add it. After adding it to the layer, we also add the new tile to the `tilesInPlay` array and remove it from the `tilesAvailable` array. By removing it from `tilesAvailable`, we ensure that we cannot select the same tile twice. After all iterations of the nested loops, the `tilesAvailable` array should be empty, and the board should be fully populated with tiles.

Adding interactivity

Now that we have our randomized grid of tiles on the board, we need to add the touch handler to let us interact with them. Since our game mechanics are pretty simple, we will use just the `ccTouchesEnded` method as follows:

Filename: `MTPlayfieldLayer.m`

```
- (void) ccTouchesEnded: (NSSet *)touches
            withEvent: (UIEvent *)event {

    // If game over, go back to the main menu on any touch
    if (isGameOver) {
        [[CCDirector sharedDirector]
                    replaceScene: [MTMenuScene node]];
    }

    UITouch *touch = [touches anyObject];

    CGPoint location = [touch locationInView: [touch view]];
    CGPoint convLoc = [[CCDirector sharedDirector]
                        convertToGL: location];

    // If the back button was pressed, we exit
    if (CGRectContainsPoint([backButton boundingBox],
                            convLoc)) {
        [[CCDirector sharedDirector]
```

```
                    replaceScene:[MTMenuScene node]];
    }

    // If we have 2 tiles face up, do not respond
    if ([tilesSelected count] == 2) {
        return;
    } else {
        // Iterate through tilesInPlay to see which tile
        // was touched
        for (MTMemoryTile *aTile in tilesInPlay) {
            if ([aTile containsTouchLocation:convLoc] &&
                [aTile isFaceUp] == NO) {
                // Flip the tile
                [aTile flipTile];
                // Hold the tile in a buffer array
                [tilesSelected addObject:aTile];

                // Call the score/fail check,
                // if it is the second tile
                if ([tilesSelected count] == 2) {
                    // We delay so player can see cards
                    [self scheduleOnce:@selector(checkForMatch)
                             delay:1.0];
                    break;
                }

            }
        }
    }
}
```

In the touch handler, the touches are provided in an NSSet. However, since we do not have multiple touches enabled, we can be sure we will only be getting a single touch that we care about. Why is there no multi-touch in this game? Multiple simultaneous touches would cause confusion for the player and really complicate the code to determine which tiles should be checked for a match. So by not enabling multiple touches, we save ourselves extra work, and reduce the confusion for the flow of the game.

The first section of the method checks to see if we have reached a game over state (as represented by a YES value in the isGameOver variable, any touch after we have reached game over will return the player to the menu screen.

The second section of the method is detecting touches on the back button. The `location` and `convLoc` variables together convert the touch into a coordinate in our game screen. We use this location to check if the `backButton` was touched. If it has been touched, we also exit to the menu screen, regardless of what else is going on in the game.

We then check to make sure the `tilesSelected` array doesn't have two items in it. The `tilesSelected` array is with the tiles that have been flipped face up. If there are two tiles already face up, that means the match checking has not yet been resolved. In those cases, we don't want to let the user keep flipping over tiles, so we simply return without responding to the touch. This will effectively throw away the touch, so we can safely move on with our game.

If we don't have two tiles selected already, then we iterate through all of the tiles in the `tilesInPlay` array and poll it to determine: a) are you being touched? and b) are you face down. If both of these are `true`, we send the message to the touched tile to flip over (`flipTile`), and we add the tile to the `tilesSelected` array. If this was our second tile added to the `tilesSelected` array, we will call the `checkForMatch` method after a delay of one second. This delay gives us two benefits: it allows the player to see the potential match they just made, and it gives plenty of time to finish iterating through the `tilesInPlay` array so we don't risk mutating the array. **Mutating** an array means you tried to change it while it was being evaluated. If we skipped the delay, the `checkForMatch` method would cause this mutation (and crash) because it can remove tiles from the `tilesInPlay` array. Go ahead and try it yourself. Actually seeing the error messages when you know what you did wrong will help you know where to look later, when you cause a crash without knowing what you did wrong.

Checking for matches

Since we have done quite a bit of preparation for the rest of the mechanics of the game, it might come as a surprise that the logic to check for matching tiles is very simple. Since we stored the name of the image used for each tile inside the `MTMemoryTile` object, it is a matter of comparing the two and see if they are the same.

Filename: MTPlayfieldLayer.m

```
-(void) checkForMatch {
    // Get the MemoryTiles for this comparison
    MTMemoryTile *tileA = [tilesSelected objectAtIndex:0];
    MTMemoryTile *tileB = [tilesSelected objectAtIndex:1];

    // See if the two tiles matched
    if ([tileA.faceSpriteName
            isEqualToString:tileB.faceSpriteName]) {
```

```
        // We remove the matching tiles
        [self removeMemoryTile:tileA];
        [self removeMemoryTile:tileB];
    } else {
        // No match, flip the tiles back
        [tileA flipTile];
        [tileB flipTile];
    }

    // Remove the tiles from tilesSelected
    [tilesSelected removeAllObjects];
}

-(void) removeMemoryTile:(MTMemoryTile*)thisTile {
    [thisTile removeFromParentAndCleanup:YES];
}
```

If you recall, in the ccTouchesEnded method we stored the face up tile in the tilesSelected array. Our logic only allows there to be two objects in the tilesSelected array, and the checkForMatch method is called only when there are two objects in that array. Because of those restrictions, we can safely assume that there are objects in that array at index 0 and index 1. (We create references to them as tileA and tileB to make the code simpler.)

It is trivial at this point to call isEqualToString on the faceSpriteName variable of tileA and pass it the value of the faceSpriteName variable from tileB. If these strings are equal, we have a match. When comparing strings, you cannot use == operations, you must use isEqualToString:.

When a match is found, we call the removeMemoryTile method that simply removes the tile passed. If we don't have a match, we send the message to each tile to flip itself back over. Since we have resolved the matching, either by making a match or by turning the tiles back over, we then remove the tiles from the tilesSelected array so we have an empty array to hold the next possible match.

Scoring and excitement

The game works well with the development we have covered, but there are a few places where we can add a little more visual flair and some excitement. Players love having a game that keeps score. They also love animation. There is excitement to be had by having the ability to lose. Let's give the player what they want.

We build the score and lives displays using CCLabelTTF labels, with the variables playerScore and livesRemaining as their label contents. These are declared as variables of the layer, so we can easily update them. When we start animating tiles, it will be useful to know where the score and lives displays are on screen.

There are two main approaches to adding text to the screen: CCLabelTTF and CCLabelBMFont. Both have their uses, which we will briefly outline here. CCLabelTTF uses a standard TTF font file. The way it draws the text on the screen is not very efficient and can cause performance issues in some uses. The other approach, CCLabelBMFont, uses a bitmap (image file) of the font and internally uses a batch node to render the text. This means it is highly efficient at drawing, with very little performance concern. Other than the use of a TTF file versus an image file, the way you code for them is very similar. One potential issue with a BMFont file is that you must have the entire font in a single bitmap. If you are using a large font size, this often causes you to need to leave out some characters that may be needed to support international keyboards. A TTF file does not have this problem. Also, it is common with the CCLabelBMFont approach to have multiple versions of the font if you want to use different font sizes. In this book, we will use CCLabelTTF labels throughout because we do not have any performance (frame rate) concerns with any of these projects.

If we were to have performance issues, we would certainly switch to using CCLabelBMFont instead of CCLabelTTF. We leave it as an exercise for the reader to convert these projects to use the CCLabelBMFont class. (For creation of the bitmaps, an excellent resource is Glyph Designer, available at http://glyphdesigner.71squared.com.)

Filename: MTPlayfieldLayer.m

```
-(CGPoint) scorePosition {
    return ccp(size.width - 10 - tileSize.width/2,
            (size.height/4) * 3);
}

-(CGPoint) livesPosition {
    return ccp(size.width - 10 - tileSize.width/2,
            size.height/4);
}
```

Rather than hardcoding the values in multiple places, it is a preferred approach to create helper methods such as scorePosition and livesPosition, which return a CGPoint reference of where those elements are onscreen. Here we see the calculations, which place the score and lives near the left edge of the screen, with the score three quarters of the way up the screen, and the lives one quarter of the way up the screen.

The creation of simple labels is very basic, using the positioning we saw above. To see how the score and lives are created, please consult the accompanying code bundle for this book.

Now we will need a way to score and animate the tiles when the player makes a successful match. When a match is scored, we will fly the tiles to the score, and then have them shrink into the score position until they disappear. Let's see how that works:

Filename: `MTPlayfieldLayer.m`

```objc
-(void) scoreThisMemoryTile:(MTMemoryTile*)aTile {
    // We set a baseline speed for the tile movement
    float tileVelocity = 600.0;

    // We calculate the time needed to move the tile
    CGPoint moveDifference = ccpSub([self scorePosition],
                                    aTile.position);
    float moveDuration = ccpLength(moveDifference) /
                                    tileVelocity;
    // Define the movement actions
    CCMoveTo *move = [CCMoveTo actionWithDuration:
                moveDuration position:[self scorePosition]];
    CCScaleTo *scale = [CCScaleTo actionWithDuration:0.5
                                            scale:0.001];
    CCDelayTime *delay = [CCDelayTime
                        actionWithDuration:0.5];
    CCCallFuncND *remove = [CCCallFuncND
                    actionWithTarget:self
                    selector:@selector(removeMemoryTile:)
                    data:aTile];

    // Run the actions
    [aTile runAction:[CCSequence actions:move, scale,
                    delay, remove, nil]];

    // Play the sound effect
    [[SimpleAudioEngine sharedEngine]
                    playEffect:SND_TILE_SCORE];

    // Remove the tile from the tilesInPlay array
    [tilesInPlay removeObject:aTile];

    // Add 1 to the player's score
    playerScore++;

    // Recalculate the number of lives left
    [self calculateLivesRemaining];
}
```

Here we leverage the cocos2d actions heavily, using the stock actions of CCMoveTo, CCScaleTo, CCDelayTime, and CCCallFuncND. One aspect of our flying-to-score effect is that we want the tiles to move at a constant rate. If we hardcoded a duration for the CCMoveTo action, the tiles closer to the score would move slowly, and those farther away would move really fast. To achieve a constant rate, we set a desired speed (tileVelocity), then calculate how far away the tile is from the score. We divide these out to arrive at the correct movement duration for this tile. After we initiate the actions, we increment the score by one (playerScore++), and call the calculateLivesRemaining method (which we will see shortly).

Animating the score

Now that we have the tile animation added, now we should do something more flashy with the score itself.

Filename: MTPlayfieldLayer.m

```
-(void) animateScoreDisplay {
    // We delay for a second to allow the tiles to get
    // to the scoring position before we animate
    CCDelayTime *firstDelay = [CCDelayTime
                actionWithDuration:1.0];
    CCScaleTo *scaleUp = [CCScaleTo
                actionWithDuration:0.2 scale:2.0];
    CCCallFunc *updateScoreDisplay = [CCCallFunc
                actionWithTarget:self
                selector:@selector(updateScoreDisplay)];
    CCDelayTime *secondDelay = [CCDelayTime
                actionWithDuration:0.2];
    CCScaleTo *scaleDown = [CCScaleTo
                actionWithDuration:0.2 scale:1.0];

    [playerScoreDisplay runAction:[CCSequence actions:
                firstDelay, scaleUp, updateScoreDisplay,
                secondDelay, scaleDown, nil]];
}

-(void) updateScoreDisplay {
    // Change the score display to the new value
    [playerScoreDisplay setString:
     [NSString stringWithFormat:@"%i", playerScore]];

    // Play the "score" sound
    [[SimpleAudioEngine sharedEngine]
                    playEffect:SND_SCORE];
}
```

We finally settled on scaling the score up, change it to the new value, and scale it back to normal. This is all done with standard cocos2d actions, so we could add in more flair with other effects. A `CCRotateTo` action might add a nice touch by spinning the score around when it updates. For this game, we will stick to this simpler animation. We leave it as a challenge to the reader to add these types of enhancements for more "visual flair."

Adding lives and game over

Now we come to the point where we decide how the player can win or lose. You win after you have successfully matched all the tiles on the board. Losing is less obvious in a one-player game like this. Our approach is to give the player a number of lives. When you take a turn and fail to match the tiles, you lose a life. Lose all of them, and it's game over. The challenge comes from deciding how many lives the player should have. After testing several approaches, we determined the most exciting way would be to have the number of lives set to half the number of tiles currently on the board. If the board has 20 tiles in play, the player has 10 lives. Once the player makes a successful match, the lives are recalculated based on the new number of tiles in play. This gives some level of excitement as the lives are dwindling, and it encourages the player to think about their moves more carefully.

Filename: `MTPlayfieldLayer.m`

```
-(void) animateLivesDisplay {
    // We delay for a second to allow the tiles to flip back
    CCScaleTo *scaleUp = [CCScaleTo
            actionWithDuration:0.2 scale:2.0];
    CCCallFunc *updateLivesDisplay = [CCCallFunc
            actionWithTarget:self
            selector:@selector(updateLivesDisplay)];
    CCCallFunc *resetLivesColor = [CCCallFunc
            actionWithTarget:self
            selector:@selector(resetLivesColor)];
    CCDelayTime *delay = [CCDelayTime
            actionWithDuration:0.2];
    CCScaleTo *scaleDown = [CCScaleTo
            actionWithDuration:0.2 scale:1.0];
    [livesRemainingDisplay runAction:[CCSequence actions:
            scaleUp, updateLivesDisplay, delay, scaleDown,
            resetLivesColor, nil]];
}

-(void) updateLivesDisplayQuiet {
    // Change the lives display without the fanfare
```

```
        [livesRemainingDisplay setString:[NSString
                stringWithFormat:@"%i", livesRemaining]];
    }


    -(void) updateLivesDisplay {
        // Change the lives display to the new value
        [livesRemainingDisplay setString:[NSString
                stringWithFormat:@"%i", livesRemaining]];
        // Change the lives display to red
        [livesRemainingDisplay setColor:ccRED];

        // Play the "wrong" sound
        [[SimpleAudioEngine sharedEngine]
                        playEffect:SND_TILE_WRONG];

        [self checkForGameOver];
    }

    -(void) calculateLivesRemaining {
        // Lives equal half of the tiles on the board
        livesRemaining = [tilesInPlay count] / 2;
    }

    -(void) resetLivesColor {
        // Change the Lives counter back to blue
        [livesRemainingDisplay setColor:ccBLUE];
    }
```

The preceding section of code looks very similar to the score methods. We leverage cocos2d actions to animate the lives display, only this time we also turn the text red when the number of lives is reduced, and then change it back to blue at the end of the CCSequence of actions. One item of note here is the updateLivesDisplayQuiet method. This method is called when the player makes a successful match to let us change the lives to their new value without the "oh-no" fanfare that we use when the player loses a life.

We now have two game over conditions to consider. If livesRemaining is zero, the player loses. If the tilesInPlay array is empty, the player has won. This feels like a good time to put the code together into a single method to check these conditions.

Filename: MTPlayfieldLayer.m

```
    -(void) checkForGameOver {
        NSString *finalText;
        // Player wins
        if ([tilesInPlay count] == 0) {
```

```
        finalText = @"You Win!";
    // Player loses
    } else if (livesRemaining <= 0) {
        finalText = @"You Lose!";
    } else {
        // No game over conditions met
        return;
    }

    // Set the game over flag
    isGameOver = YES;

    // Display the appropriate game over message
    CCLabelTTF *gameOver = [CCLabelTTF
                labelWithString:finalText
                fontName:@"Marker Felt" fontSize:60];
    [gameOver setPosition:ccp(size.width/2,size.height/2)];
    [self addChild:gameOver z:50];
}
```

Bringing it all together

We have added extra flash and flair in the code, but we haven't tied it all together yet. Most of the new code is integrated into the checkForMatch method, so let's see how that looks with everything integrated:

Filename: MTPlayfieldLayer.m

```
-(void) checkForMatch {
    // Get the MemoryTiles for this comparison
    MTMemoryTile *tileA = [tilesSelected objectAtIndex:0];
    MTMemoryTile *tileB = [tilesSelected objectAtIndex:1];

    // See if the two tiles matched
    if ([tileA.faceSpriteName
            isEqualToString:tileB.faceSpriteName]) {
        // We start the scoring, lives, and animations
        [self scoreThisMemoryTile:tileA];
        [self scoreThisMemoryTile:tileB];
        [self animateScoreDisplay];
        [self calculateLivesRemaining];
        [self updateLivesDisplayQuiet];
        [self checkForGameOver];

    } else {
        // No match, flip the tiles back
        [tileA flipTile];
```

```
        [tileB flipTile];

        // Take off a life and update the display
        livesRemaining--;
        [self animateLivesDisplay];
    }

    // Remove the tiles from tilesSelected
    [tilesSelected removeAllObjects];
}
```

Now we have a fully functional game, complete with scoring, lives, a way to win and a way to lose. There is only one necessary element still missing.

It's quiet...too quiet

A major mistake some casual game designers make is to downplay the importance of audio. When you are playing a quiet game without the aid of a computer, there are always subtle sounds. Playing cards give a soft "thwap" sound when playing solitaire. Tokens in board games click as they tap their way around the board. Video games should have these "incidental" sound effects, too. These are the button clicks, the buzzers when something goes wrong, and so forth.

We will be using CocosDenshion, the audio engine that is bundled with cocos2d. CocosDenshion includes a very easy to use interface appropriately named SimpleAudioEngine. To initialize it, you need to import it into your classes (including the AppDelegate.m file) and add one line near the end of the application:didFinishLaunchingWithOptions: method (before the return YES; line).

Filename: AppDelegate.m

```
        // Initialize the SimpleAudioEngine
        [SimpleAudioEngine sharedEngine];
```

For our implementation, we want to preload all of our sound effects so there is no lag the first time the sound effect is played. We do this with a method that is called from the initWithRows:andColumns: method of our MTPlayfieldLayer.

Filename: MTPlayfieldLayer.m

```
    -(void) preloadEffects {
        // Preload all of our sound effects
        [[SimpleAudioEngine sharedEngine]
                        preloadEffect:SND_TILE_FLIP];
        [[SimpleAudioEngine sharedEngine]
                        preloadEffect:SND_TILE_SCORE];
```

```
[[SimpleAudioEngine sharedEngine]
                  preloadEffect:SND_TILE_WRONG];
[[SimpleAudioEngine sharedEngine]
                  preloadEffect:SND_SCORE];
}
```

The `preloadEffect` method of `SimpleAudioEngine` actually takes an `NSString` as an argument. We have defined constants to hold the names of the sound files. (These constants are at the top of the `MTPlayfieldLayer.m` file, above the `@implementation` statement.)

```
#define SND_TILE_FLIP @"button.caf"
#define SND_TILE_SCORE @"whoosh.caf"
#define SND_TILE_WRONG @"buzzer.caf"
#define SND_SCORE @"harprun.caf"
```

Why do we do this? By using `#define` statements in a single location, we can easily change the sound files we are using in one place, rather than relying on find-and-replace functionality to change the filenames throughout our code. Having done this, anywhere we want to play the `button.caf` file, we can simply refer to it as `SND_TILE_FLIP` (no quotes around it), and Xcode takes care of the rest.

We have peppered the code with various playing of these sound effects, but we won't go into detail on where each sound is triggered. When you want to play a sound effect, you can call it with a single line of code, as follows:

```
[[SimpleAudioEngine sharedEngine]
                    playEffect:SND_SCORE];
```

It doesn't get much simpler than that!

Summary

We've covered a lot of ground with this memory game. At this point you should be familiar with the methodology we will continue you use throughout the book regarding `CCScene` and `CCLayer` organization. We have used a custom `init` method to make our game engine more flexible. We have also covered effective use of actions, `SimpleSoundEngine`, a couple ways of handling touches, and some basic game flow intelligence. And this is just the beginning! In the next chapter, we tackle a modern favorite, a Match-3 game. We'll explore a couple ways to solve the match detection problem, and build a fun game along the way.

2
Match 3 and Recursive Methods

We will now move to a modern classic game that features addictive gameplay, predictive coding, and artificial randomness. We will also work with recursive methods—methods that call themselves repeatedly.

In this chapter, we cover the following:

- Basic state machines
- Detecting matches
- Predictive logic
- Artificial randomness

The project is…

We will be building a Match 3 game in this chapter. This game is heavily influenced by several of the extremely popular games of the genre, but we will be sticking to core mechanics in this chapter. What is being left out? We will not be including any special modes for matching four or five gems in a row, though those matches will still be scored. We will explore one approach to avoiding a "no more moves" situation using predictive logic and artificial randomness. We will assume you have familiarity with the basic structural concepts from *Chapter 1, Thanks for the Memory Game*, so we will dive directly into the Match 3-specific code.

We will be using classes with names such as MAMenuLayer, MAPlayfieldLayer, MAMenuScene, and MAPlayfieldScene throughout the book. The two-letter prefix will be different for each game (MT for *Chapter 1, Thanks for the Memory Game*, MA for this chapter, and so on), but the role each class plays will be the same. This structure is our foundational nomenclature, so we should assume we have classes named in this fashion in each project.

Basic gem interaction

In this game, we only really have one type of object to play with — we will refer to these playing pieces as gems, since that is the most commonly used image in Match 3 games. We will look at some of the internals of the MAGem class, and then move on to how we actually handle the gems before tackling the more intricate logic.

The MAGem header

We start out by looking at the header for the MAGem class, which is a subclass of CCSprite. We have a couple of new things here. We are using the @class statement to tell this class that there is another class called MAPlayfieldLayer that exists, but we don't want to import that class here. MAGem will be imported by MAPlayfieldLayer, and we don't want to get stuck in an infinite "import" loop.

Filename: MAGem.h

```
@class MAPlayfieldLayer;

typedef enum {
    kGemAnyType = 0,
    kGem1,
    kGem2,
    kGem3,
    kGem4,
    kGem5,
    kGem6,
    kGem7
} GemType;

typedef enum {
    kGemIdle = 100,
    kGemMoving,
    kGemScoring,
```

```
    kGemNew
} GemState;

@interface MAGem : CCSprite {
    NSInteger _rowNum; // Row number for this gem
    NSInteger _colNum; // Column number for this gem
    GemType _gemType; // The enum value of the gem
    GemState _gemState; // The current state of the gem
    MAPlayfieldLayer *gameLayer; // The game layer
}

@property (nonatomic, assign) NSInteger rowNum;
@property (nonatomic, assign) NSInteger colNum;
@property (nonatomic, assign) GemType gemType;
@property (nonatomic, assign) GemState gemState;
@property (nonatomic, assign) MAPlayfieldLayer *gameLayer;

-(BOOL) isGemSameAs:(MAGem*)otherGem;
-(BOOL) isGemInSameRow:(MAGem*)otherGem;
-(BOOL) isGemInSameColumn:(MAGem*)otherGem;
-(BOOL) isGemBeside:(MAGem*)otherGem;

-(void) highlightGem;
-(void) stopHighlightGem;

- (BOOL) containsTouchLocation:(CGPoint)pos;
@end
```

You will notice we begin the class with two sections of `typedef enum`. This is a C construct that is basically an integer constant. Inside the curly braces is a comma-separated list of all of the named elements we want to use, and after the closing curly brace, we give a name to this enumerated value. In the first `typedef` statement, we are establishing that we have a new object type called `GemType`. Valid values for this are `kGemAnyType`, `kGem1`, `kGem2`, and so on. You will also notice that the first value is assigned to an integer, `0`. If you omit this assignment, the named values will automatically be assigned unique integer values. Because we have explicitly declared that the first value is `0`, the compiler will automatically assign incremental integers to the remaining values. This gives a small peek at the flexibility of these values. Even though we use the named values for them, we can also treat them as integers if there is a need. For example, `kGem1` and the integer value `1` are identical and can be used interchangeably.

Once we have built these `typedef` sections, we can treat the `GemType` and `GemState` types the same as any other valid data type, as we have done in the variable declarations. These will also be valid to use in any other class that imports the `MAGem` class.

One important feature we have added to the `MAGem` class is a primitive state machine. We use the `gemState` variable to hold the current state of the gem. The gem can only be in a single state at a time. The possible states are `kGemNew`, `kGemIdle`, `kGemScoring`, and `kGemMoving` (as defined in the second `typedef enum` statement). These could also be handled by a series of `BOOL` variables for each state, but that gets confusing very quickly. Since the states are mutually exclusive, using a single state variable is the preferred way to handle this.

The MAGem class

Now we turn our attention to the `MAGem.m` file. Because `MAGem` is a subclass of `CCSprite`, we have intentionally avoided overriding any methods. Although it is common to override the `init` method, we are taking an alternate approach here. All of our instance variables will be set by the calling method, not by the `init` method. This illustrates the fact that there is not a single right answer to any situation. This approach actually leads to slightly fewer lines of code, since the gems will only be created by a single method in our `MAPlayfieldLayer` class. Functionally, there is no difference between setting these values in a custom `init` method versus the approach taken here.

Filename: `MAGem.m`

```
@implementation MAGem

@synthesize rowNum = _rowNum;
@synthesize colNum = _colNum;
@synthesize gemType = _gemType;
@synthesize gemState = _gemState;

@synthesize gameLayer;

-(BOOL) isGemSameAs:(MAGem*)otherGem {
    // Is the gem the same type as the other Gem?
    return (self.gemType == otherGem.gemType);
}

-(BOOL) isGemInSameRow:(MAGem*)otherGem {
    // Is the gem in the same row as the other Gem?
    return (self.rowNum == otherGem.rowNum);
```

```
}

-(BOOL) isGemInSameColumn:(MAGem*)otherGem {
    // Is the gem in the same column as the other gem?
    return (self.colNum == otherGem.colNum);
}
```

We have a few helper methods in this class that will make the matching logic easier. Look at the method isGemSameAs in this class. Since this is in the MAGem class, we can pass it another MAGem instance as an argument, and it compares the gemType variables to determine whether they are the same type of gem. If they are the same, we return YES. If they are different, we return NO. We follow the same pattern for the isGemInSameRow and isGemInSameColumn methods. The code in these methods is extremely simple but will allow us to simplify how we interact with the gems.

Filename: MAGem.m

```
-(BOOL) isGemBeside:(MAGem*)otherGem {
    // If the row is the same, and the other gem is
    // +/- 1 column, they are neighbors
    if ([self isGemInSameRow:otherGem] &&
        ((self.colNum == otherGem.colNum - 1) ||
        (self.colNum == otherGem.colNum + 1))
        ) {
        return YES;
    }
    // If the column is the same, and the other gem is
    // +/- 1 row, they are neighbors
    else if ([self isGemInSameColumn:otherGem] &&
                ((self.rowNum == otherGem.rowNum - 1) ||
                 (self.rowNum == otherGem.rowNum + 1))
                ) {
        return YES;
    } else {
        return NO;
    }
}
```

The isGemBeside method is a little more involved. We first check to see whether the two gems in question (the current gem and otherGem) are in the same row, using the method we just saw. We also check to see whether the colNum variable of the otherGem object is either one greater or one less than the current gem. If this is true, we return YES. We then check to see whether otherGem is in the same column and whether they are in adjacent rows, in the same manner. This method (with the other isGem methods) will make comparisons between gems trivial to implement later.

Filename: `MAGem.m`

```
-(void) highlightGem {
    // Build a simple repeating "wobbly" animation
    CCMoveBy *moveUp = [CCMoveBy actionWithDuration:0.1
                        position:ccp(0,3)];
    CCMoveBy *moveDown = [CCMoveBy actionWithDuration:0.1
                        position:ccp(0,-3)];
    CCSequence *moveAround = [CCSequence actions:moveUp,
                        moveDown, nil];
    CCRepeatForever *gemHop = [CCRepeatForever
                        actionWithAction:moveAround];

    [self runAction:gemHop];
}

-(void) stopHighlightGem {
    // Stop all actions (the wobbly) on the gem
    [self stopAllActions];

    // We call to the gameLayer itself to make sure we
    // haven't left the gem a little off-base
    // (from the highlightGem movements)
    [gameLayer performSelector:@selector(resetGemPosition:)
                        withObject:self];
}
```

In the preceding code, we see the `highlightGem` and `stopHighlightGem` methods. These will be used when the player touches a gem. The gem will hop up and down when it is selected. `stopHighlightGem` makes a call to the `resetGemPosition` method in the `GameLayer` class. We do this because the gem itself has no knowledge of where it is supposed to be on the screen. We could migrate the positioning code into the `MAGem` class to avoid this cross-class calling, but this works well, so we will leave it this way.

Generating gems

We will build a new subclass of `CCLayer`, called `MAPlayfieldLayer`, and we will set up a couple of methods to control all gem creation.

Filename: `MAPlayfieldLayer.m`

```
-(MAGem*) generateGemForRow:(NSInteger)rowNum
    andColumn:(NSInteger)colNum ofType:(GemType)newType {
```

```
    GemType gemNum;

    if (newType == kGemAnyType) {
        // If we passed a kGemAnyType, randomize the gem
        gemNum = (arc4random() % totalGemsAvailable) + 1;
    } else {
        // If we passed another value, use that gem type
        gemNum = newType;
    }

    // Generate the sprite name
    NSString *spritename = [NSString stringWithFormat:
                            @"gem%i.png", gemNum];

    // Build the MAGem, which is just an enhanced CCSprite
    MAGem *thisGem = [MAGem
                     spriteWithSpriteFrameName:spritename];

    // Set the gem's vars
    [thisGem setRowNum:rowNum];
    [thisGem setColNum:colNum];
    [thisGem setGemType:(GemType)gemNum];
    [thisGem setGemState:kGemNew];
    [thisGem setGameLayer:self];

    // Set the position for this gem
    [thisGem setPosition:[self positionForRow:rowNum
                                    andColumn:colNum]];

    // Add the gem to the array
    [gemsInPlay addObject:thisGem];

    // We return the newly created gem, which is already
    // added to the gemsInPlay array
    // It has NOT been added to the layer yet.
    return thisGem;
}

-(void) addGemForRow:(NSInteger)rowNum
           andColumn:(NSInteger)colNum
              ofType:(GemType)newType {

    // Add a replacement gem
    MAGem *thisGem = [self generateGemForRow:rowNum
```

```
                       andColumn:colNum ofType:newType];

    // We reset the gem above the screen
    [thisGem setPosition:ccpAdd(thisGem.position,
                                ccp(0,size.height))];

    // Add the gem to the scene
    [self addChild:thisGem];

    // Drop it to the correct position
    [self moveToNewSlotForGem:thisGem];
}
```

Combined, these two methods take care of creating a new gem, assigning all variables (including the `GameLayer` variable we use to refer to the layer from the `MAGem` class), and putting the gem into play. Why two methods? The `addGemForRow:` method takes control over three aspects of the addition: adding the gem to the layer, setting the position to a position higher than the screen, and calling the method to drop the gem into its proper position. The `generateGemsForRow:` method does everything except putting the gem into play. We do this because there are situations where we want to create a gem without making it visible, such as when we build the initial board.

Since we are keeping a reference to the playfield layer inside the `MAGem` class (in the `setGameLayer:` line in the `generate` methods), we need to be memory-conscious and set that property to `nil` when the gem's `dealloc` method is run.

Filename: `MAGem.m`

```
-(void) dealloc {
    [self setGameLayer:nil];

    [super dealloc];

}
```

Building the playfield

The creation of a basic playfield is very similar to the setup for the Memory game in *Chapter 1, Thanks for the Memory Game*, with some slight variations. We do not want the playfield to start with three-in-a-row matches, so we want to check for matching situations and change the gems around to make sure the board is "clean" when the game starts.

Filename: `MAPlayfieldLayer.m`

```objc
-(void) generatePlayfield {
    // Randomly select gems and place on the board
    // Iterate through all rows and columns
    for (int row = 1; row <= boardRows; row++) {
        for (int col = 1; col <= boardColumns; col++) {
            // Generate a gem for this slot
            [self generateGemForRow:row andColumn:col
                                ofType:kGemAnyType];
        }
    }


    // We check for matches now, and remove any gems
    // from starting in the scoring position
    [self fixStartingMatches];

    // Add the gems to the layer
    for (MAGem *aGem in gemsInPlay) {
        [aGem setGemState:kGemIdle];
        [matchsheet addChild:aGem];
    }
}
```

In this method, we iterate through all positions and call `generateGemForRow:` for each slot on the board. As you recall, the `generateGemForRow:` method does not add the gems to the layer, so we can manipulate the board before we introduce it to the player. We call the `fixStartingMatches` method to correct any starting three-in-a-row situations, and then we iterate through all of the gems in the `gemsInPlay` array and add them to the board. (You may notice that, when a gem is first added, it is set to the state `kGemNew`, and when it is added to the board, it is changed to `kGemIdle`. This is to avoid any accidental matches occurring when a new gem has been created but is not yet visible. By the time we add it to the board, it is ready to play, so `kGemIdle` is the correct state at that time.) Now we need to see how the `fixStartingMatches` method works.

Filename: `MAPlayfieldLayer.m`

```objc
-(void) fixStartingMatches {
    // This method checks for any possible matches
    // and will remove those gems. After fixing the gems,
    // we call this method again (from itself) until we
    // have a clean result
    [self checkForMatchesOfType:kGemNew];
```

```
        if ([gemMatches count] > 0) {

            // get the first matching gem
            MAGem *aGem = [gemMatches objectAtIndex:0];

            // Build a replacement gem
            [self generateGemForRow:[aGem rowNum] andColumn:
                    [aGem colNum] ofType:kGemAnyType];

            // Destroy the original gem
            [gemsInPlay removeObject:aGem];
            [gemMatches removeObject:aGem];

            // We recurse so we can see if the board is clean
            // When we have no gemMatches, we stop recursion
            [self fixStartingMatches];
        }
    }
```

This method starts with the `checkForMatchesOfType` method, which we will cover shortly. For now, we only need to know that it reviews all gems in the `gemsInPlay` array and any three-in-a-row matching gems are added to the `gemMatches` array. This method calls that check, and if there are any gems in the `gemMatches` array, it destroys the first gem in the `gemMatches` array and creates a new replacement. After it has replaced this *one* gem, it calls itself, so it can check the entire board again. Why not fix all of them at once? The `gemMatches` array contains *all* matches, which means that if there is only a single three-in-a-row match on the board, there are three gems in the array. We only need to replace one of those gems to "fix" this match on the board, so the other two gems in that match will be unchanged. To help visually explain this, look at the following comparison:

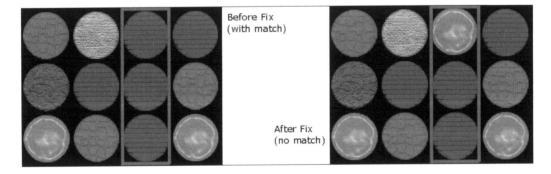

Before Fix
(with match)

After Fix
(no match)

When the board was first generated, it created an instant match, as seen within the red box in the left image. After the `fixStartingMatches` method was run, it replaced the first gem in the match (the top one, in this case) and replaced it with a new, randomly generated gem. There is no longer a three-in-a-row match, so we are done. The `fixStartingMatches` method will run itself again after this one gem is changed, just to make sure we don't have another match situation. When all three-in-a-row match conditions have been fixed in this manner, the game setup can continue.

For the remainder of the book, we will be focusing on the implementation (`.m`) files. With a few exceptions, we will not be spending time going over the details of the headers, so you will want to consult the code bundle for this book if you are uncertain about a variable or property that is used within the code presented here. Our goal is primarily to understand how the various methods and objects power the games, and most of the important details are in the implementation files.

Checking for matches

There is only one method left to see the initial board built. The method `checkForMatchesOfType` takes a `desiredGemState` value as a parameter. We do this because, during the initial board setup, we only want to check gems that are in the state `kGemNew`. Later, during actual gameplay, we only want to check for matches when the gems are in the state `kGemIdle`. (During gameplay, the gems in the `kGemNew` state will be outside the visible screen before they are dropped on to the screen, and we definitely do not want to include them in matches until they drop into position.) Let's look at the method now, in two parts:

Filename: `MAPlayfieldLayer.m` (`checkForMatchesOfType`, part 1)

```
-(void) checkForMatchesOfType:(GemType)desiredGemState {
  // Let's look for horizontal matches
  for (MAGem *aGem in gemsInPlay) {
    // Let's grab the first gem
    if (aGem.gemState == desiredGemState) {
      // If it is the desired state, let's look
      // for a matching neighbor gem
      for (MAGem *bGem in gemsInPlay) {
        // If the gem is the same type and state,
        // in the same row, and to the right
        if ([aGem isGemSameAs:bGem] &&
          [aGem isGemInSameRow:bGem] &&
            aGem.colNum == bGem.colNum - 1 &&
            bGem.gemState == desiredGemState) {
```

```
        // Now we loop through again,
        // looking for a 3rd in a row
        for (MAGem *cGem in gemsInPlay) {
          // If this is the 3rd gem in a row
          // in the desired state
          if (aGem.colNum == cGem.colNum - 2 &&
              cGem.gemState == desiredGemState) {
              // Is the gem the same type
              // and in the same row?
              if ([aGem isGemSameAs:cGem] &&
            [aGem isGemInSameRow:cGem]) {
                  // Add gems to match array
            [self addGemToMatch:aGem];
             [self addGemToMatch:bGem];
            [self addGemToMatch:cGem];
                  break;
              }
          }
        }
      }
    }
  }
}
```

This method looks a little daunting, so let's take it apart. We have two main sections, one for the horizontal matches and one for vertical matches. What we see in the preceding code is just the horizontal match checking. The outer *for* loop iterates through all of the gems in the gemsInPlay array, naming this gem aGem. We immediately check to make sure aGem has the desiredGemState value we are looking for. If not, the rest of this section is skipped. If the gemState has the desiredGemState value, we start a second *for* loop on the same gemsInPlay array, this time calling the gem being evaluated bGem. We check to see whether the following conditions are true:

- aGem is the same type as bGem (using the isGemSameAs method)
- aGem is in the same row as bGem
- aGem's colNum is equal to the bGem's colNum – 1
- bGem is in the desiredGemState

If all these conditions are true, it means that the aGem being evaluated has an identical gem to the right of it. So, we have a two-in-a-row situation. Now we start a third *for* loop using the gemsInPlay array, the same as the other two loops. With the third loop, we break the conditions into two separate *if* statements:

- aGem's colNum is equal to cGem's colNum – 2

- cGem's gem state is equal to the desiredGemState

And in the second *if* statement, we check these statements:

- aGem is of the same type as cGem

- aGem is in the same row as cGem

If all of these conditions are true, we have made a three-in-a-row match. All three gems involved in the matching are then added to the gemMatches array. Instead of adding the gems directly to the array, we use the method addGemToMatch.

Filename: MAPlayfieldLayer.m

```
-(void) addGemToMatch:(MAGem*)thisGem {
    // Only adds it to the array if it isn't already there
    if ([gemMatches indexOfObject:thisGem] == NSNotFound) {
        [gemMatches addObject:thisGem];
    }
}
```

Because we are checking the whole board, we often find multiple matches that involve the same gem. Since we only want each matching gem represented once, the addGemToMatch method checks to make sure the gem is not already in the array before adding it.

Now we can take a look at the second half of the method:

Filename: MAPlayfieldLayer.m (checkForMatchesOfType, part 2)

```
    // Let's look for vertical matches
    for (MAGem *aGem in gemsInPlay) {
      // Let's grab the first gem
      if (aGem.gemState == desiredGemState) {
        // If it is the desired state, let's look for a
        // matching neighbor gem
        for (MAGem *bGem in gemsInPlay) {
          // If the gem is the same type and state,
          // in the same column, and above
          if ([aGem isGemSameAs:bGem] &&
            [aGem isGemInSameColumn:bGem] &&
```

```
                     aGem.rowNum == bGem.rowNum - 1 &&
                bGem.gemState == desiredGemState) {
                  // Now we looking for a 3rd in the column
                  for (MAGem *cGem in gemsInPlay) {
                      // If this is the 3rd gem in a row
                      if (bGem.rowNum == cGem.rowNum - 1 &&
                          cGem.gemState == desiredGemState) {
                              // Is the gem the same type and
                      // in the same column?
                          if ([bGem isGemSameAs:cGem] &&
                              [bGem isGemInSameColumn:cGem]) {
                                  // Add gems to match array
                                  [self addGemToMatch:aGem];
                          [self addGemToMatch:bGem];
                          [self addGemToMatch:cGem];
                                  break;

                          }
                      }
                  }
              }
          }
      }
  }
}
```

The second half of this method checks for vertical matches. You will notice that the code looks strikingly similar to the horizontal check we just reviewed in detail. The vertical check is almost the same as the horizontal, except that all references to rows and columns are reversed. Everything else is in the same structure.

Collecting touches

Now that we have a board built, we need to add some mechanics to move the gems so we can make matches. Let's look at the touch handlers, starting with the ccTouchBegan method:

Filename: MAPlayfieldLayer.m

```
-(BOOL) ccTouchBegan:(UITouch *)touch withEvent:(UIEvent *)event {

    CGPoint location = [touch locationInView:[touch view]];
    CGPoint convLoc = [[CCDirector sharedDirector]
                    convertToGL:location];
```

```
    // If we reached game over, any touch returns to menu
    if (isGameOver) {
        [[CCDirector sharedDirector]
                replaceScene:[MAMenuScene scene]];
        return YES;
    }

    // If the back button was pressed, we exit
    if (CGRectContainsPoint([backButton boundingBox],
                            convLoc)) {
        [[CCDirector sharedDirector]
         replaceScene:[MAMenuScene node]];
        return YES;
    }

    // If we have only 0 or 1 gem in gemsTouched, track
    if ([gemsTouched count] < 2) {
        // Check each gem
        for (MAGem *aGem in gemsInPlay) {
            // If the gem was touched AND the gem is idle,
            // return YES to track the touch
            if ([aGem containsTouchLocation:convLoc] &&
                        aGem.gemState == kGemIdle) {
                return YES;
            }
        }
    }

    // If we failed to find any good touch, return
    return NO;
}
```

The ccTouchBegan method controls whether we track a specific touch. If we have reached a "game over" condition (indicated by the gameOver variable), we go back to the menu. We also trigger the same replaceScene method if backButton is touched. We handle these situations in ccTouchBegan, so we can override any other logic that might be going on and can leave the game whenever we want to.

This is the first time we have encountered the gemsTouched array, so we will explain it here. When the player touches any gem, we add that gem to the gemsTouched array. When we have two gems in the gemsTouched array, we swap the position of the gems and check for a match. If there are two gems in the array, we know something else is happening in the game (swapping gems, checking for matches, moving gems around, and so on), so we stop tracking the touch at that point. If we have less than two gems in the array, we iterate through the gemsInPlay array to determine which (if any) gem was touched. When we find one, we return YES to allow the touch to be tracked.

Now that we have a touch being tracked, the handler continues with the
ccTouchMoved method.

Filename: MAPlayfieldLayer.m

```
-(void) ccTouchMoved:(UITouch *)touch withEvent:(UIEvent *)event {
    // Swipes are handled here.
    [self touchHelper:touch withEvent:event];
}
```

There is not much here. This method passes everything along to our own
touchHelper method.

Filename: MAPlayfieldLayer.m

```
-(void) touchHelper:(UITouch *)touch withEvent:(UIEvent *)event {
    // If we're already checking for a match, ignore
    if ([gemsTouched count] >= 2 || gemsMoving == YES) {
        return;
    }

    CGPoint location = [touch locationInView:[touch view]];
    CGPoint convLoc = [[CCDirector sharedDirector]
                        convertToGL:location];

    // Let's figure out which gem was touched (if any)
    for (MAGem *aGem in gemsInPlay) {
        if ([aGem containsTouchLocation:convLoc] &&
            aGem.gemState == kGemIdle) {
            // We can't add the same gem twice
            if ([gemsTouched containsObject:aGem] == NO) {
                // Add the gem to the array
                [self playDing];
                [gemsTouched addObject:aGem];
                [aGem highlightGem];
            }
        }
    }

    // We now have touched 2 gems.  Let's swap them.
    if ([gemsTouched count] >= 2) {
        MAGem *aGem = [gemsTouched objectAtIndex:0];
        MAGem *bGem = [gemsTouched objectAtIndex:1];

        // If the gems are adjacent, we can swap
```

```
            if ([aGem isGemBeside:bGem]) {
                [self swapGem:aGem withGem:bGem];
            } else {
                // They're not adjacent, so let's drop
                // the first gem
                [aGem stopHighlightGem];
                [gemsTouched removeObject:aGem];
            }
        }
    }
```

As the player slides their finger on the board, ccTouchMoved will be triggered constantly, which in turn will call the touchHelper method repeatedly. The first check is to make sure that we don't already have two objects in the gemsTouched array (the same "protection" as in ccTouchBegan) and to make sure we don't have any gems moving (where the gemsMoving variable is YES). If we do, we call return, to stop tracking this touch.

If the touch comes in contact with a gem, and the gem is not already in the gemsTouched array, we play a sound, add it to the gemsTouched array, and send a message to the gem to run the highlightGem method. Since this code is called from the ccTouchMoved method, each gem will be added to the array (up to the stated maximum of two) as we swipe across multiple gems. We have swipe detection without needing any gesture detection code.

The final *if* statement is to check whether we have gathered two gems in the gemsTouched array. If we have, we first check to make sure the gems are adjacent (the isGemBeside method). If they are adjacent, we call swapGem and pass the two gems to that method. If not, we stop highlighting the first gem in the array and remove it from the gemsTouched array, so the second touch is now the only gem in the gemsTouched array.

Now let's look at the final touch handler method, ccTouchEnded.

Filename: MAPlayfieldLayer.m

```
-(void) ccTouchEnded:(UITouch *)touch withEvent:(UIEvent *)event {
    // Taps are handled here.
    [self touchHelper:touch withEvent:event];
}
```

What's going on here? The checks that we needed in the ccTouchEnded method are exactly the same checks that we used in the ccTouchMoved method, so we can call the same code, rather than copying all the code into both methods; this is why we created the touchHelper method. Looking at both the ccTouchMoved and ccTouchEnded methods together, we have the flexibility to be able to swipe or tap on gems to select them. ccTouchMoved is only called when the touch moves (that is, a swipe), so a simple tap will not activate the code in that method. The ccTouchEnded method is only called when the touch ends (that is, the finger is lifted off the screen). By triggering the same code in both places, we can cover both styles of player interaction.

Moving gems

Let's briefly look at the methods we use to handle gem movements:

Filename: MAPlayfieldLayer.m

```
- (void) swapGem: (MAGem*) aGem withGem: (MAGem*) bGem {
    NSInteger tempRowNumA;
    NSInteger tempColNumA;

    // Stop the highlight
    [aGem stopHighlightGem];
    [bGem stopHighlightGem];

    // Grab the temp location of aGem
    tempRowNumA = [aGem rowNum];
    tempColNumA = [aGem colNum];

    // Set the aGem to the values from bGem
    [aGem setRowNum:[bGem rowNum]];
    [aGem setColNum:[bGem colNum]];

    // Set the bGem to the values from the aGem temp vars
    [bGem setRowNum:tempRowNumA];
    [bGem setColNum:tempColNumA];
    // Move the gems
    [self moveToNewSlotForGem:aGem];
    [self moveToNewSlotForGem:bGem];
}
```

The `swapGem` method is very basic. We use temporary variables to assist with swapping the `rowNum` and `colNum` values of the two gems passed to the method. After they are changed, we call the `moveToNewSlotForGem` method on both gems.

Filename: `MAPlayfieldLayer.m`

```
-(void) moveToNewSlotForGem:(MAGem*)aGem {
    // Set the gem's state to moving
    [aGem setGemState:kGemMoving];

    // Move the gem, play sound, let it rest
    CCMoveTo *moveIt = [CCMoveTo
            actionWithDuration:0.2
            position:[self positionForRow:[aGem rowNum]
                            andColumn:[aGem colNum]]];
    CCCallFunc *playSound = [CCCallFunc
            actionWithTarget:self
                selector:@selector(playSwoosh)];
    CCCallFuncND *gemAtRest = [CCCallFuncND
            actionWithTarget:self
            selector:@selector(gemIsAtRest:) data:aGem];
    [aGem runAction:[CCSequence actions:moveIt,
                    playSound, gemAtRest, nil]];
}
```

The `moveToNewSlotForGem` method first sets the gem's state to `kGemMoving`, so this gem will not take part in any matching logic while in motion. Then, we use a `CCMoveTo` action to move the gem where it should be (based on the new `rowNum` and `colNum` variables we just assigned to it), play a sound effect, and then call the `gemIsAtRest` method.

Filename: `MAPlayfieldLayer.m`

```
-(void) gemIsAtRest:(MAGem*)aGem {
    // Reset the gem's state to Idle
    [aGem setGemState:kGemIdle];

    // Identify that we need to check for matches
    checkMatches = YES;
}
```

The `gemIsAtRest` method resets the gem's state, so it is now `kGemIdle`. This means it will now be allowed to participate in any matching checks that are performed on the board. We also set the `checkMatches` variable to YES. This is the trigger we use to identify that the board is now stable enough to check for a potential match.

Checking moves

We are close to completing a basic Match 3 game. Let's look at a couple more methods we need to finish it.

Filename: `MAPlayfieldLayer.m`

```
-(void) checkMove {
    // A move was made, so check for potential matches
    [self checkForMatchesOfType:kGemIdle];

    // Did we have any matches?
    if ([gemMatches count] > 0) {
        // Iterate through all matched gems
        for (MAGem *aGem in gemMatches) {
            // If the gem is not already in scoring state
            if (aGem.gemState != kGemScoring) {
                // Trigger the scoring & removal of gem
                [self animateGemRemoval:aGem];
            }
        }
        // All matches processed.  Clear the array.
        [gemMatches removeAllObjects];
    // If we have any selected/touched gems, we must
    // have made an incorrect move
    } else if ([gemsTouched count] > 0) {
        // If there was only one gem, grab it
        MAGem *aGem = [gemsTouched objectAtIndex:0];

        // If we had 2 gems in the touched array
        if ([gemsTouched count] == 2) {
            // Grab the second gem
            MAGem *bGem = [gemsTouched objectAtIndex:1];
            // Swap them back to their original slots
            [self swapGem:aGem withGem:bGem];
        } else {
            // If we only had 1 gem, stop highlighting it
            [aGem stopHighlightGem];
        }
```

```
    }
    // Touches were processed.  Clear the touched array.
    [gemsTouched removeAllObjects];
}
```

By now, you should be familiar enough with the way the gem arrays are handled in this code, and so you should find this method pretty simple. First, we call the `checkForMatchesOfType` method to populate the `gemMatches` array with matching gems (if any are found). If we find any matches, all matching gems are sent to the `animateGemRemoval` method. Once that loop is complete, we remove all gems from the `gemMatches` array. If we have any gems in the `gemsTouched` array, we call `stopHighlightGem` on them. If there were two gems in that array, it means we had a move that did not make a match, so we call `swapGem` to move them back to where they started from. After that has been resolved, we clear the `gemsTouched` array. By the end of this method, the two temporary arrays are empty and all matches have been resolved.

Removing gems

Now let's look at the methods used to remove gems from the board:

Filename: `MAPlayfieldLayer.m`

```
-(void) animateGemRemoval:(MAGem*)aGem {
    // We swap the image to "boom", and animate it out
    CCCallFuncND *changeImage = [CCCallFuncND
            actionWithTarget:self
            selector:@selector(changeGemFace:) data:aGem];
    CCCallFunc *updateScore = [CCCallFunc
            actionWithTarget:self
            selector:@selector(incrementScore)];
    CCCallFunc *addTime = [CCCallFunc
            actionWithTarget:self
            selector:@selector(addTimeToTimer)];
    CCMoveBy *moveUp = [CCMoveBy actionWithDuration:0.3
            position:ccp(0,5)];
    CCFadeOut *fade = [CCFadeOut actionWithDuration:0.2];
    CCCallFuncND *removeGem = [CCCallFuncND
            actionWithTarget:self
            selector:@selector(removeGem:) data:aGem];

    [aGem runAction:[CCSequence actions:changeImage,
            updateScore, addTime, moveUp, fade,
            removeGem, nil]];
}
-(void) changeGemFace:(MAGem*)aGem {
    // Swap the gem texture to the "boom" image
```

```
        [aGem setDisplayFrame:[[CCSpriteFrameCache
                          sharedSpriteFrameCache]
                      spriteFrameByName:@"boom.png"]];
}


-(void) removeGem:(MAGem*)aGem {
    // Clean up after ourselves and get rid of this gem
    [gemsInPlay removeObject:aGem];
    [aGem setGemState:kGemScoring];
    [self fillHolesFromGem:aGem];
    [aGem removeFromParentAndCleanup:YES];
    checkMatches = YES;
}
```

These three methods, taken together, handle everything we need to neatly animate
a matched gem. changeGemFace uses a method we haven't seen before. Since all
of our images are part of the same CCSpriteBatchNode, we are able to use the
setDisplayFrame method to change the image of the sprite on the fly. Here, we
replace the gem's image with the "boom" image. We move it up the screen and fade it
out, so it disappears from the board neatly. (We also update the score and add time to
the timer, but we won't be discussing those features of the game here. If you don't use
a score or a timer, you can easily remove those actions.) There is one important method
called from the removeGem method, fillHolesFromGem. Let's see what it does:

Filename: MAPlayfieldLayer.m

```
-(void) fillHolesFromGem:(MAGem*)aGem {
    // aGem passed is one that is being scored.
    // We know we will need to fill in the holes, so
    // this method takes care of that.

    for (MAGem *thisGem in gemsInPlay) {
        // If thisGem is in the same column and ABOVE
        // the current matching gem, we reset the
        // position down, so we can fill the hole
        if (aGem.colNum == thisGem.colNum &&
            aGem.rowNum < thisGem.rowNum) {
            // Set thisGem to drop down one row
            [thisGem setRowNum:thisGem.rowNum - 1];
            [self moveToNewSlotForGem:thisGem];
        }
    }


    // Call the smart fill method.
    [self smartFill];
}
```

This method looks for any gems that are in the same column as the passed gem, aGem. We iterate through the gemsInPlay array, looking for any gems in a row above aGem, reset their rowNum variable to one row lower, and then trigger the moveToNewSlotForGem method. This will effectively fill in any gaps in the board. It doesn't add any new gems to the board, but collapses them all downward so any remaining holes are at the top of the board. (The smartFill method is covered in the *Predictive logic* section of this chapter.)

The update method

We now turn our attention to the update method, which will tie it all together.

Filename: MAPlayfieldLayer.m

```
-(void) update:(ccTime)dt {

    gemsMoving = NO;

    // See if we have any gems currently moving
    for (MAGem *aGem in gemsInPlay) {
        if (aGem.gemState == kGemMoving) {
            gemsMoving = YES;
            break;
        }
    }

    // If we flagged that we need to check the board
    if (checkMatches) {
        [self checkMove];
        [self checkMovesRemaining];
        checkMatches = NO;
    }

    // Too few gems left.  Let's fill it up.
    // This will avoid any holes if our smartFill left
    // gaps, which is common on 4 and 5 gem matches.
    if ([gemsInPlay count] < boardRows * boardColumns &&
        gemsMoving == NO) {
        [self addGemsToFillBoard];
    }

    // Update the timer value & display

    // Game Over / Time's Up

    }
}
```

Now we tie together a couple of loose ends in the code. We start with the gemsMoving BOOL, which we used in the touch handler. We set the value in the update method by iterating through all the gems to determine whether there are any gems in the state kGemMoving. If any gems are moving, gemsMoving is set to YES.

The BOOL checkMatches is next. If this variable has been set to YES, we run the checkMove method. As we saw earlier, this method takes care of handling all the matching logic and removal of matched gems. At the end of this *if* statement, we reset the checkMatches variable to NO to indicate the matches are resolved. (We will discuss checkMovesRemaining in the next section).

The final portion of the core update method checks to see if we don't have enough gems on the board and if nothing is moving. If both of these conditions are true, we call the addGemsToFillBoard method to fill in any missing gems. (There are also the timer update and the game-over checks at the end. We will not be discussing those here, so the code details have been omitted. Please see the accompanying code for those portions of the update method.)

Filename: MAPlayfieldLayer.m

```
-(void) addGemsToFillBoard {
    // Loop through all positions, see if we have a gem
    for (int i = 1; i <= boardRows; i++) {
        for (int j = 1; j <= boardColumns; j++) {

            BOOL missing = YES;

            // Look for a missing gem in each slot
            for (MAGem *aGem in gemsInPlay) {
                if (aGem.rowNum == i && aGem.colNum == j
                    && aGem.gemState != kGemScoring) {
                    // Found a gem, not missing
                    missing = NO;
                }
            }
            // We didn't find anything in this slot.
            if (missing) {
                [self addGemForRow:i andColumn:j
                        ofType:kGemAnyType];
            }
        }
    }
    // We possibly changed the board, trigger match check
    checkMatches = YES;
}
```

We iterate through all the spaces on the board, and then, through all the gems in the `gemsInPlay` array. If we find a gem in that slot, we set the `missing` variable to `NO`. If we do not find a gem in a given slot (that is, `missing = YES`), we call the `addGemForRow` method to add a new random gem to fill in that slot.

Predictive logic

So far, we have mostly covered straightforward code that takes care of basic game mechanics. There is one problem, though. The game can produce a board that is impossible to make a move on. Worse, we have no way of knowing that there are no more moves remaining. We aim to correct that deficiency now, in a rather dense method called `checkMovesRemaining`. First, we should cover the basic concept of how this is accomplished.

If you recall, the `checkForMatchesOfType` method we reviewed earlier did a good job of finding any actual matches on the board. We could code this predictive method in that style, but it quickly gets confusing since you need to be able to determine matches up to five gems in a row to get an accurate count of moves remaining. Here, we take another approach by writing the `gemType` values into a "C-style" array, so we can easily get a single view of the whole board without massive nested loops.

The challenge is determining all the possible ways a player can legally move a gem and how the board would look after the move. We iterate through all positions from the bottom left corner, and we will test what happens if the gem is moved to the right, and also what happens if the gem is moved up. Even though the player can also move left and down, those will already be taken care of because swapping one gem downwards is the same as swapping the one below it upwards.

We start our test scenarios by creating a "letter map" of the board area, with the letter "a" representing the board slot being evaluated, like so:

		j			
		h	i		
k	l	e	f	g	
m	n	a	b	c	d
		o	p		
		q	r		

We will use this letter map and assign variables to represent the value at each specified position in the array. For example, the variable f is at location row+1 and col+1, relative to the letter *a*. From there, we will test a "deformed" version of the map, first with the *a* and *b* positions swapped, and then by testing *a* and *e* swapped. From there, we count up all the matches that can be made with a single move, and we set that as the movesRemaining variable. (This code is pretty long, but there's no good way to break it up here.)

Filename: `MAPlayfieldLayer.m`

```
-(void) checkMovesRemaining {

    NSInteger matchesFound = 0;
    NSInteger gemsInAction = 0;

    // Create a temporary C-style array
    NSInteger map[12][12];

    // Make sure it is cleared
    for (int i = 1; i< 12; i++) {
        for (int j = 1; j < 12; j++) {
            map[i][j] = 0;
        }
    }

    // Load all gem types into it
    for (MAGem *aGem in gemsInPlay) {
        if (aGem.gemState != kGemIdle) {
            // If gem is moving or scoring, fill with zero
            map[aGem.rowNum][aGem.colNum] = 0;
            gemsInAction++;
        } else {
            map[aGem.rowNum][aGem.colNum] = aGem.gemType;
        }
    }

    // Loop through all slots on the board
    for (int row = 1; row <= boardRows; row++) {
        for (int col = 1; col <= boardColumns; col++) {

            // Grid variables look like:
            //
            //           j
            //          h i
            //      k l e f g
            //      m n a b c d
```

```
//        o p
//        q r

// where "a" is the root gem we're testing
// The swaps we test are a/b and a/e
// So we need to identify all possible matches
// that those swaps could cause
GemType a = map[row][col];
GemType b = map[row][col+1];
GemType c = map[row][col+2];
GemType d = map[row][col+3];
GemType e = map[row+1][col];
GemType f = map[row+1][col+1];
GemType g = map[row+1][col+2];
GemType h = map[row+2][col];
GemType i = map[row+2][col+1];
GemType j = map[row+3][col];
GemType k = map[row+1][col-2];
GemType l = map[row+1][col-1];
GemType m = map[row][col-2];
GemType n = map[row][col-1];
GemType o = map[row-1][col];
GemType p = map[row-1][col+1];
GemType q = map[row-2][col];
GemType r = map[row-2][col+1];

// deform the board-swap of a and b, test
GemType newA = b;
GemType newB = a;

matchesFound = matchesFound +
    [self findMatcheswithA:h andB:e
              andC:newA andD:o andE:q];
matchesFound = matchesFound +
    [self findMatcheswithA:i andB:f
              andC:newB andD:p andE:r];
matchesFound = matchesFound +
    [self findMatcheswithA:m andB:n
              andC:newA andD:0 andE:0];
matchesFound = matchesFound +
    [self findMatcheswithA:newB andB:c
              andC:d andD:0 andE:0];

// Now we swap a and e, then test
newA = e;
GemType newE = a;
```

```
        matchesFound = matchesFound +
            [self findMatcheswithA:m andB:n
                        andC:newA andD:b andE:c];
        matchesFound = matchesFound +
            [self findMatcheswithA:k andB:l
                        andC:newE andD:f andE:g];
        matchesFound = matchesFound +
            [self findMatcheswithA:newA andB:o
                        andC:q andD:0 andE:0];
        matchesFound = matchesFound +
            [self findMatcheswithA:newE andB:h
                        andC:j andD:0 andE:0];
    }
}


    // See if we have gems in motion on the board
    // Set the BOOL so other methods don't try to fix
    // any "problems" with a moving board
    gemsMoving = (gemsInAction > 0);

    movesRemaining = matchesFound;
}
```

To keep the positioning straight, you can see that we have put in a textual version of the letter map into the code. This is a convenience, since trying to read the patterns from the code itself is rather tiresome and challenging. When we look at possible matches after deforming the board, there are four possible ways we can match for each of the deformations, as illustrated here:

if a and b swap	if a and e swap
checks needed for:	checks needed for:
h, e, a, o, q	m, n, a, b, c
i, f, b, p, r	k, l, e, f, g
m, n, a	a, o, q
b, c, d	j, h, e

To assist with this checking, we add a helper method.

Filename: `MAPlayfieldLayer.m`

```
-(NSInteger) findMatcheswithA:(NSInteger)a
                        andB:(NSInteger)b
                        andC:(NSInteger)c
                        andD:(NSInteger)d
                        andE:(NSInteger)e {
    NSInteger matches = 0;

    if (a == b && b == c && c == d && d == e &&
                        a + b + c + d + e != 0) {
        // 5 match
        matches++;
    } else if (a == b && b == c && c == d  &&
                        a + b + c + d != 0) {
        // 4 match (left)
        matches++;
    } else if (b == c && c == d && d == e &&
                        b + c + d + e != 0) {
        // 4 match (right)
        matches++;
    } else if (a == b && b == c && a + b + c != 0) {
        // 3 match (left)
        matches++;
    } else if (b == c && c == d && b + c + d != 0) {
        // 3 match (mid)
        matches++;
    } else if (c == d && d == e && c + d + e != 0) {
        // 3 match (right)
        matches++;
    }
    return matches;
}
```

Any combination of five gems could result in a match of three, four, or five in a row. We pass five gems in a row to this method, and it checks for five in a row first, then four in a row, and then three in a row. It is an *if...else-if* structure because a five-in-a-row match would also trigger as four-in-a-row and three-in-a-row matches, so we let it act as a waterfall to avoid over-counting the matches. You will also notice that we are making sure that one of the variables is not 0. As we saw in the `checkMovesRemaining` method itself, we only record the gem type for gems that are in the `kGemIdle` state. All other gem states (`kGemMoving`, `kGemScoring`, and `kGemNew`), as well as positions off the board, will be represented as 0 in the map.

Artificial randomness

So now, we can evaluate the board to see all potential moves. Then what? We could put in a trigger in the `update` method to flash a "no more moves" message and cause game over, but that's no fun, is it? Our goal is to make a game that will keep going forever. This is where we are finally ready to find out details of the `smartFill` method we saw in the code earlier. This is a really long method, listed in its entirety. It is a critical method to the process, so please bear with us.

Filename: `MAPlayfieldLayer.m`

```
-(void) smartFill {
    // In case we were scheduled, unschedule it first
    [self unschedule:@selector(smartFill)];

    // If anything is moving, we don't want to fill yet
    if (gemsMoving) {
        // We reschedule so we retry when gems not moving
        [self schedule:@selector(smartFill) interval:0.05];
        return;
    }

    // If we have plenty of matches, use a random fill
    if (movesRemaining >= 6) {
        [self addGemsToFillBoard];
        return;
    }

    // Create a temporary C-style array
    // We make it bigger than the playfield on purpose
    // This way we can evaluate past the edges
    NSInteger map[12][12];

    // Make sure it is cleared
    for (int i = 1; i< boardRows + 5; i++) {
        for (int j = 1; j < boardColumns + 5; j++) {
            if (i > boardRows || j > boardColumns) {
                // If row or column is bigger than board,
                // assign a -1 value
                map[i][j] = -1;
            } else {
                // If it is on the board, zero it
                map[i][j] = 0;
            }
```

```
        }
    }

    // Load all gem types into it
    for (MAGem *aGem in gemsInPlay) {
        // We don't want to include scoring gems
        if (aGem.gemState == kGemScoring) {
            map[aGem.rowNum][aGem.colNum] = 0;
        } else {
            // Assign the gemType to the array slot
            map[aGem.rowNum][aGem.colNum] = aGem.gemType;
        }
    }

    // Parse through the map, looking for zeroes
    for (int row = 1; row <= boardRows; row++) {
        for (int col = 1; col <= boardColumns; col++) {

            // We use "intelligent randomness" to fill
            // holes when close to running out of matches

            // Grid variables look like:
            //
            //          h
            //         e   g
            //        n a b c
            //        s o p t
            //

            // where "a" is the root gem we're testing

            GemType a = map[row][col];
            GemType b = map[row][col+1];
            GemType c = map[row][col+2];
            GemType e = map[row+1][col];
            GemType g = map[row+1][col+2];
            GemType h = map[row+2][col];
            GemType n = map[row][col-1];
            GemType o = map[row-1][col];
            GemType p = map[row-1][col+1];
            GemType s = map[row-1][col-1];
            GemType t = map[row-1][col+2];

            // Vertical hole, 3 high
```

```
if (a == 0 && e == 0 && h == 0) {
    if ((int)p >= 1) {
        [self addGemForRow:row andColumn:col
                    ofType:p];
        [self addGemForRow:row+1 andColumn:col
                    ofType:p];
        [self addGemForRow:row+2 andColumn:col
                    ofType:kGemAnyType];
        [self checkMovesRemaining];
        [self smartFill];
        return;
    }

    if ((int)s >= 1) {
        [self addGemForRow:row andColumn:col
                    ofType:s];
        [self addGemForRow:row+1 andColumn:col
                    ofType:s];
        [self addGemForRow:row+2 andColumn:col
                    ofType:kGemAnyType];
        [self checkMovesRemaining];
        [self smartFill];
        return;
    }

    if ((int)n >= 1) {
        [self addGemForRow:row andColumn:col
                    ofType:kGemAnyType];
        [self addGemForRow:row+1 andColumn:col
                    ofType:n];
        [self addGemForRow:row+2 andColumn:col
                    ofType:n];
        [self checkMovesRemaining];
        [self smartFill];
        return;
    }

    if ((int)b >= 1) {
        [self addGemForRow:row andColumn:col
                    ofType:kGemAnyType];
        [self addGemForRow:row+1 andColumn:col
                    ofType:b];
        [self addGemForRow:row+2 andColumn:col
                    ofType:b];
```

```
        [self checkMovesRemaining];
        [self smartFill];
        return;
    }
}


// Horizontal hole, 3 high
if (a == 0 && b == 0 && c == 0) {
    if ((int)o >= 1) {
        [self addGemForRow:row andColumn:col
                    ofType:kGemAnyType];
        [self addGemForRow:row andColumn:col+1
                    ofType:o];
        [self addGemForRow:row andColumn:col+2
                    ofType:o];
        [self checkMovesRemaining];
        [self smartFill];
        return;
    }

    if ((int)t >= 1) {
        [self addGemForRow:row andColumn:col
                    ofType:t];
        [self addGemForRow:row andColumn:col+1
                    ofType:t];
        [self addGemForRow:row andColumn:col+2
                    ofType:kGemAnyType];
        [self checkMovesRemaining];
        [self smartFill];
        return;
    }

    if ((int)e >= 1) {
        [self addGemForRow:row andColumn:col
                    ofType:kGemAnyType];
        [self addGemForRow:row andColumn:col+1
                    ofType:e];
        [self addGemForRow:row andColumn:col+2
                    ofType:e];
        [self checkMovesRemaining];
        [self smartFill];
        return;
    }
```

```
        if ((int)g >= 1) {
            [self addGemForRow:row andColumn:col
                    ofType:g];
            [self addGemForRow:row andColumn:col+1
                    ofType:g];
            [self addGemForRow:row andColumn:col+2
                    ofType:kGemAnyType];
            [self checkMovesRemaining];
            [self smartFill];
            return;
        }
    }
  }
 }
}
```

This structure of code should look familiar to you, as it uses the same design structure as the checkMovesRemaining method. It uses the same "map" array concept, albeit with fewer variables needed for this method. There are two subtle differences in the top portion of the code. The first is that if the gemsMoving variable is YES, we schedule the smartFill method with an interval of 0.05 and immediately exit the method (with the return statement). The first thing the method does, in fact, is unschedule itself if it was already scheduled. This causes the smartFill method to wait until the board has stabilized with nothing moving. This allows us to always check a static board without worrying about the difference between an empty slot and a slot with a moving gem.

The second interesting portion of the top of the method is the check for whether movesRemaining is greater than or equal to six. If that is true, we have plenty of moves remaining, so the addGemsToFillBoard method we saw earlier will be called, which will generate random gems to fill in the board. Why six? Ideally, we would want to be able to kick in this smartFill method only when we are down to one or two moves remaining, but since a single move has the potential of eliminating several other moves (by shifting the board, or by using gems that were also potentially part of another match), testing showed six is a safe number to use to avoid a deadlocked board.

We also have one difference in the way the map is populated. In this case, we check if any position is outside of the actual board area and assign a value of -1. If it is a "hole in the board", it will be assigned 0. In this way, we can make sure we are only filling in the board itself, and not areas outside the board. (These external -1 values are sometimes called **sentinel values** because they guard the edges of the board.)

Here is our fill-in map for the `smartFill` method:

The goal is to fill in the holes in the board with something that will be usable in making a match. We do this by copying a nearby gem, so we can guarantee a match. However, depending on where on the board the hole is, we cannot always guarantee there will be a single gem we can always clone (relative to the hole), so we iterate through a few likely possibilities until we find one and then call `smartFill` again to take care of any further holes. You will notice that, in all situations, we clone two gems and leave the third gem to be set as `kGemAnyType`—randomized. This gives us some level of randomness that adds spice to the situation, even as we spoon feed the player a viable board.

This `smartFill` method does not do a complete job by itself; it can leave small 1- or 2-gem holes if there is a four-in-a-row or five-in-a-row match. The remaining holes will be filled in by the call to the `addGemsToFillBoard` method in the update loop. This is by design, since we did not want to add even more code to handle artificial randomness for 4- and 5-gem holes. The added calculations required are not necessary to fulfill our goal of keeping the game going. As a final note, if you want to remove all of the "artificial randomness", you only have to comment out the call to the `smartFill` method at the end of the `fillHolesFromGem` method. Of course, then you will need to add a "no more moves" handler to react to that situation.

Summary

We have covered a lot of ground in a short period of time, and we've covered more than one approach to some of the challenges this game presents to us. We have learned how to control a grid of gems with the appearance of gravity (in other words, filling in holes), we have learned how to match by using nested *for* loops. We have also learned how to check for matches and how to check for predictive matches using a "C-style" array without forcing ourselves to use C-style arrays throughout the code. Finally, we addressed the idea of artificial randomness to give the player an ongoing game experience without risking a "no more moves" situation.

The code bundle for this chapter also includes both scoring and a progress timer, which we saw traces of but didn't really discuss here. The implementation is very simple, so we leave it to you, the reader, to explore these features on your own. The example "tests" contained within the sample projects included with the cocos2d download are a great resource for lesser-known classes, such as `CCProgressTimer`.

In the next chapter, we will tackle a classic mole-whacking game, and learn how to trick the player's eye.

3
Thumping Moles for Fun

We will be continuing our journey through classic gameplay styles in this chapter. We will talk a little about different approaches to solve the design challenges in this chapter. In game programming, there are always many ways to solve the same problem, there is no single right answer.

In this chapter, we will cover:

- Tricking the eye with Z-ordering
- Reusing objects
- Detecting touch on the part of a sprite
- Animations and movement actions
- Randomized objects

The project is…

In this chapter, we will be building a mole thumping game. Inspired by mechanical games of the past, we will build molehills on the screen and randomly cause animated moles to pop their heads out. The player taps them to score. Simple in concept, but there are a few challenging design considerations in this deceptively easy game. To make this game a little unusual, we will be using a penguin instead of a mole for the graphics, but we will continue to use the mole terminology throughout, since a molehill is easier to consider than a penguin-hill.

Design approach

Before diving into the code, let's start with a discussion of the design of the game. First, we will need to have molehills on the screen. To be aesthetically pleasing, the molehills will be in a 3 x 4 grid. Another approach would be to use random molehill positions, but that doesn't really work well on the limited screen space of the iPhone. Moles will randomly spawn from the molehills. Each mole will rise up, pause, and drop down. We will need touch handling to detect when a mole has been touched, and that mole will need to increase the player's score and then go away.

How do we make the mole come up from underground? If we assume the ground is a big sprite with the molehills drawn on it, we would need to determine where to make the "slot" from which the mole emerges, and somehow make the mole disappear when it is below that slot. One approach is to adjust the size of the mole's displayed frame by clipping the bottom of the image so that the part below the ground is not visible. This needs to be done as a part of every update cycle for every mole for the entire game. From a programming standpoint this will work, but you may experience performance issues. Another consideration is that this usually means the hole in the molehill will always appear to be a straight-edged hole, if we trim the sprite with a straight line. This lacks the organic feel we want for this game.

The approach we will take is to use Z-ordering to trick the eye into seeing a flat playfield when everything is really on staggered Z-orders. We will create a "stair step" board, with multiple "sandwiches" of graphics for every row of molehills on the board.

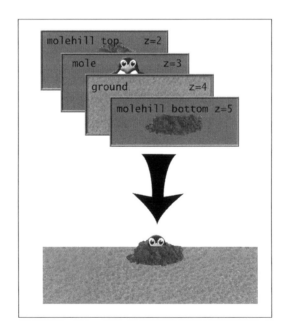

For each "step" of the "stair step", we have a sandwich of Z-ordered elements in this order, from back to front: molehill top, mole, ground, and molehill bottom. We need to have everything aligned so that the molehill top graphic overlaps the ground of the next "step" further towards the top of the screen. This will visually contain the mole, so it appears to be emerging from inside the molehill.

We intentionally skipped the Z value of 1, to provide an extra expansion space if we later decide that we need another element in the "sandwich". It is easier to leave little holes like this than to worry about changing everything later, if we enhance our design. So throughout our layout, we will consider it as a sandwich of five Z values, even though we only use four elements in the sandwich.

As we said, we need this to be a "stair step" board. So for each row of molehills, from the top of the screen to the bottom, we will need to increase the Z-ordering between layers to complete the illusion. This is needed so that each mole will actually pass in front of the ground layer that is closer to the top of the screen, yet will hide completely behind the ground layer in its own sandwich of layers.

Designing the spawn

That covers the physical design of the game, but there is one additional design aspect we need to discuss: spawning moles. We need to spawn the moles whenever we need one to be put into the play. Just as we reviewed two approaches to the hiding mole problem earlier, we will touch on two approaches to mole spawning.

The first approach (and most common) is to create a new mole from scratch each time you need one. When you are done with it, you destroy it. This works fine for games with a small number of objects or games of more limited complexity, but there is a performance penalty to create and destroy a lot of objects in a short amount of time. Strictly speaking, our mole thumping game would likely work fine with this approach. Even though we will be creating and destroying quite a few moles all the time, we only have a dozen possible moles, not hundreds.

The other approach is to create a spawning pool. This is basically a set number of the objects that are created when you start up. When you need a mole, in our case, you ask the pool for an unused "blank mole", set any parameters that are needed, and use it. When you are done with it, you reset it back to the "blank mole" state, and it goes back into the pool.

For our game the spawning pool might be a little more heavily coded than needed, as it is doubtful that we would run into any performance issues with this relatively simple game. Still, if you are willing to build the additional code as we are doing here, it does provide a strong foundation to add more performance-heavy effects later on.

To clarify our design approach, we will actually implement a variation of the traditional spawning pool. Instead of a general pool of moles, we will build our "blank mole" objects attached to their molehills. A more traditional spawning pool might have six "blank moles" in the pool, and they are assigned to a molehill when they are needed. Both approaches are perfectly valid.

Portrait mode

The default orientation supported by cocos2d is landscape mode, which is more commonly used in games. However, we want our game to be in portrait mode. The changes are very simple to make this work. If you click once on the project name (and blue icon) in the **Project Navigator** pane (where all your files are listed), and then click on the name of your game under **TARGETS**, you will see the **Summary** pane. Under the **Supported Interface Orientations**, select **Portrait**, and deselect **Landscape Left** and **Landscape Right**. That will change your project to portrait. The one adjustment to the cocos2d template code we need is in the IntroLayer.m. After it sets the background to Default.png, there is a command to rotate the background. Remove, or comment out this line, and everything will work correctly.

Custom TTF fonts

In this project we will be using a custom TTF font. In cocos2d 1.x, you could simply add the font to your project and use it. Under cocos2d 2.0, which we are using, we have to approach this a little differently. We add the font to our project (we are using anudrg.ttf). Then we edit the Info.plist for our project, and add a new key to the list, like this:

▼ Fonts provided by application	Array	(1 item)
Item 0	String	anudrg.ttf

This tells the project that we need to know about this font. To actually use the font, we need to call it by the proper name for the font, not the filename. To find out this name, in **Finder**, select the file and choose **File Info**. In the info box, there is an entry for **Full Name**. In our case, the file name is AnuDaw. Any time we create a label with CCLabelTTF, we simply need to use this as the font name, and everything works perfectly.

Defining a molehill

We have created a new subclass of CCNode to represent the MXMoleHill object. Yes, we will be using a subclass of CCNode, not a subclass of CCSprite. Even though we initially would consider the molehill to be a sprite, referring back to our design, it is actually made up of *two* sprites, one for the top of the hill and one for the bottom. We will use CCNode as a container that will then contain two CCSprite objects as variables inside the MXMoleHill class.

Filename: MXMoleHill.h

```
@interface MXMoleHill : CCNode {

  NSInteger moleHillID;
  CCSprite *moleHillTop;
  CCSprite *moleHillBottom;
  NSInteger moleHillBaseZ;
  MXMole *hillMole;
  BOOL isOccupied;
}

@property (nonatomic, assign) NSInteger moleHillID;
@property (nonatomic, retain) CCSprite *moleHillTop;
@property (nonatomic, retain) CCSprite *moleHillBottom;
@property (nonatomic, assign) NSInteger moleHillBaseZ;
@property (nonatomic, retain) MXMole *hillMole;
@property (nonatomic, assign) BOOL isOccupied;

@end
```

If this seems rather sparse to you, it is. As we will be using this as a container for everything that defines the hill, we don't need to override any methods from the standard CCNode class. Likewise, the @implementation file contains nothing but the @synthesize statements for these variables.

It is worth pointing out that we could have used a CCSprite object for the hillTop sprite, with the hillBottom object as a child of that sprite, and achieved the same effect. However, we prefer consistency in our object structure, so we have opted to use the structure noted previously. This allows us to refer to the two sprites in exactly the same fashion, as they are both children of the same parent.

Building the mole

When we start building the playfield, we will be creating "blank mole" objects for each hill, so we need to look at the MXMole class before we build the playfield. Following the same design decision as we did with the MXMoleHill class, the MXMole class is also a subclass of CCNode.

Filename: MXMole.h

```
#import <Foundation/Foundation.h>
#import "cocos2d.h"
#import "MXDefinitions.h"
#import "SimpleAudioEngine.h"

// Forward declaration, since we don't want to import it here
@class MXMoleHill;

@interface MXMole : CCNode <CCTargetedTouchDelegate> {
  CCSprite *moleSprite;  // The sprite for the mole
    MXMoleHill *parentHill;  // The hill for this mole
  float moleGroundY;  // Where "ground" is
    MoleState _moleState; // Current state of the mole
    BOOL isSpecial; // Is this a "special" mole?
}

@property (nonatomic, retain) MXMoleHill *parentHill;
@property (nonatomic, retain) CCSprite *moleSprite;
@property (nonatomic, assign) float moleGroundY;
@property (nonatomic, assign) MoleState moleState;
@property (nonatomic, assign) BOOL isSpecial;

-(void) destroyTouchDelegate;

@end
```

We see a forward declaration here (the @class statement). Use of forward declaration avoids creating a circular loop, because the MXMoleHill.h file needs to import MXMole.h. In our case, MXMole needs to know there is a valid class called MXMoleHill, so we can store a reference to an MXMoleHill object in the parentHill instance variable, but we don't actually need to import the class. The @class declaration is an instruction to the compiler that there is a valid class called MXMoleHill, but doesn't actually import the header while compiling the MXMole class. If we needed to call the methods of MXMoleHill from the MXMole class, we could then put the actual #import "MXMoleHill.h" line in the MXMole.m file. For our current project, we only need to know the class exists, so we don't need that additional line in the MXMole.m file.

We have built a simple state machine for `MoleState`. Now that we have reviewed the `MXMole.h` file, we have a basic idea of what makes up a mole. It tracks the state of the mole (dead, alive, and so on), it keeps a reference to its parent hill, and it has `CCSprite` as a child where the actual mole sprite variable will be held. There are a couple of other variables (`moleGroundY` and `isSpecial`), but we will deal with these later.

Filename: `MXDefinitions.h`

```
typedef enum {
    kMoleDead = 0,
    kMoleHidden,
    kMoleMoving,
    kMoleHit,
    kMoleAlive
} MoleState;

#define SND_MOLE_NORMAL @"penguin_call.caf"
#define SND_MOLE_SPECIAL @"penguin_call_echo.caf"
#define SND_BUTTON @"button.caf"
```

Unlike in the previous chapter, we do not have `typedef enum` that defines the `MoleState` type inside this header file. We have moved our definitions to the `MXDefinitions.h` file, which helps to maintain slightly cleaner code. You can store these "universal" definitions in a single header file, and include the header in any `.h` or `.m` files where they are needed, without needing to import classes just to gain access to these definitions. The `MXDefinitions.h` file only includes the definitions; there are no `@interface` or `@implementation` sections, nor a related `.m` file.

Making a molehill

We have our molehill class and we've seen the mole class, so now we can look at how we actually build the molehills in the `MXPlayfieldLayer` class:

Filename: `MXPlayfieldLayer.m`

```
-(void) drawHills {
    NSInteger hillCounter = 0;
    NSInteger newHillZ = 6;

    // We want to draw a grid of 12 hills
    for (NSInteger row = 1; row <= 4; row++) {
        // Each row reduces the Z order
        newHillZ--;
```

```
for (NSInteger col = 1; col <= 3; col++) {
    hillCounter++;

    // Build a new MXMoleHill
    MXMoleHill *newHill = [[MXMoleHill alloc] init];
    [newHill setPosition:[self
        hillPositionForRow:row andColumn:col]];
    [newHill setMoleHillBaseZ:newHillZ];
    [newHill setMoleHillTop:[CCSprite
        spriteWithSpriteFrameName:@"pileTop.png"]];
    [newHill setMoleHillBottom:[CCSprite
        spriteWithSpriteFrameName:@"pileBottom.png"]];
    [newHill setMoleHillID:hillCounter];

    // We position the two moleHill sprites so
    // the "seam" is at the edge.  We use the
    // size of the top to position both,
    // because the bottom image
    // has some overlap to add texture
    [[newHill moleHillTop] setPosition:
        ccp(newHill.position.x, newHill.position.y +
        [newHill moleHillTop].contentSize.height
            / 2)];
    [[newHill moleHillBottom] setPosition:
        ccp(newHill.position.x, newHill.position.y -
        [newHill moleHillTop].contentSize.height
            / 2)];

    //Add the sprites to the batch node
    [molesheet addChild:[newHill moleHillTop]
                    z:(2 + (newHillZ * 5))];
    [molesheet addChild:[newHill moleHillBottom]
                    z:(5 + (newHillZ * 5))];

    //Set up a mole in the hill
    MXMole *newMole = [[MXMole alloc] init];
    [newHill setHillMole:newMole];
    [[newHill hillMole] setParentHill:newHill];
    [newMole release];

    // This flatlines the values for the new mole
    [self resetMole:newHill];

    [moleHillsInPlay addObject:newHill];
    [newHill release];
    }
  }
}
```

This is a pretty dense method, so we'll walk through it one section at a time. We start by creating two nested `for` loops so we can iterate over every possible row and column position. For clarity, we named our loop variables as `row` and `column`, so we know what each represents. If you recall from the design, we decided to use a 3 x 4 grid, so we will have three columns and four rows of molehills. We create a new hill using an `alloc/init`, and then we begin filling in the variables. We set an ID number (1 through 12), and we build `CCSprite` objects to fill in the `moleHillTop` and `moleHillBottom` variables.

Filename: `MXPlayfieldLayer.m`

```
-(CGPoint) hillPositionForRow:(NSInteger)row
                 andColumn:(NSInteger)col {
    float rowPos = row * 82;
    float colPos = 54 + ((col - 1) * 104);
    return ccp(colPos,rowPos);
}
```

We also set the position using the helper method, `hillPositionForRow:andColumn:`, that returns a `CGPoint` for each molehill. (It is important to remember that `ccp` is a cocos2d shorthand term for a `CGPoint`. They are interchangeable in your code.) These calculations are based on experimentation with the layout, to create a grid that is both easy to draw as well as being visually appealing.

The one variable that needs a little extra explaining is `moleHillBaseZ`. This represents which "step" of the Z-order stair-step design this hill belongs to. We use this to aid in the calculations to determine the proper Z-ordering across the entire playfield. If you recall, we used Z-orders from 2 to 5 in the illustration of the stack of elements. When we add the `moleHillTop` and `moleHillBottom` as children of the `moleSheet` (our `CCSpriteBatchNode`), we add the Z-order of the piece of the sandwich to the "base Z" times 5. We will use a "base Z" of 5 for the stack at the bottom of the screen, and a "base Z" of 2 at the top of the screen. This will be easier to understand the reason if we look at the following chart, which shows the calculations we use for each row of molehills:

moleHillID	base Z	moleHillTop	mole	ground	moleHillBottom
1	5	z = (2 + (5 * 5)) = 27	z = (3 + (5 * 5)) = 28	z = (4 + (5 * 5)) = 29	z = (5 + (5 * 5)) = 30
4	4	z = (2 + (4 * 5)) = 22	z = (3 + (4 * 5)) = 23	z = (4 + (4 * 5)) = 24	z = (5 + (4 * 5)) = 25
7	3	z = (2 + (3 * 5)) = 17	z = (3 + (3 * 5)) = 18	z = (4 + (3 * 5)) = 19	z = (5 + (3 * 5)) = 20
10	2	z = (2 + (2 * 5)) = 12	z = (3 + (2 * 5)) = 13	z = (4 + (2 * 5)) = 14	z = (5 + (2 * 5)) = 15

As we start building our molehills at the bottom of the screen, we start with a higher Z-order first. In the preceding chart, you will see that the mole in hole 4 (second row of molehills from the bottom) will have a Z-order of 23. This will put it behind its own ground layer, which is at a Z-order of 24, but in front of the ground higher on the screen, which would be at a Z-order of 19.

It is worth calling out that since we have a grid of molehills in our design, all Z-ordering will be identical for all molehills in the same row. This is why the decrement of the `baseHillZ` variable occurs only when we are iterating through a new row.

If we refer back to the `drawHills` method itself, we also see a big calculation for the actual position of the `moleHillTop` and `moleHillBottom` sprites. We want the "seam" between these two sprites to be at the top edge of the ground image of their stack, so we set the `y` position based on the position of the `MXMoleHill` object. At first it may look like an error, because both `setPosition` statements use `contentSize` of the `moleHillTop` sprite as a part of the calculation. This is intentional, because we have a little jagged overlap between those two sprites to give it a more organic feel.

To wrap up the `drawHills` method, we allocate a new `MXMole`, assign it to the molehill that was just created, and set the cross-referencing `hillMole` and `parentHill` variables in the objects themselves. We add the molehill to our `moleHillsInPlay` array, and we clean everything up by releasing both the `newHill` and the `newMole` objects. Because the array retains a reference to the molehill, and the molehill retains a reference to the mole, we can safely release both the `newHill` and `newMole` objects in this method.

Drawing the ground

Now that we have gone over the Z-ordering "trickery", we should look at the `drawGround` method to see how we accomplish the Z-ordering in a similar fashion:

Filename: `MXPlayfieldLayer.m`

```
-(void) drawGround {
    // Randomly select a ground image
    NSString *groundName;
    NSInteger groundPick = CCRANDOM_0_1() * 2;

    switch (groundPick) {
        case 1:
            groundName = @"ground1.png";
            break;
        default: // Case 2 also falls through here
            groundName = @"ground2.png";
            break;
    }

    // Build the strips of ground from the selected image
    for (int i = 0; i < 5; i++) {
        CCSprite *groundStrip1 = [CCSprite
                spriteWithSpriteFrameName:groundName];
```

```
        [groundStrip1 setAnchorPoint:ccp(0.5,0)];
        [groundStrip1 setPosition:ccp(size.width/2,i*82)];
        [molesheet addChild:groundStrip1 z:4+((5-i) * 5)];
    }


    // Build a skybox
    skybox = [CCSprite
            spriteWithSpriteFrameName:@"skybox1.png"];
    [skybox setPosition:ccp(size.width/2,5*82)];
    [skybox setAnchorPoint:ccp(0.5,0)];
    [molesheet addChild:skybox z:1];
}
```

This format should look familiar to you. We create five CCSprite objects for the five stripes of ground, tile them from the bottom of the screen to the top, and assign the Z-order as z:4+((5-i) * 5). We do include a randomizer with two different background images, and we also include a skybox image at the top of the screen, because we want some sense of a horizon line above the mole-thumping area.

We saw anchorPoints briefly in *Chapter 1, Thanks for the Memory Game* but we should revisit them here, as they will become more important in later projects. anchorPoint is the point that is basically "center" for the sprite. The acceptable values are floats between 0 and 1. For the x axis, an anchorPoint of 0 is the left edge, and 1 is the right edge (0.5 is centered). For the y axis, an anchorPoint of 0 is the bottom edge, and 1 is the top edge. This anchorPoint is important here because that anchorPoint is the point on the object to which the setPosition method will refer. So in our code, the first groundStrip1 created will be anchored at the bottom center. When we call setPosition, the coordinate passed to setPosition needs to relate to that anchorPoint; the position set will be the bottom center of the sprite. If this is still fuzzy for you, it is a great exercise to change anchorPoint of your own CCSprite objects and see what happens on the screen.

Mole spawning

The only piece of the "sandwich" of elements we haven't seen in detail is the mole itself, so let's visit the mole spawning method to see how the mole fits in with our design:

Filename: MXPlayfieldLayer.m

```
-(void) spawnMole:(id)sender {
    // Spawn a new mole from a random, unoccupied hill
    NSInteger newMoleHill;
    BOOL isApprovedHole = FALSE;
    NSInteger rand;
```

```
if (molesInPlay == [moleHillsInPlay count] ||
      molesInPlay == maxMoles) {
  // Holes full, cannot spawn a new mole
} else {
  // Loop until we pick a hill that isn't occupied
  do {
    rand = CCRANDOM_0_1() * maxHills;

    if (rand > maxHills) { rand = maxHills; }

        MXMoleHill *testHill = [moleHillsInPlay
                                    objectAtIndex:rand];

        // Look for an unoccupied hill
    if ([testHill isOccupied] == NO) {
      newMoleHill = rand;
      isApprovedHole = YES;
      [testHill setIsOccupied:YES];
    }
  } while (isApprovedHole == NO);

  // Mark that we have a new mole in play
  molesInPlay++;

  // Grab a handle on the mole Hill
  MXMoleHill *thisHill = [moleHillsInPlay
                    objectAtIndex:newMoleHill];

  NSInteger hillZ = [thisHill moleHillBaseZ];

  // Set up the mole for this hill
  CCSprite *newMoleSprite = [CCSprite
          spriteWithSpriteFrameName:@"penguin_forward.png"];

  [[thisHill hillMole] setMoleSprite:newMoleSprite];
  [[thisHill hillMole] setMoleState:kMoleAlive];

  // We keep track of where the ground level is
  [[thisHill hillMole] setMoleGroundY:
                            thisHill.position.y];

  // Set the position of the mole based on the hill
```

```
    float newMolePosX = thisHill.position.x;
    float newMolePosY = thisHill.position.y -
        (newMoleSprite.contentSize.height/2);

    [newMoleSprite setPosition:ccp(newMolePosX,
                                    newMolePosY)];

    // See if we need this to be a "special" mole
    NSInteger moleRandomizer = CCRANDOM_0_1() * 100;

    // If we randomized under 5, make this special
    if (moleRandomizer < 5) {
            [[thisHill hillMole] setIsSpecial:YES];
    }

    //Trigger the new mole to raise
    [molesheet addChild:newMoleSprite
                        z:(3 + (hillZ * 5))];
    [self raiseMole:thisHill];
    }
}
```

The first thing we check is to make sure we don't have active moles in every molehill, and that we haven't reached the maximum number of simultaneous moles we want on screen at the same time (the maxMoles variable). If we have enough moles, we skip the rest of the loop. If we need a new mole, we enter a do...while loop that will randomly pick a molehill and check if it has the isOccupied variable set to NO (that is, no active mole in this molehill). If the randomizer picks a molehill that is already occupied, the do...while loop will pick another molehill and try again. When we find an unoccupied molehill, the code breaks out of the loop and starts to set up the mole.

As we saw earlier, there is already a "blank mole" attached to every molehill. At this point we build a new sprite to attach to the moleSprite variable of MXMole, change the moleState to kMoleAlive, and set up the coordinates for the mole to start. We want the mole to start from underground (hidden by the ground image), so we set the mole's y position as the position of the molehill minus the height of the mole.

Once we have set up the mole, we assign our calculated Z-order for this mole (based on the moleHillBaseZ variable we stored earlier for each molehill), and call the raiseMole method, which controls the animation and movement of the mole.

Special moles

We have seen two references to the `isSpecial` variable from the `MXMole` class, so now is a good time to explain how it is used. In order to break the repetitive nature of the game, we have added a "special mole" feature. When a new mole is requested to spawn in the `spawnMole` method, we generate a random number between 1 and 100. If the resulting number is less than five, then we set the `isSpecial` flag for that mole. This means that roughly 5 percent of the time the player will get a special mole. Our special moles use the same graphics as the standard mole, but we will make them flash a rainbow of colors when they are in the play. It is a small difference, but enough to set up the scoring to give extra points for the "special mole". To implement this special mole, we only need to adjust coding in three logic areas:

- When `raiseMole` is setting the mole's actions (to make it flashy)
- When we hit the mole (to play a different sound effect)
- When we score the mole (to score more points)

This is a very small task, but it is the small variations in the gameplay that will draw the players in further. Let's see the game with a special mole in the play:

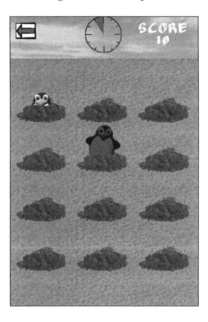

Moving moles

When we call the `raiseMole` method, we build all of the mole's behavior. The absolute minimum we need is to raise the mole from the hill and lower it again. For our game, we want to add a little randomness to the behavior, so that we don't see exactly the same motions for every mole. We use a combination of pre-built animations with actions to achieve our result. As we haven't used any `CCAnimate` calls before, we should talk about them first.

The animation cache

Cocos2d has many useful caches to store frequently used data. When we use a `CCSpriteBatchNode`, we are using the `CCSpriteFrameCache` to store all of the sprites we need by name. There is an equally useful `CCAnimationCache` as well. It is simple to use. You build your animation as a `CCAnimation`, and then load it to the `CCAnimationCache` by whatever name you would like.

When you want to use your named animation, you can create a `CCAnimate` action that loads directly from `CCAnimationCache`. The only caution is that if you load two animations with the same name to the cache, they will collide in the cache, and the second one will replace the first.

For our project, we preload the animation during the `init` method by calling the `buildAnimations` method. We only use one animation here, but you could preload as many as you need to the cache ahead of time.

Filename: `MXPlayfieldLayer.m`

```objc
-(void) buildAnimations {
    // Load the Animation to the CCSpriteFrameCache
    NSMutableArray *frameArray = [NSMutableArray array];

    // Load the frames
    [frameArray addObject:[[CCSpriteFrameCache
            sharedSpriteFrameCache]
            spriteFrameByName:@"penguin_forward.png"]];
    [frameArray addObject:[[CCSpriteFrameCache
            sharedSpriteFrameCache]
            spriteFrameByName:@"penguin_left.png"]];
    [frameArray addObject:[[CCSpriteFrameCache
            sharedSpriteFrameCache]
            spriteFrameByName:@"penguin_forward.png"]];
    [frameArray addObject:[[CCSpriteFrameCache
            sharedSpriteFrameCache]
            spriteFrameByName:@"penguin_right.png"]];
```

```
[frameArray addObject:[[CCSpriteFrameCache
        sharedSpriteFrameCache]
        spriteFrameByName:@"penguin_forward.png"]];
[frameArray addObject:[[CCSpriteFrameCache
        sharedSpriteFrameCache]
        spriteFrameByName:@"penguin_forward.png"]];


// Build the animation
CCAnimation *newAnim = [CCAnimation
        animationWithSpriteFrames:frameArray delay:0.4];


// Store it in the cache
[[CCAnimationCache sharedAnimationCache]
        addAnimation:newAnim name:@"penguinAnim"];
}
```

We only have three unique frames of animation, but we load them multiple times into the `frameArray` to fit our desired animation. We create a `CCAnimation` object from the `frameArray`, and then commit it to `CCAnimationCache` under the name `penguinAnim`. Now that we have loaded it to the cache, we can reference it anywhere we want it, just by requesting it from `CCAnimationCache`, like this:

```
[[CCAnimationCache sharedAnimationCache]
            animationByName:@"penguinAnim"]]
```

Combining actions and animation

For the behavior of the moles, we will be combining actions and animation at the same time to give more of a feeling of life to the game. In all, we define six behaviors for a normal mole, and one specific behavior for a special mole.

Filename: `MXPlayfieldLayer.m`

```
-(void) raiseMole:(MXMoleHill*)aHill {
  // Grab the mole sprite
  CCSprite *aMole = [[aHill hillMole] moleSprite];

    float moleHeight = aMole.contentSize.height;

  // Define the hole wobble/jiggle
  CCMoveBy *wobbleHillLeft = [CCMoveBy
          actionWithDuration:.1 position:ccp(-3,0)];
  CCMoveBy *wobbleHillRight =[CCMoveBy
          actionWithDuration:.1 position:ccp(3,0)];
```

```
// Run the actions for the hill
[[aHill moleHillBottom] runAction:
        [CCSequence actions:wobbleHillLeft,
         wobbleHillRight, wobbleHillLeft,
         wobbleHillRight, nil]];


// Define some mole actions.
  // We will only use some of them on each mole
CCMoveBy *moveUp = [CCMoveBy
        actionWithDuration:moleRaiseTime
        position:ccp(0,moleHeight*.8)];
CCMoveBy *moveUpHalf = [CCMoveBy
        actionWithDuration:moleRaiseTime
        position:ccp(0,moleHeight*.4)];
CCDelayTime *moleDelay = [CCDelayTime
        actionWithDuration:moleDelayTime];
CCMoveBy *moveDown = [CCMoveBy
        actionWithDuration:moleDownTime
        position:ccp(0,-moleHeight*.8)];
CCCallFuncND *delMole = [CCCallFuncND
        actionWithTarget:self
        selector:@selector(deleteMole:data:)
        data:(MXMoleHill*)aHill];
  CCAnimate *anim = [CCAnimate
        actionWithAnimation:[[CCAnimationCache
        sharedAnimationCache]
        animationByName:@"penguinAnim"]];
  CCRotateBy *rot1 = [CCRotateBy
        actionWithDuration:moleDelayTime/3 angle:-20];
  CCRotateBy *rot2 = [CCRotateBy
        actionWithDuration:moleDelayTime/3 angle:40];
  CCRotateBy *rot3 = [CCRotateBy
        actionWithDuration:moleDelayTime/3 angle:-20];

  // We have 6 behaviors to choose from. Randomize.
  NSInteger behaviorPick = CCRANDOM_0_1() * 6;

  // If this is a special mole, let's control him better
  if ([aHill hillMole].isSpecial) {

      // Build some more actions for specials
      CCTintTo *tintR = [CCTintTo actionWithDuration:0.2
                    red:255.0 green:0.2 blue:0.2];
      CCTintTo *tintB = [CCTintTo actionWithDuration:0.2
```

```
                                    red:0.2 green:0.2 blue:255.0];
            CCTintTo *tintG = [CCTintTo actionWithDuration:0.2
                            red:0.2 green:255.0 blue:0.2];


            // Set a color flashing behavior
            [aMole runAction:[CCRepeatForever
                    actionWithAction:[CCSequence actions:
                    tintR, tintB, tintG, nil]]];
            // Move up and down and rotate/wobble
            [aMole runAction:[CCSequence actions:moveUp, rot1,
                    rot2, rot3, rot1, rot2, rot3, moveDown,
                    delMole, nil]];
        } else {
            switch (behaviorPick) {
                case 1:
                    // Move up and down and rotate/wobble
                    [aMole runAction:[CCSequence actions:
                        moveUp, rot1, rot2, rot3, moveDown,
                        delMole, nil]];
                    break;
                case 2:
                    // Move up and then down without pausing
                    [aMole runAction:[CCSequence actions:
                        moveUp, moveDown, delMole, nil]];
                    break;
                case 3:
                    // Move up halfway and then down
                    [aMole runAction:[CCSequence actions:
                        moveUpHalf, moleDelay, moveDown,
                        delMole, nil]];
                    break;
                case 4:
                    // Move up halfway and then down, no pause
                    [aMole runAction:[CCSequence actions:
                        moveUpHalf, moveDown, delMole, nil]];
                    break;
                case 5:
                    // Move up halfway, look around, then down
                    [aMole runAction:[CCSequence actions:
                        moveUpHalf, anim, moveDown, delMole,
                        nil]];
                    break;
                default:
                    // Play the look around animation
```

```
        [aMole runAction:anim];
        // Move up and down
        [aMole runAction:[CCSequence actions:
            moveUp, moleDelay, moveDown, delMole,
            nil]];
        break;
    }
  }
}
```

This method takes one big shortcut to keep from repeating code. We define nine separate actions for a standard mole, even though we will not use them all on the same mole. We do this because there is a lot of overlap between the different behaviors, and we don't want to repeat the same line of code again and again. If we look at just two of the actions, moveUp and moveUpHalf, half of the mole behaviors use the first, and half use the second. Instead of the path we have taken here, the alternative would be to include seven individual CCMoveBy definitions in this method to accommodate the six normal mole move up behaviors plus the special mole behavior. On the surface this isn't a big concern, but it does matter if we wanted to alter the behavior of how far a mole is raised up from the moveUp action, we would have to change that in four places. If we only defined the necessary actions after the behavior was determined, this would mean 31 lines to maintain instead of our current 9 lines. If performance is not negatively affected, it is a good idea to always take the maintainable approach.

We also define the special mole behavior in this method. If the isSpecial flag is set, we use one set behavior, in two distinct actions. The CCRepeatForever action loops over our tinting, which tints the mole to red, then blue, and then green. At the same time, we are also running CCSequence of moveUp, rotating side to side a couple of times, and then moving it down again.

For a standard mole, we use a similar parallel action in the default section of the switch statement. We play the animation (named anim), which does not impact the moving up and down run by the second runAction.

Simultaneous actions

This running of multiple simultaneous actions is a source of confusion for new developers. Some actions cannot be run in parallel in this fashion. For example, trying to run CCMoveTo and CCMoveBy at the same time will result in only the second run action being run. Why? Both are affecting the position of the sprite, and are therefore incompatible. The last one that is run "wins" and the former is discarded. Earlier we were able to run CCTintTo at the same time as a full CCSequence of movement and rotation actions. None of these other commands affected the color of the sprite, so they were able to be run in parallel.

When developing more complex sets of actions, it is important to evaluate what the desired outcome is, and which actions could conflict. A good rule of thumb is that you cannot run two of the "same" action on the "same" sprite at the "same" time. If you need to use two CCMoveBy statements, for example, you either need to chain them with CCSequence so they will run in order, or you need to revise your logic to combine the parameters so you can make a single CCMoveBy action that integrates both.

> The final level of complexity would be to abandon actions for that behavior and instead manually change the positioning in your update method. This is powerful, but nothing we need to delve into at this time.

Deleting moles

At the end of all of the mole actions, there was a CCCallFuncND action named delMole called. CCCallFuncND is a very powerful action, yet it is extremely simple at the same time. This action is used to call any selector and pass any data object to it. In our case, we call the deleteMole:data: method, and pass it a pointer to the current MXMoleHill. Using CCCallFuncND (and its similar brethren CCCallFunc and CCCallFuncN), you can integrate other methods into an action sequence.

Filename: MXPlayfieldLayer.m

```
-(void)deleteMole:(id)sender data:(MXMoleHill*)moleHill {
    molesInPlay--;
    [self resetMole:moleHill];
}
```

Because we implemented the "blank mole" model into our design, we aren't actually deleting the moles. We reduce the counter molesInPlay and call the method to reset the mole to become a "blank mole". This is the same resetMole we called when we first created the "blank moles" in the beginning.

Filename: MXPlayfieldLayer.m

```
-(void) resetMole:(MXMoleHill*)moleHill {
    // Reset all mole-related values.
    // This allows us to keep reusing moles in the hills
    [[moleHill hillMole] stopAllActions];
    [[[moleHill hillMole] moleSprite]
                    removeFromParentAndCleanup:NO];
    [[moleHill hillMole] setMoleGroundY:0.0f];
    [[moleHill hillMole] setMoleState:kMoleDead];
    [[moleHill hillMole] setIsSpecial:NO];
    [moleHill setIsOccupied:NO];
}
```

That's all it takes to completely clean a mole when we're ready to make a "blank mole" out of it. We reset everything to default values, and we remove the sprite attached to it.

Touching moles

By this point, we have moles that can be spawned, animated, and reset. What about the real fun, the mole thumping? For that, we look at the MXMole.m file, where all of the mole touch handling is coded:

Filename: MXMole.m

```
#import "MXMole.h"

@implementation MXMole

@synthesize parentHill;
@synthesize moleSprite;
@synthesize moleGroundY;
@synthesize moleState = _moleState;
@synthesize isSpecial;

-(id) init {
    if(self = [super init]) {
            self.moleState = kMoleDead;
            [[[CCDirector sharedDirector] touchDispatcher]
                    addTargetedDelegate:self priority:0
                    swallowsTouches:NO];
    }
  return self;
}

- (BOOL)ccTouchBegan:(UITouch *)touch withEvent:(UIEvent *)event {
    CGPoint location = [touch locationInView:[touch view]];
    CGPoint convLoc = [[CCDirector sharedDirector]
                        convertToGL:location];

    if (self.moleState == kMoleDead) {
        return NO;
    } else if (self.moleSprite.position.y +
                (self.moleSprite.contentSize.height/2)
                <= moleGroundY) {
    self.moleState = kMoleHidden;
    return NO;
    } else {
```

```
        // Verify touch was on this mole and above ground
        if (CGRectContainsPoint(self.moleSprite.boundingBox,
                                convLoc) &&
            convLoc.y >= moleGroundY)
        {
            // Set the mole's state
            self.moleState = kMoleHit;

            // Play the "hit" sound
            if (isSpecial) {
                [[SimpleAudioEngine sharedEngine]
                        playEffect:SND_MOLE_SPECIAL];
            } else {
                [[SimpleAudioEngine sharedEngine]
                        playEffect:SND_MOLE_NORMAL];
            }
        }
        return YES;
    }
}

-(void) destroyTouchDelegate {
    [[[CCDirector sharedDirector] touchDispatcher]
                        removeDelegate:self];
}

@end
```

We have registered the MXMole class with the CCTouchDispatcher as a Targeted Delegate. This means that the mole will be notified of every touch individually. As we are looking for a single touch per mole, this is perfect for our needs. We registered with the dispatcher in the init method, and we built the matching destroyTouchDelgate method, which is called in the dealloc method of MXPlayfieldLayer. If we don't remove the delegate, the mole will be a leaked object and will cause memory issues.

When the game design was reviewed at the beginning of the chapter, we discussed the approach we would take with the Z-order "trick" to make the mole disappear when it went behind the ground image. If we left it at that, there would be a serious gameplay flaw. The normal touch handling would also accept the touch when the mole was touched below the ground level. How do we fix this?

Correcting this issue is the reason we created the `moleGroundY` variable. When we spawn a new mole, we set this variable to match the molehill's y position. Since we also use the molehill's y value in the placement of the molehill graphics, this represents the exact y position where the mole emerges from the ground. In our `ccTouchBegan` method inside the `MXMole` class, we only accept the touch if the mole is being touched and the touch has a y value greater than or equal to the `moleGroundY` position. This will effectively limit the touched mole parts to those above ground level. (It's not pixel-perfect, because the `moleHillBottom` sprite has a few pixels above this "horizon" line, but it is so small a coordinate variation that it does not affect the playability of the game).

When the mole is touched, it changes the `moleState` variable to a value of `kMoleHit` and plays a sound.

Tying it together

There are only two important methods left to review to tie this all together. First is the `update` method. Let's look at the applicable portions of the `update` method (we have left placeholders for the other portions of the `update` method, but those will not be addressed here. Please refer the code bundle for this book to see those details):

Filename: `MXPlayfieldLayer.m`

```
-(void)update:(ccTime)dt {

  for (MXMoleHill *aHill in moleHillsInPlay) {

    if (aHill.hillMole.moleState == kMoleHit) {
          [[aHill hillMole] setMoleState:kMoleMoving];
      [self scoreMole:[aHill hillMole]];
    }
  }

    if (molesInPlay < maxMoles && spawnRest > 10) {
        [self spawnMole:self];
        spawnRest = 0;
    } else {
        spawnRest++;
    }

    // Update the timer value & display
```

```
// Protection against overfilling the timer

// Update the timer visual

// Game Over / Time's Up
}
```

On every loop of the update method, we iterate through the moleHillsInPlay array. We check each mole to see if we have one in the kMoleHit state. If a hit mole is found, we change the state of that mole to kMoleMoving, and call the scoreMole method. As we only set the moleState to kMoleHit within the touch handler, and then immediately change it to kMoleMoving when we first trap it in this loop, we can be assured that this is the first (and only) time we have seen this particular scoring event. If we did not change the moleState here, we would trigger scoreMole every time the update method ran, and the game would grind to a halt.

The second section of the update method controls the spawning of new moles. As we want to have a little delay between new moles being created, we use the spawnRest variable to act as a timer to leave at least 10 update loops between calls to spawnMole. We also make sure we don't have the maximum number of desired moles in the play already. Combined, these two simple checks provide a very natural spawn feeling. The player is never bored waiting for moles to spawn, and the moles themselves don't appear in any synchronized pattern.

Scoring the mole

We haven't addressed the details of the scoring system because it is trivially simple. There is a variable called playerScore, and a label that displays that score. (For details on the scoring, please see the code bundle for this book.) In this game, the more interesting aspect of "scoring the mole" is the visual way we show that it was scored.

Filename: MXPlayfieldLayer.m

```
-(void) scoreMole:(MXMole*)aMole {
  // Make sure we don't have a dead mole
  if (aMole.moleState == kMoleDead) {
    return;
  }

  // Get the hill
  MXMoleHill *aHill = [aMole parentHill];

    // Add the score
    if (aMole.isSpecial) {
```

```
            // Specials score more points
            playerScore = playerScore + 5;
            // You get 5 extra seconds, too
            [self addTimeToTimer:5];
        } else {
            // Normal mole.  Add 1 point.
            playerScore++;
        }

        // Update the score display
        [self updateScore];

        // Set up the mole's move to the score
        CCMoveTo *moveMole = [CCMoveTo actionWithDuration:0.2f
                position:[self scorePosition]];
        CCScaleTo *shrinkMole = [CCScaleTo
                actionWithDuration:0.2f scale:0.5f];
        CCSpawn *shrinkAndScore = [CCSpawn
                actionOne:shrinkMole two:moveMole];
        CCCallFuncND *delMole = [CCCallFuncND
                actionWithTarget:self
                selector:@selector(deleteMole:data:)
                data:(MXMoleHill*)aHill];

        [aHill.hillMole.moleSprite stopAllActions];
        [aHill.hillMole.moleSprite runAction:[CCSequence
                actions: shrinkAndScore, delMole,  nil]];
    }
```

Most of this code should look familiar by now. After a "safety net" check to prevent scoring a dead mole, we increment the score itself. After we update the score, we build some new actions to move the mole to the score location, scale it down, and then delete it when we're done.

Here we see one type of action we haven't touched on before: CCSpawn. Despite the name, it is completely unrelated to the mole spawning we built in this game. Instead, a CCSpawn action allows two actions to be performed on the same target at the same time. This is an alternate behavior compared to CCSequence, which will run the actions one at a time. For our use, we want the sprite to move and scale down by 50 percent at the same time. There are a couple of limitations of CCSpawn. The first is that it must be a finite interval action. No CCRepeatForever actions can be used inside a CCSpawn, for example. The other limitation is that both actions inside the CCSpawn action should have the same duration. If their duration is different, it will run until the longer of the two actions is complete. With that in mind, we set the duration for both the CCMoveTo and CCScaleTo actions to 0.2f so the move and scale is quick and pleasant.

Summary

We have navigated the challenges of a mole thumping game, and survived intact. In this chapter we have covered a few interesting concepts. We learned how to use Z-ordering to trick the eye. We created persistent objects that can be reused (the moles). We have also worked with using instances of `CCNode` as containers for other objects for both the molehills and the moles. We have spent considerable time discussing actions and animations, both of which are core to a successful cocos2d game design.

In the next chapter, we will explore a snake game. From snakes eating mice to scaling difficulty levels, the chapter will cover some familiar ground and some new terrain.

4

Give a Snake a Snack…

One of the challenges of object-oriented design for a game is how to build fully cohesive objects that function as needed for a game. We will build this project with that focus in mind. The main class for the player will be as self-contained and self-sufficient as possible.

In this chapter we will cover:

- Overriding methods
- Self-contained classes
- Difficulty levels
- Scaling level progression
- Object lifespan control

The project is…

This chapter will take on the often copied game that has graced pretty much every possible computing platform, from early cell phones to current consoles: the snake game. There are many variations under a variety of names, but the mechanics are generally the same. You control a snake that is always moving forward. You can turn the snake right or left (at right angles only), avoiding walls and eating mice (or other food). Each time you eat something, your snake gets longer. You can go on eating (and growing) until you run into a wall or your own tail.

Design approach

The "classic" way to handle the snake's movement in a snake game is to draw a new body segment in the direction the snake is moving, and erase the one at the end. While this approach works, we want to use a more object-oriented approach in our design.

We will focus on letting the snake be as autonomous as possible. We want a snake class that we can simply instruct to move, and the snake object will handle the movement itself. The snake class will also be able to handle what to do when we pass it a message to "turn left" or "turn right".

The levels should be generated with a variable number of walls inside the playfield, as well as drawing outer walls around the edge of the screen. Finally, we need to have mice appear on the playfield as the food. These mice should have a limited lifespan, so they will disappear if they are not eaten in a given amount of time. When a mouse is eaten or runs out of life, we will replace it with another. Let's see what it should look like:

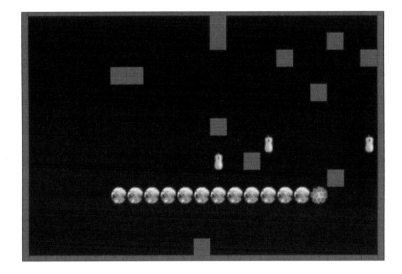

We will also establish three difficulty levels, and incrementing game levels for each difficulty. Since the game is based primarily on random elements, we need to use the difficulty and the level number in setting the variable elements in the game (for example, high levels are faster with more mice and more walls), as well as the snake's movement speed. That doesn't sound too difficult, does it?

Building a better snake

The first thing we need to keep in mind is that the snake is of a variable length. The snake could be as short as one segment or as long as 100 segments (in theory—we won't get that long in our game). As we said during the design, the snake should be as autonomous as possible. With that in mind, let's look at the SNSnake.h file to see what we need.

Filename: FileSNSnake.h

```
#import "SNSnakeSegment.h"

@class SNPlayfieldLayer;

@interface SNSnake : CCNode {

    SNPlayfieldLayer *parentLayer; // Parent layer
    NSMutableArray *snakebody; // Contains the snake
    NSInteger headRow; // Starting row for snake head
    NSInteger headColumn; // Starting col for snake head

    SnakeHeading _snakeDirection;  // Direction facing
    float _snakeSpeed; // Current rate of movement
}

@property (nonatomic, retain) NSMutableArray *snakebody;
@property (nonatomic, assign) SnakeHeading snakeDirection;
@property (nonatomic, assign) float snakeSpeed;

+(id) createWithLayer:(SNPlayfieldLayer*)myLayer
         withLength:(NSInteger)startLength;

-(void) addSegment;
-(void) move;
-(void) turnLeft;
-(void) turnRight;
-(void) deathFlash;

@end
```

We need to track how fast the snake should move (snakeSpeed) and what direction it is moving in (snakeDirection). But what is this SnakeHeading variable type? We will again be placing our common definitions in a separate definitions file, SNDefinitions.h. Even though we did not import that file in this header, it is imported in the SNSnakeSegment.h file, which is then imported here, so we can use it freely. The definition of SnakeHeading is:

Filename: SNDefinitions.h

```
typedef enum {
    kUp = 1,
    kRight,
    kLeft,
    kDown
} SnakeHeading;
```

The SnakeHeading type uses these four directional values (which are integers in disguise) to keep track which direction, relative to the playfield, the snake is facing. This is easier than trying to remember that one means "up".

The entire snake's body, including the head, will be stored in the NSMutableArray snakeBody. This array will contain objects of type SNSnakeSegment, but we don't have to provide those specifics in the header.

One aspect worth pointing out is that we declare some of these variables as properties. Why only some, and not others? When you declare a property, it can be accessed from outside the class. A variable without a property declaration will be only usable inside the class in which it is defined. So here, we know we will want the main playfield to be able to use the snakeSpeed, snakeDirection, and snakeBody, so we declare those as properties.

The headRow and headColumn are convenience variables to keep track of where we want the head of the snake to start in our playing grid. These could be done away with entirely and hardcode the starting values, but this allows us to easily relocate the snake's starting position without digging through the code to identify the values to change.

We will be handling all of the segment creation within this class (using the addSegment method), so we need to keep a reference to the game layer itself. This is stored in the parentLayer variable, which is of type SNPlayfieldLayer. As we discussed in *Chapter 3, Thumping Moles for Fun*, the @class declaration at the top of the header file tells the compiler "we have a class called SNPlayfieldLayer, but that's all you need to know for now". Unlike our use of a forward declaration in *Chapter 3*, we do need to call a method from that class, so we will add the line #import "SNPlayfieldLayer.h" into the SNSnake.m file.

We also provide several exposed methods in the header. These should all be fairly self-explanatory. We do need to point out the one class method, `createWithLayer:withLength:`. In earlier chapters, we often took the approach of using default `init` structures, and filled in the variables after the object was instantiated. While this does work, it is often cleaner to build your own class methods to ensure that no required parameters are overlooked. This approach also allows us to pursue our goal with this game of making the snake as self-contained as possible.

Anatomy of a snake segment

Before we dive into the `SNSnake` implementation, let's turn our attention to the `SNSnakeSegment`. This is the object that will represent each segment of the snake, both head and body. This class is a mostly unmodified subclass of `CCSprite`, but we will make a small, yet important change to its behavior.

Filename: `SNSnakeSegment.h`

```
@interface SNSnakeSegment : CCSprite {
    CGPoint _priorPosition;
    SNSnakeSegment *_parentSegment;
}

@property (nonatomic, assign) CGPoint priorPosition;
@property (nonatomic, assign) SNSnakeSegment *parentSegment;

@end
```

We establish a property named `priorPosition`, which is the position where this sprite was before the last time it moved. We also keep a property for `parentSegment`. The `parentSegment` is the segment of the snake directly in front of the current segment. In this way, each snake segment has a direct connection to the segment in front of it.

Filename: `SNSnakeSegment.m`

```
@implementation SNSnakeSegment

@synthesize priorPosition = _priorPosition;
@synthesize parentSegment = _parentSegment;

-(void) setPosition:(CGPoint)position {
    // override the method to let us keep the prior position
    self.priorPosition = self.position;
    [super setPosition:position];
}

@end
```

This class is very brief, yet it will make our game a lot easier to build. In most ways this will behave as a normal CCSprite, except when the setPosition method is used. We are overriding setPosition to provide new behavior. First, we store our current position in the priorPosition variable, and then we call the super setPosition method, which actually calls the standard CCSprite setPosition method. All told, this will behave like a standard setPosition, except that it is quietly storing the coordinates of its last position before the move. To understand why, we will need to look at the snake's implementation.

Dissecting the snake

Let's begin with the createWithLayer:withLength: class method, and the related initWithLayer:withLength: instance method.

Filename: SNSnake.m

```
+(id) createWithLayer:(SNPlayfieldLayer*)myLayer
          withLength:(NSInteger)startLength {
    return [[[self alloc] initWithLayer:myLayer
          withLength:startLength] autorelease];
}

-(id) initWithLayer:(SNPlayfieldLayer*)myLayer
             withLength:(NSInteger)startLength {
    if (self = [super init]) {

        // Keep a reference to the parent, so we can use
        // the parent layer's positioning method
        parentLayer = myLayer;

        // Set up the snakebody array
        snakebody = [[NSMutableArray alloc]
                    initWithCapacity:30];

        // Set the starting defaults
        headRow = 2;
        headColumn = 2;
        self.snakeSpeed = 0.3;
        self.snakeDirection = kUp;

        // Add the head
        [self addHead];

        // Add the requested number of body segments
```

```
        for (int i = 1; i < startLength; i++) {
            [self addSegment];
        }
    }
    return self;
}
```

We keep a reference to the layer passed (as `parentLayer`), initialize the `NSMutableArray snakeBody`, and set some default values for the rest of the variables. We then call `addHead` to add the snake's head. This must be called before we make any calls to `addSegment`, because we need the head to be the first element in the array. We then use the `startLength` variable to determine how many times we need to call the `addSegment` method. Notice that the `addSegment` loop will iterate one time less than the passed `startLength`. We do this because the head does count as a part of the snake length, so if we requested a `snakeLength` of five, we only need to generate four body segments.

Building the head

Now let's look at the `addHead` method.

Filename: `SNSnake.m`

```
-(void) addHead {
    // Create the snake head
    SNSnakeSegment *newSeg = [SNSnakeSegment
            spriteWithSpriteFrameName:@"snakehead.png"];

    // We use the parent layer's positioning method, so we
    // will still be in lockstep with the other objects
    CGPoint newPos = [parentLayer positionForRow:headRow
                                 andColumn:headColumn];

    // Set up the snake's initial head position
    [newSeg setPosition:newPos];
    [newSeg setPriorPosition:newSeg.position];

    // The head has no parent segment
    [newSeg setParentSegment:nil];

    // Add the head to the array and parent
    [snakebody addObject:newSeg];
    [parentLayer addChild:newSeg z:100];
}
```

We begin this method by using the standard `CCSprite` `spriteWithSpriteFrameName` convenience method to create the sprite. Next we see one of the reasons we keep a reference to the `parentLayer`. To set the value of the `CGPoint newPos`, we call the `positionForRow:andColumn:` method directly from the parent layer. Calling the method from the parent layer guarantees we are using the same grid formula for all object position calculations, without having to maintain multiple versions of the same `positionForRow:` method in different classes. This is the only piece of code that uses the `headRow` and `headColumn` variables, so we could have avoided those variables and embedded the values directly in this method call if we wanted to tighten up the code. We set the position for our `newSeg` to the value of `newPos`, and then we set the value of `priorPosition` to the same value.

The next line is the only real substantial difference between the head and a body segment: we set the `parentSegment` to nil. If the segment does not have a `parentSegment`, we can be sure it is the head segment.

After adding the snake's head to the `snakeBody` array, we add the head as a child of the `parentLayer`. Notice we use a `z` order of 100. When we create the snake, we want the head to overlap the next body segment, so we start with a high `z` value for the head.

Building the body segments

We now turn our attention to the `addSegment` method, which adds a single body segment to the snake.

Filename: `SNSnake.m`

```
-(void) addSegment {
    // Create a new segment
    SNSnakeSegment *newSeg = [SNSnakeSegment
            spriteWithSpriteFrameName:@"snakebody.png"];

    // Get a reference to the last segment of the snake
    SNSnakeSegment *priorSeg = [snakebody objectAtIndex:
                                ([snakebody count] - 1)];

    // The new segment is positioned at the prior
    // position as stored in priorSeg
    [newSeg setPosition:[priorSeg position]];

    // We start with same position for both variables
    [newSeg setPriorPosition:[newSeg position]];
```

```
        // Connect this segment to the one in front of it
        [newSeg setParentSegment:priorSeg];
        // Add the segment to the array and layer
        [snakebody addObject:newSeg];
        [parentLayer addChild:newSeg z:100-[snakebody count]];
    }
```

At first glance, this looks very similar to the addHead method. Let's take a closer look. We use a different image for the body segments. Then we look up the last segment in the snakeBody array. Here we use the prior segment's position as the position for our new segment. We also set the parentSegment variable to point to the prior segment. So each segment now has a connection to the one in front of it, and it identifies its own position as being in the prior location of the parent segment. (For the initial building of the snake, these will all share the same coordinates, but this design will be essential when we are calling this method during gameplay.)

We add this segment to the snakeBody array, and then add this segment to the parentLayer. You will notice we assign the z order as 100 - [snakeBody count]. This will essentially slip each segment under the segment in front of it, since a higher z order is drawn on top of lower z orders.

Moving the snake

We now turn our attention to the way we move the snake. Since we want as much of the snake's control inside the snake object, we will be generating our own move method, instead of using setPosition.

Filename: SNDefinition.h

```
    #define gridSize 22
```

In the SNDefinitions.h file we have created a gridSize definition that works well with the graphics we have defined for this project. Having a centralized gridSize definition allows us to alter the dimensions of the playfield in one place. With that definition fresh in our minds, let's look at the move method.

Filename: SNSnake.m

```
    -(void) move {
        CGPoint moveByCoords;
        // Based on the direction, set the coordinate change
        switch (self.snakeDirection) {
            case kUp:
                moveByCoords = ccp(0,gridSize);
                break;
```

```
        case kLeft:
            moveByCoords = ccp(-gridSize,0);
            break;
        case kDown:
            moveByCoords = ccp(0,-gridSize);
            break;
        case kRight:
            moveByCoords = ccp(gridSize,0);
            break;
        default:
            moveByCoords = ccp(0,0);
            break;
    }

    // Iterate through each segment and move it
    for (SNSnakeSegment *aSeg in snakebody) {
        if (aSeg.parentSegment == nil) {
            // Move the head by the specified amount
            [aSeg setPosition:ccpAdd(aSeg.position,
                                moveByCoords)];
        } else {
            // Body segments move to the prior position
            // of the segment ahead of it
            [aSeg setPosition:
                    aSeg.parentSegment.priorPosition];
        }
    }
}
```

We use the snakeDirection variable and the defined gridSize to determine where to move the head of the snake. All of the snake's movements will be constrained to the grid. If we allowed free movement, it would be extremely easy to run into the edges of a wall. By constraining the snake's movements to a grid, we allow the snake to have "close calls" with walls without dying because they were one pixel too close.

We then iterate through all members of the snakeBody array. If the segment does not have a parentSegment defined, it is the head. We use the ccpAdd function to add the new moveByCoords to the head's current position. The ccpAdd function takes two ccp coordinates as arguments and adds them together into a new ccp value. The end result is a new position for the head segment, moved in the desired direction.

If there is a `parentSegment` defined, it is a normal body segment. Here is where we take advantage of the extra variables we added to the `SNSnakeSegment` class. We set the segment's position to the prior position of their parent segment. This means for each segment, it will move to the same position just vacated by the segment in front of it. In this way, the snake's body will follow the same path as the head, even through multiple turns.

Turning the snake

Now that we have addressed moving the snake, we need to make it turn. As we just saw in the `move` method, the movement is completely driven by the `snakeDirection` variable. All we need to do is adjust that variable, and the snake will move in the new direction.

Filename: `SNSnake.m`

```
-(void) turnLeft {
    switch (self.snakeDirection) {
        case kUp:
            self.snakeDirection = kLeft;
            break;
        case kLeft:
            self.snakeDirection = kDown;
            break;
        case kDown:
            self.snakeDirection = kRight;
            break;
        case kRight:
            self.snakeDirection = kUp;
            break;
        default:
            break;
    }
}
```

If the snake is sent the message to `turnLeft`, and the snake is currently facing up, the new direction will be facing left. We check each of the four movement directions, and change the snake's direction appropriately. Since the `switch` statements are using the integer values underlying the `SnakeHeading` type, it is very efficient and lightweight code. We repeat the same structure in the `turnRight` command, except we change the `snakeDirection` to turn in the correct "turn right" direction. (See the code bundle if you need to see how `turnRight` differs from `turnLeft`.)

Death of a snake

There is one method left to complete the snake. At some point, the player will do something unfortunate and run into a wall (or their own tail). The snake dies, and game is over. We include the visual "death" in the snake class.

Filename: SNSnake.m

```
-(void) deathFlash {
    // Establish a flashing/swelling animation of head
    CCTintTo *flashA = [CCTintTo actionWithDuration:0.2
                            red:255.0 green:0.0 blue:0.0];
    CCTintTo *flashB = [CCTintTo actionWithDuration:0.2
                            red:255.0 green:255.0 blue:255.0];
    CCScaleBy *scaleA = [CCScaleBy actionWithDuration:0.3
                            scale:2.0];
    CCScaleBy *scaleB = [CCScaleBy actionWithDuration:0.3
                            scale:0.5];

    SNSnakeSegment *head = [snakebody objectAtIndex:0];

    [head runAction:[CCRepeatForever actionWithAction:
            [CCSequence actions:flashA, flashB, nil]]];
    [head runAction:[CCRepeatForever actionWithAction:
            [CCSequence actions:scaleA, scaleB, nil]]];
}
```

We leverage cocos2d actions to give a nice death sequence. We set up two separate CCRepeatForever sequences that are run simultaneously on the snake's head. We flash red and then back to normal sprite color (setting the color to pure white gives the original sprite coloring). We also scale the head to twice its own size, and then back to normal. We set these with slightly different durations, so the two behaviors are not in lockstep with each other. Together, these provide a nice appearance of throbbing pain, perfect for the death of the snake.

Building the environment

The snake is now functionally complete, so we turn our attention to building an interesting environment for the snake to live in. All of our game objects use the same positioning method we saw when designing the snake.

Filename: SNPlayfieldLayer.m

```
-(CGPoint) positionForRow:(NSInteger)rowNum
            andColumn:(NSInteger)colNum {
    float newX = (colNum * gridSize) - 2;
    float newY = (rowNum * gridSize) - 4;
    return ccp(newX, newY);
}
```

This method takes the designated row and column values and multiplies them by the gridSize. The additional modifiers (-2 and -4) are used to better align the walls so there is an equal size of partial walls on the outside edges of the screen. This is because the gridSize value of 22 does not exactly fit the dimensions of the iPhone screen. With this slight adjustment, it looks visually centered after we add the outer walls.

Outer walls

The first part of the environment to build are the outer walls, since the snake needs to be contained on the screen. Let's look at that method.

Filename: SNPlayfieldLayer.m

```
-(void) createOuterWalls {
    // Left and Right edges of screen
    for (int row = 0; row <= size.height/gridSize+1; row++) {
        // Build a new wall on the left edge
        CGPoint newPosLeft = [self positionForRow:row
                                        andColumn:0];
        CCSprite *newWallLeft = [CCSprite
                spriteWithSpriteFrameName:@"wall.png"];
        [newWallLeft setPosition:newPosLeft];
        [self addChild:newWallLeft];
        [wallsOnField addObject:newWallLeft];

        // Build a new wall on the right edge
        CGPoint newPosRight = [self positionForRow:row
                andColumn:(size.width/gridSize)+1];
        CCSprite *newWallRight = [CCSprite
                spriteWithSpriteFrameName:@"wall.png"];
        [newWallRight setPosition:newPosRight];
        [self addChild:newWallRight];
        [wallsOnField addObject:newWallRight];
    }
```

```
    // Top and Bottom edges of screen
    for (int col = 1; col < size.width/gridSize; col++) {
        // Build a new wall at bottom edge of screen
        CGPoint newPosBott = [self positionForRow:0
                                     andColumn:col];
        CCSprite *newWallBottom = [CCSprite
                spriteWithSpriteFrameName:@"wall.png"];
        [newWallBottom setPosition:newPosBott];
        [self addChild:newWallBottom];
        [wallsOnField addObject:newWallBottom];

        // Build a new wall at the top edge of screen
        CGPoint newPosTop = [self positionForRow:
                (size.height/gridSize)+1 andColumn:col];
        CCSprite *newWallTop = [CCSprite
                spriteWithSpriteFrameName:@"wall.png"];
        [newWallTop setPosition:newPosTop];
        [self addChild:newWallTop];
        [wallsOnField addObject:newWallTop];
    }
}
```

We have two separate loops, one for each pair of edges on the screen. The loop for the left and right edges is the same, as is the top and bottom edge loop. We iterate from the minimum grid position through the maximum grid position for that edge of the screen. We base the maximum on the size of the screen divided by the `gridSize`, so we will always be at the outside edges, even if we change the `gridSize`.

For each position (and side of the screen), we create a new `CCSprite`, set its position, and add it to the layer. We also add it to the `wallsOnField` array. The `wallsOnField` array is critical to the collision handling routines we will address shortly.

Inner walls

When we move to building the inner walls, we have a couple of additional details to consider. We need to make sure the position is not already occupied by another object. We also want to make sure we don't build a wall in front of the snake.

Filename: `SNPlayfieldLayer.m`

```
-(void) createWall {
    BOOL approvedSpot = YES;
    SNSnakeSegment *head = [[snake snakebody]
```

```
objectAtIndex:0];

    CGRect snakeline = CGRectMake(head.boundingBox.origin.x -
        head.contentSize.width/2, 0,
        head.boundingBox.origin.x + head.contentSize.width/2,
        size.height);

    // Randomly generate a position
    NSInteger newRow = CCRANDOM_0_1()*(size.height/gridSize);
    NSInteger newCol = CCRANDOM_0_1()*(size.width/gridSize);
    CGPoint newPos = [self positionForRow:newRow
                                andColumn:newCol];

    // Build a new wall, add it to the layer
    CCSprite *newWall = [CCSprite
                spriteWithSpriteFrameName:@"wall.png"];
    [newWall setPosition:newPos];
    [self addChild:newWall];

    // Check to make sure we aren't on top of the snake
    for (SNSnakeSegment *aSeg in [snake snakebody]) {
        if (CGRectIntersectsRect([newWall boundingBox],
                                  [aSeg boundingBox])) {
            approvedSpot = NO;
            break;
        }
    }
    // Checks for a clear path in front of the snake
    // Assumes the snake is facing up
    if (CGRectIntersectsRect([newWall boundingBox],
                              snakeline)) {
        approvedSpot = NO;
    }
    // Check to make sure there are no walls overlapping
    for (CCSprite *aWall in wallsOnField) {
        if (CGRectIntersectsRect([newWall boundingBox],
                                  [aWall boundingBox])) {
            approvedSpot = NO;
            break;
        }
    }
    // Check to make sure there are no mice in the way
    for (CCSprite *aMouse in miceOnField) {
        if (CGRectIntersectsRect([newWall boundingBox],
```

```
                                            [aMouse boundingBox]])) {
                approvedSpot = NO;
                break;
            }
        }
    }
    // If we passed everything, keep the wall
    if (approvedSpot) {
        [wallsOnField addObject:newWall];
    // If we detected an overlap, build a replacement
    } else {
        [self removeChild:newWall cleanup:YES];
        [self createWall];
        return;
    }
}
```

We start this method by creating a CGRect that is directly in front of the snake. This CGRect assumes the snake is facing up, which is the default we established in the SNSnake class. Our design does not allow for adding extra walls during a level, so we can be sure the snake is facing up when the environment is built.

We generate a random position, based on the screen size divided by the gridSize. We go ahead and build a new wall and add it to the layer. At this point, we don't know if the wall is in a good position or not, but we add it anyway. We then proceed to iterate through all of our arrays to see if the new wall we just created is overlapping an existing object, using a call to CGRectIntersectsRect. We also check to see if the new wall is in the "line of sight" of the snake. If the wall is in an empty position, we add it to the wallsOnField array. If it is in a bad (occupied) position, we remove the wall from the layer and then call the createWall method again to build a replacement.

Building snake food

We only have one type of object left to complete the environment: mice to eat. If you recall from our original design, we want the mice to have a limited lifespan before they disappear from the playfield. We do this by creating SNMouse, a subclass of CCSprite.

Filename: SNMouse.m

```
+(id) spriteWithSpriteFrameName:(NSString *)spriteFrameName {
    return [[[self alloc] initWithSpriteFrameName:
            spriteFrameName] autorelease];
}
```

```
-(id) initWithSpriteFrameName:(NSString*)spriteFrameName {
    if (self = [super initWithSpriteFrameName:spriteFrameName]) {
        // Lifespan is between 10 and 20
        lifespan = 10 + (CCRANDOM_0_1() * 10);
    }
    return self;
}
```

We are using a new variable, lifespan, and we set it to a random value between 10 and 20 (this is in seconds). This is defined when the mouse is instantiated, so it will be different for each mouse. (Note that we use a class convenience method that overrides the spriteWithSpriteFrameName. This is needed in cocos2d 2.0 because the init method is not called during instantiation.) The actual creation of the mouse is nearly the same as the createWall method.

Filename: SNPlayfieldLayer.m

```
-(void) createMouse {
    BOOL approvedSpot = YES;

    // Randomly generate a position
    NSInteger newRow = CCRANDOM_0_1()*(size.height/gridSize);
    NSInteger newCol = CCRANDOM_0_1()*(size.width/gridSize);
    CGPoint newPos = [self positionForRow:newRow
                                andColumn:newCol];
    // Build a new mouse, add it to the layer
    SNMouse *newMouse = [SNMouse
                spriteWithSpriteFrameName:@"mouse.png"];
    [newMouse setPosition:newPos];
    [self addChild:newMouse];
    // Check to make sure we aren't on top of the snake
    for (SNSnakeSegment *aSeg in [snake snakebody]) {
        if (CGRectIntersectsRect([newMouse boundingBox],
                                 [aSeg boundingBox])) {
            approvedSpot = NO;
            break;
        }
    }
    // Check to make sure there are no walls here
    for (CCSprite *aWall in wallsOnField) {
        if (CGRectIntersectsRect([newMouse boundingBox],
                                 [aWall boundingBox])) {
            approvedSpot = NO;
            break;
        }
```

```
    }
    // Check to make sure there are no mice in the way
    for (SNMouse *aMouse in miceOnField) {
        if (CGRectIntersectsRect([newMouse boundingBox],
                                 [aMouse boundingBox])) {
            approvedSpot = NO;
            break;
        }
    }
    // If we passed everything, keep the mouse
    if (approvedSpot) {
        [miceOnField addObject:newMouse];
    // If we detected an overlap, build a replacement
    } else {
        [self removeChild:newMouse cleanup:YES];
        [self createMouse];
        return;
    }
}
```

The only structural difference between this method and the createWall method is
that we don't check for the snake's "line of sight" CGRect, since there's no harm in
putting a mouse directly in front of the snake. That's all it takes to make snake food.

Collisions and eating

Now that we have all of the visible objects on the screen, we can move to the collision
detection. Collision detection is actually the easy part. We have already written code
that looks suspiciously like collision detection in the createWall and createMouse
methods. The checks we perform are nearly the same, except we are concerned only
with collisions involving the head of the snake, since it is the only part of the snake
that can collide with another surface. Let's look at the checkForCollisions method
in two sections. The first section contains the checking for game ending crashes.

Filename: SNPlayfieldLayer.m (checkForCollisions, part 1)

```
-(void) checkForCollisions {
    // Get the head
    SNSnakeSegment *head = [[snake snakebody]
                                       objectAtIndex:0];
    // Check for collisions with the snake's body
    for (SNSnakeSegment *bodySeg in [snake snakebody]) {
        if (CGRectIntersectsRect([head boundingBox],
            [bodySeg boundingBox]) && head != bodySeg) {
```

```
            [self snakeCrash];
            break;
        }
    }
    // Check for collisions with the walls
    for (CCSprite *aWall in wallsOnField) {
        if (CGRectIntersectsRect([aWall boundingBox],
                                    [head boundingBox])) {
            [self snakeCrash];
            break;
        }
    }
```

First we get the head segment to use in all of our collision checking. We compare it against all segments in the snakebody array. If the CGRectIntersectsRect is true (that is, the two CGRects are overlapping at least a bit), and the segment it is testing is not the head, then it has crashed into its own tail. The second check is the same boundingBox check we used earlier against all the walls in the wallsOnField array. Any positive hits in these routines will cause the snakeCrash method to be called.

The second half is concerned with eating mice. It is a little more involved, but still fairly simple.

Filename: SNPlayfieldLayer.m (checkForCollisions, part 2)

```
        // Check for mice eaten
        CCSprite *mouseToEat;
        BOOL isMouseEaten = NO;
        for (CCSprite *aMouse in miceOnField) {
            if (CGRectIntersectsRect([head boundingBox],
                                        [aMouse boundingBox])) {
                isMouseEaten = YES;
                mouseToEat = aMouse;
                [[SimpleAudioEngine sharedEngine]
                                    playEffect:SND_GULP];
                break;
            }
        }
        if (isMouseEaten) {
            // Replace the mouse, longer snake, score
            [mouseToEat removeFromParentAndCleanup:YES];
            [miceOnField removeObject:mouseToEat];
            [self createMouse];
            [snake addSegment];
            [self incrementScore];
        }
    }
```

Here we look for collisions between the snake's head and the mice on the playfield. Because we want to eat the mice, not crash into them, we care more about which mouse is being eaten. In this case, we retain the mouse that has just been eaten in the mouseToEat variable. We do this because part of the process we must go through to remove the mouse would cause the array to mutate while iterating through it, which would cause the game to crash. So we set mouseToEat to reference the mouse in question, and set the isMouseEaten BOOL to YES.

Once we are safely outside of the loop through the miceOnField array, we can remove the mouse from the layer (removeFromParentAndCleanup) as well as removing it from the miceOnField array. We then trigger the creation of a new mouse. Since each mouse eaten should lengthen the snake by one, we then call the snake's addSegment method. This is the same method we used in the initial build of the snake.

Levels and difficulties

You can play on the same level for only a limited time before your snake becomes so long that it is impossible to continue. To solve that issue, we will implement levels. Additionally, not everyone likes to play at the same speed to begin with, so we will also add difficulty or skill levels. We address this need by another custom init method for the SNPlayfieldLayer class, as shown in the following shortened form:

Filename: SNPlayfieldLayer.m

```
+(id)  initForLevel:(NSInteger)startLevel
    andDifficulty:(SNSkillLevel)skillLevel {
            return [[[self alloc]initForLevel:startLevel
                andDifficulty:skillLevel] autorelease];
}


-(id)  initForLevel:(NSInteger)startLevel
    andDifficulty:(SNSkillLevel)skillLevel {

  if (self = [super init]) {
    levelNum = startLevel;
      currentSkill = skillLevel;

  // See code bundle for complete initForLevel method
```

When we create the scene (and subsequently the layer), we pass it to the starting level and skill level. We store those passed values in the variables: levelNum and currentSkill. We want the level and skill-based parameters all centralized, so all of the level-control values are set in one method, createSnake.

Filename: `SNPlayfieldLayer.m`

```
-(void) createSnake {
    NSInteger snakeLength = 4 + currentSkill;
    snake = [[SNSnake createWithLayer:self
                          withLength:snakeLength] retain];
    snake.snakeSpeed = .3 -((levelNum+currentSkill)*0.02);

    wallCount = 3 + (levelNum * currentSkill);
    mouseCount = currentSkill;
}
```

Here we see how we are setting a few important variables based on the `levelNum` and `currentSkill`. Part of the "behind the scenes" is our use of mathematical operations using the `currentSkill`. It is of type `SNSkillLevel`, which is another custom type.

Filename: `SNDefinitions.h`

```
typedef enum {
    kSkillEasy = 1,
    kSkillMedium,
    kSkillHard
} SNSkillLevel;
```

From this you can see that any reference to the `currentSkill` type is actually representing values of 1, 2, or 3. So the number of walls we would create for a game on `kSkillHard` and level 10 would be `3 + (10 * 3) = 33`. This allows the game to slowly ramp up in difficulty, with the skill level determining not only that level 1 begins slightly harder, but the actual difficulty scales up faster on the harder skill levels.

The snake speed needs a little explanation. The speed is actually the delay between movements. So the lower the number, the faster it moves. Our calculation starts at `.3` and uses a formula to speed up as the levels increase. So the previously cited example of `kSkillHard` on level 10 would result in a snake speed of `0.3 - (13 * 0.02)`, which is a pretty fast value of `0.04`. All of this logic was centralized in this method so we can tweak the parameters side-by-side as we approach our optimal gameplay experience.

The main loop

Much of the remaining functionality is in the `update` method. There are three distinct sections of the loop, and we will look at them in turn. The first section handles the movement updates.

Filename: SNPlayfieldLayer.m (update, part 1)

```
-(void)update:(ccTime)dt {
    stepTime += dt;
    if (stepTime > snake.snakeSpeed) {
        stepTime = 0;
        [snake move];
        [self checkForCollisions];
    }
```

We use a standard delta time counter to keep adding to the stepTime variable. On each loop, we check if the stepTime is greater than the snakeSpeed variable. If it is, then we need to move the snake. As discussed in the previous sections of the chapter, all we have to do is call the snake's move method. The only time we need to check for collisions is after the snake's move method is called, so we call that method next.

Level-up checking

Filename: SNPlayfieldLayer.m (update, part 2)

```
    if (playerScore >= 8) {
        [self showLevelComplete];
    }
```

Here we have hard-coded the value of 8 as being the total number of mice needed to be eaten per level before we advance. Although we don't reproduce the showLevelComplete method here, it unschedules the update, gives a "Level Complete" display, and then makes the following call:

Filename: SNPlayfieldLayer.m

```
    [[CCDirector sharedDirector] replaceScene:
        [SNPlayfieldScene sceneForLevel:levelNum + 1
                        andDifficulty:currentSkill]];
```

We call replaceScene, requesting the current scene to be replaced with a fresh one that is exactly the same, except one level higher. The level-based variables we saw in the createSnake method will make the next level just a little bit harder, and the level up process can continue for as long as the player can keep up with it.

Dead mice

The third and final piece of the update loop handles the lifespan we discussed for the mice. Every mouse already has a semi-random lifespan, but we haven't done anything with it yet.

Filename: SNPlayfieldLayer.m (update, part 3)

```
for (SNMouse *aMouse in miceOnField) {
    aMouse.lifespan = aMouse.lifespan - dt;

    if (aMouse.lifespan <= 0) {
        [deadMice addObject:aMouse];
        [aMouse removeFromParentAndCleanup:YES];
    }
}
[miceOnField removeObjectsInArray:deadMice];

// Add new mice as replacements
for (int i = 0; i < [deadMice count]; i++) {
    [self createMouse];
}

[deadMice removeAllObjects];
}
```

We again use the delta time, but this time we subtract the delta from the lifespan of every mouse on the field. If a mouse's lifespan reaches zero, it died of old age. We add it to the deadMice array so we can get rid of it outside of the loop. We use an array in this method because there could be more than one mouse whose lifespan expires in the same iteration. We remove the dead mice from the miceOnField array, clear them from the layer, and create new mice in their place. This assures that the correct number of mice are on-screen at all times.

But…how do we control the snake?

The most basic question of all has been completely ignored until now. We have dealt with how the game works internally, but we have actually left the player out in the cold. It is precisely because we have done so much "under the hood" work on the snake and its environment that makes the touch handler really anti-climatic. We will focus on the direct user interaction. (There is additional code that handles the game over and some basic splash screens that are outside of the scope of this chapter.)

Filename: SNPlayfieldLayer.m

```
-(BOOL) ccTouchBegan:(UITouch *)touch
        withEvent:(UIEvent *)event {

    CGPoint location = [touch locationInView:[touch view]];
    CGPoint convLoc = [[CCDirector sharedDirector]
```

```
        convertToGL:location];

    if (convLoc.x < size.width/2) {
        // Touched left half of the screen
        [snake turnLeft];
        return YES;
    } else {
        // Touched right half of the screen
        [snake turnRight];
        return YES;
    }

    // If we did not claim the touch.
    return NO;
}
```

We start by using a standard conversion of the touch to OpenGL coordinate space. We evaluate the converted touch location and compare its x value to determine which half of the screen has been touched. If the left half of the screen was touched, we instruct the snake to turn left. For the right side, we instruct the snake to turn right. You will notice that we are using ccTouchBegan, rather than ccTouchEnded. We want responsiveness as soon as the screen is touched, not relying on the player lifting their finger off or moving it around. If they want to turn, we want to respond as fast as possible, and only trigger once. The touch will not trigger again until their finger is raised and tapped again.

Summary

In this chapter, we have focused more on internal structure than we have on complex gameplay. By designing each object as fully contained as possible, it insulates the layer from the object. If we wanted to change the way the snake's movement is handled, for example, we could make those changes in the SNSnake class without touching the SNPlayfieldLayer at all. We have experimented with overriding the setPosition method to control the serpentine nature of the snake's movement. We have implemented easy collision detection. We have also built our first game that includes several difficulty levels with increasingly more difficult playable levels. Finally, we have seen how adding a single variable can be all we really need to turn a CCSprite into a mouse with a life of its own (and how to get rid of dead ones).

In the next chapter we will move on to a brick-breaking game using the Box2D physics engine. We will use plists to store level data and even build some simple power-ups that will change the physics of the game while the game is running.

5

Brick Breaking Balls
with Box2D

There is a lot you can do with cocos2d by itself. However, when you combine it with a true physics engine, such as Box2D or Chipmunk, you can do so much more. There is a steep learning curve, so this chapter will be both a new project and a basic primer on Box2D for the beginner.

In this chapter, we will cover:

- Box2D basics
- Building Box2D objects
- Using mouse joints
- Singleton classes
- Separate HUD layer
- Using plists to store level data
- Changing game physics during play

The project is…

In this chapter we will discuss the classic brick breaking game. Dating back to the early days of Atari, this game is a wonderful way to start exploring physics engines, because there aren't too many objects moving at the same time. If you are not familiar with this game, it is fairly easy to explain. The player controls a paddle at the bottom of the screen that can move side-to-side. The top portion of the screen has a number of bricks in fixed positions. There is a small ball bouncing around, and the player's job is to break all of the bricks without letting the ball past the paddle. Of course, the ball bounces around everywhere, so there are actually quite a lot of physics-based calculations needed to make it work.

Let's take a look at the final game:

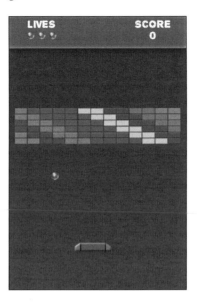

Box2D – a primer

Before we can even begin to think about our project, we need to review the basics of Box2D. There is a lot of depth to the Box2D engine, and we will only be scratching the surface in this book. This section aims to give an overview of the parts of the engine that we will need to interact with for this game.

Box2D – what is it?

To quote the manual, "Box2D is a 2D rigid body simulation library for games. Programmers can use it in their games to make objects move in believable ways and make the game world more interactive." That's a pretty straightforward description of what Box2D is, except for the "rigid body" term. What does that mean? Rigid body means that Box2D is built to simulate hard objects such as balls, walls, stone, metal, and so on. Box2D was not built to simulate "soft body" objects such as pillows, jelly, and so on.

We will briefly go through the basic terms of the Box2D environment here, and we will deal with everything in more detail when we build the game. The official documentation for Box2D is available at: http://box2d.org/documentation.html

One important aspect of Box2D to be pointed out here is that it is written in C++, so there is a little bit of a language translation aspect when using Box2D with a game written primarily in Objective-C. For the most part, the two play together nicely, but you will have to gain some familiarity with C++ notation to make sense out of the Box2D-specific code. (If the C++ notation looks alien to you, we would advise consulting your favorite search engine to learn the basics of C++.)

Basic parts of Box2D

The widest-reaching component of the Box2D environment is called a **world**. All objects created in Box2D will be contained in the world. This is where all movement, collisions, and so on take place. The world is also where we set the gravity of the environment. Normally, a given simulation will have only one Box2D world.

The next object that we have is called a **body**. A body represents a thing of some sort in the world. The body controls the position of the object, as well as other attributes necessary for the simulation, such as the body type. The body type lets you identify whether it is a static (non-moving) or dynamic (movable) body.
A body does not directly "know" how big it is, how dense it is, and so on.

A **shape** describes the geometry of the object. There are several different types of shapes supported by Box2D. The most commonly used are the circle shape, the polygon shape, and the edge shape. For a complete list of supported shapes, please refer to the Box2D documentation.

A **fixture** can be thought of as the "glue" between the shape and the body. However, it is more than that. A fixture also defines core attributes of the object, such as density, friction, and restitution (aka bounciness).

Box2D supports a wide variety of **joints** to connect bodies together. There are distance joints, pulley joints, revolute joints, and so on. The only joints we will be concerned with in this game are the mouse joint and the prismatic joint, both used in the paddle controls.

As you might imagine, there is also a collision handler. One of the core components we use is called a **contact listener**. This is a very complex piece of software, and the one that makes us dive into C++ the most. We will only scratch the surface with a basic collision handler in this game.

A very important value is the PTM_RATIO. This is the Points-To-Meters Ratio. Internally, Box2D represents everything as meters. The default value for this ratio is 32, which represents 32 points as 1 meter in the simulation world. For most games, this will work perfectly. In our code, we will have to apply this PTM_RATIO to many calculations when we are converting locations between the cocos2D layer and the Box2D world.

On to the game!

We start our game from the Cocos2D + Box2D template, so it has all the libraries we need. To prepare for this project, we still go through the same motions from the template, namely removing HelloWorldLayer.h/.mm, and changing the references in the IntroLayer.mm to our menu class. There are a couple of additional classes in the template, GLES-Render and PhysicsSprite. We will deal with them later. We also need to switch the supported orientation to portrait only, as we did in the previous chapter. (Don't forget to also remove the background rotation line in the IntroLayer.mm file.)

With a Box2D project, it is important to note that all our implementation classes will need names that end in .mm instead of .m. This tells the compiler that we will be using a mixture of Objective-C and C++. You must do this with Box2D, because Box2D is written in C++. So where do we start?

World building

We will start with building the Box2D world itself.

Filename: BRPlayfieldLayer.mm

```
-(void) setupWorld {
    // Define the gravity vector.
    b2Vec2 gravity;
    gravity.Set(0.0f, 0.0f);

    // Construct a world object
    world = new b2World(gravity);

    world->SetAllowSleeping(true);
    world->SetContinuousPhysics(true);

    // Create contact listener
    contactListener = new BRContactListener();
    world->SetContactListener(contactListener);
}
```

As you can see, the world is pretty easy to set up. Here we are defining `gravity` as zero, as we don't want our ball to slow down and we don't want our bricks falling off the screen. We then set up the world, which is assigned to a variable called `world`, which is a `b2World` variable type. When you set up the `b2World`, you define the gravity for the world. We will allow objects to sleep. Sleeping means that objects that are at rest will "sleep", so the simulation won't spend a lot of time calculating movements of a body at rest. However, if something else interacts with it (that is, runs into it), the body will wake up immediately and react appropriately. We set the continuous physics to be `true`. This allows for a more accurate simulation, but requires more computing power. We also establish the contact listener we will use for this world. We won't get into the details here – we will save that for our discussion about the collision handler.

If you're confused by the C++ syntax here, it is helpful to know that the lines with the arrow (->) symbol are calling functions from the object to the left-hand side of the arrow. So the line `world->SetContactListener(contactListener);` would look like `[world setContactListener:contactListener];`, if Box2D was written in Objective-C.

> Although there are some wrappers that allow you to use Box2D with Objective-C syntax, as of this writing none of the projects are mature enough to be recommended here.

On the edge

Now that we have a world, we can start defining "stuff" to go in our world. Let's start with some edges for the screen:

Filename: `BRPlayfieldLayer.mm`

```
-(void) buildEdges {
    // Define the wall body
    b2BodyDef wallBodyDef;
    wallBodyDef.position.Set(0, 0);

    // Create a body for the walls
    wallBody = world->CreateBody(&wallBodyDef);

    // This defines where the bottom edge of the HUD is
    float maxY = 424;

    // Define the 4 corners of the playfield
    b2Vec2 bl(0.0f, 0.0f); // bottom left corner
```

```
    b2Vec2 br(size.width/PTM_RATIO,0); // bottom right
    b2Vec2 tl(0,maxY/PTM_RATIO); // top left corner
    b2Vec2 tr(size.width/PTM_RATIO,maxY/PTM_RATIO); // top right

    b2EdgeShape bottomEdge;
    b2EdgeShape leftEdge;
    b2EdgeShape rightEdge;
    b2EdgeShape topEdge;

    // Set the edges
    bottomEdge.Set(bl, br);
    leftEdge.Set(bl, tl);
    rightEdge.Set(br, tr);
    topEdge.Set(tl, tr);

    // Define the fixtures for the walls
    wallBody->CreateFixture(&topEdge,0);
    wallBody->CreateFixture(&leftEdge,0);
    wallBody->CreateFixture(&rightEdge,0);

    // Keep a reference to the bottom wall
    bottomGutter = wallBody->CreateFixture(&bottomEdge,0);
}
```

We've written quite a bit of new code here, so let's break it down. First we defined a new body definition (b2BodyDef), called wallBodyDef. It is an extremely basic body. We then tell the world to create a body using the b2BodyDef we just created, and we keep a reference to it. Our world now has one formless, shapeless body in it.

We fix the "shapeless" problem next. We begin by defining the positions for each of the four corners of our playing area, using a shorthand naming pattern (that is, bl = bottom left, br = bottom right, and so on). There are two important things we need to point out here. For all non-zero positions, we divide the "normal" screen position by the PTM_RATIO. This is the standard way we can convert the ccp value we normally would use into a Box2D-friendly coordinate. As you recall, PTM means Points-To-Meters, so 32 screen points equals 1 meter in the simulation world. Doing this conversion keeps our display and our Box2D simulation in sync. You may also notice we are using the maxY value of 424, rather than the top of the screen. Our game has a Heads-Up Display covering the top portion of the screen, and a y value of 424 places this top edge at the bottom of that display HUD. We really don't want our player losing their ball under the Heads-Up Display, do we?

We then create four `b2EdgeShape` objects, for each side of the screen. We use our corner variables to define their positions, using the `Set` function. We then instruct the `wallBody` to create a fixture for each of these walls. You will notice that we set the variable `bottomGutter` to the returned value of the `CreateFixture` command. We will use this later in the collision handler to determine when the player lost his ball.

Having a ball

So far we have a world with walls, but we don't have any moving parts yet. Let's build a ball to bounce around:

Filename: `BRPlayfieldLayer.mm`

```
-(void) buildBallAtStartingPosition:(CGPoint)startPos
                withInitialImpulse:(b2Vec2)impulse {
    // Create sprite and add it to layer
    PhysicsSprite *ball = [PhysicsSprite
                spriteWithSpriteFrameName:@"ball.png"];
    ball.position = startPos;
    ball.tag = kBall;
    [bricksheet addChild:ball z:50];

    // Create ball body
    b2BodyDef ballBodyDef;
    ballBodyDef.type = b2_dynamicBody;
    ballBodyDef.position.Set(startPos.x/PTM_RATIO,
                        startPos.y/PTM_RATIO);
    ballBodyDef.userData = ball;
    b2Body *ballBody = world->CreateBody(&ballBodyDef);

    // Link the body to the sprite
    [ball setPhysicsBody:ballBody];

    //Create a circle shape
    b2CircleShape circle;
    circle.m_radius = 7.0/PTM_RATIO;

    //Create fixture definition and add to body
    b2FixtureDef ballFixtureDef;
    ballFixtureDef.shape = &circle;
    ballFixtureDef.density = 1.0f;
    ballFixtureDef.friction = 0.0f;
    ballFixtureDef.restitution = 1.0f;
```

```
        ballBody->CreateFixture(&ballFixtureDef);
        ballBody->ApplyLinearImpulse(impulse,
                                ballBody->GetPosition());
        isBallInPlay = YES;
    }
```

Building a dynamic object is a little more involved than building the edges, but the same basic concepts still apply. Because the ball will have a visible sprite associated with the body, we first build a PhysicsSprite object. PhysicsSprite is one of the classes in the cocos2d + Box2D template we used to create the project. It is a subclass of CCSprite, but includes a couple of extra methods that will automatically keep the sprite locked in position with the physics body connected to it. The only thing we need to do differently than a normal CCSprite is to call setPhysicsBody on it, which connects the Box2D body to the sprite. The end result is that we do not have to manually move (or rotate) the sprite. Without this "helper" class, we would be responsible for updating the position and rotation of the sprite ourselves.

You will also notice that we assign a tag value to the ball. This will be useful later, when we are dealing with collisions. (The tag definitions are contained in typedef enum in the BRDefinitions.h file.)

We then build a body for the ball. We assign it a type of b2_dynamicBody, to let Box2D know that this is a body that can move. We set the position of the body to correspond to the position of the sprite. A body is by default anchored in the middle, just like a CCSprite. We can use the same coordinates for the body (divided by the PTM_RATIO).

The userData is a flexible part of the body definition; userData can hold anything you want to store in it. userData is customarily used to hold a reference to the CCSprite object (or the PhysicsSprite object, in our case) that represents the actor. Following this convention makes it a trivial matter to get to the sprite from the body.

After we instruct the world to create a body with this definition, we define a shape. Since we are using a round ball, the b2CircleShape is perfect. We define the shape's radius by taking the radius of the ball (half the sprite width) and dividing by the PTM_RATIO.

We then build the fixture to represent the "guts" that accompany the body. We assign the circle shape we just defined, and then we set the density, friction, and restitution. Density is used in the calculation of mass. The higher the density, the more massive the object is. Friction is used to control how the objects slide along each other. Friction is normally set between 0 and 1. Higher friction values will slow objects down as they slide against each other. We don't want any friction on the ball to keep it moving nicely. The final parameter here is restitution.

The term restitution is less familiar than the other two, but you can think of it as how bouncy the object is. A value of zero means the object will not bounce at all. A value of 1 means the object is perfectly bouncy, and will not lose any of its velocity when it impacts another object. We don't want the ball to lose any velocity when it collides, so we use a value of 1 for the restitution of the ball.

After we define the fixture, we create it with the `ballBody`. As a final step, we add a linear impulse to the ball, based on the message passed to this method. An impulse is basically a kick, with the strength and direction of the impulse controlled by the `b2Vec2` parameter, here called `impulse`. The second argument `ballBody->GetPosition()` returns the center of the `ballBody`. This will apply the impulse to the center of the body, so we get a straight application of the impulse.

Now we need a `newBall` method that will always start the ball in the same position, and give it a decent impulse to set it in motion.

Filename: `BRPlayfieldLayer.mm`

```
-(void) newBall {
    [self buildBallAtStartingPosition:ccp(150,200)
                    withInitialImpulse:b2Vec2(0.2,-1.5)];
}
```

As we see from the `newBall` method, we give the ball a very slight "kick" with the initial impulse, down and to the right.

 A `b2Vec2()` is equivalent to a `ccp()`, and uses the same bottom-left origin point.

Setting everything in motion

At this point we have a world, we have edges to hold everything in, and we have a ball. Now we need to get it all moving. As you might expect, we handle this in the `update` method.

Filename: `BRPlayfieldLayer.mm`

```
-(void)update:(ccTime)dt {
    // Step the world forward
  world->Step(dt, 10, 10);

    // Iterate through all bodies in the world
    for(b2Body *b = world->GetBodyList(); b;b=b->GetNext()) {
    if (b->GetUserData() != NULL) {
```

```
                    // Get the sprite for this body
        PhysicsSprite *sprite =
  (PhysicsSprite*)b->GetUserData();


            // Speed clamp for balls
            if (sprite.tag == kBall) {
        static int maxSpeed = 15;

        b2Vec2 velocity = b->GetLinearVelocity();
        float32 speed = velocity.Length();

        if (speed > maxSpeed) {
          b->SetLinearDamping(0.5);
        } else if (speed < maxSpeed) {
          b->SetLinearDamping(0.0);
        }
      }
    }
  }
}
```

This is an abbreviated form of our final `update` method, with just the ball movement handling in place. We start by instructing the world to step forward in its simulation. The three parameters sent to the `Step` function are, in order, the **time step**, the **velocity iterations**, and the **position iterations**. In this game, we are using a variable time step (using the delta value `dt`), which works well in our case. More intensive and detailed simulations are better suited to use a fixed time step. (Point your favorite search engine to the topic to learn more about how to implement a fixed time step.) The velocity iterations and position iterations control how detailed the simulation is. A value of 10 for both iteration values is a good starting point for most projects. Higher values will result in more accuracy, but the trade-off is more of a processor load to calculate the simulation.

Now that we have made one step forward in time for the world, we evaluate all of the bodies in the world to determine what we should do with them. We iterate through the world's bodies with `world->GetBodyList()`, and advance to the next body with `b->GetNext()`. For each body we find, we evaluate whether or not it has a sprite attached by checking that `userData` is not null. When we find a body with a sprite, we get a sprite reference from that body's `userData`. (We already have the variable `b` to represent the body, from the `for` loop.)

Because the ball might pick up speed during the game, we put in a speed clamping check next. If the sprite is a ball, and the speed is over the set value of 15, the body has **linear damping** applied, which will affect the velocity of the ball on the next step of the simulation. Damping is essentially applying the brakes on the object. We use a value of 0.5, which will slow the ball down, but not stop it completely. This acts the same as tapping the brakes in a car, decreasing the forward velocity a little bit at a time.

You will notice that we don't actually move the ball sprite at all. Because we are using a PhysicsSprite object instead of a CCSprite object, it will automatically take care of that for us.

Collision handling

The code we have reviewed so far will make the ball bounce around the screen, but nothing interesting will happen when the ball hits the wall, except it will bounce around. What we need is to add a way to take some action when certain objects collide with others. We do this by implementing a contact listener. A contact listener has four components: BeginContact, EndContact, PreSolve, and PostSolve. Going into detail on each of these is beyond the scope of this book. For our project, we will only be implementing a simplified contact listener with code for BeginContact and EndContact only. Let's look at the header first:

Filename: BRContactListener.h

```
#import "Box2D.h"
#import <vector>
#import <algorithm>

struct BRContact {
  b2Fixture *fixtureA;
  b2Fixture *fixtureB;
  bool operator ==(const BRContact& other) const
  {
    return (fixtureA == other.fixtureA) &&
            (fixtureB == other.fixtureB);
  }
};

class BRContactListener : public b2ContactListener {

public:
  std::vector<BRContact>_contacts;

  BRContactListener();
```

```
~BRContactListener();

virtual void BeginContact(b2Contact* contact);
virtual void EndContact(b2Contact* contact);
virtual void PreSolve(b2Contact* contact,
                      const b2Manifold* oldManifold);
virtual void PostSolve(b2Contact* contact,
                       const b2ContactImpulse* impulse);
};
```

Now we can look at the implementation file for this class:

Filename: `BRContactListener.mm`

```
#import "BRContactListener.h"

BRContactListener::BRContactListener() : _contacts() {
}

BRContactListener::~BRContactListener() {
}

void BRContactListener::BeginContact(b2Contact* contact) {
  // We need to copy the data because b2Contact is reused.
  BRContact brContact = { contact->GetFixtureA(),
                          contact->GetFixtureB() };
  _contacts.push_back(brContact);
}

void BRContactListener::EndContact(b2Contact* contact) {
  BRContact brContact = { contact->GetFixtureA(),
                          contact->GetFixtureB() };
  std::vector<BRContact>::iterator pos;
  pos = std::find(_contacts.begin(), _contacts.end(),
                  brContact);
  if (pos != _contacts.end()) {
    _contacts.erase(pos);
  }
}

void BRContactListener::PreSolve(b2Contact* contact,
                 const b2Manifold* oldManifold) {
}

void BRContactListener::PostSolve(b2Contact* contact,
                 const b2ContactImpulse* impulse) {
}
```

This is the simplified contact listener published as part of a tutorial by Ray Wenderlich (`http://raywenderlich.com`), so any credit for this approach belongs to Ray. The basic design of this contact listener is to get the fixtures that are in contact (that is, colliding), and copy them out to `_contacts`, so we can evaluate them in our `BRPlayfieldLayer` instead of here. This copying is done in the `BeginContact`. `EndContact` removes the contact from `_contacts`, so that we are not evaluating outdated contacts.

One nice aspect of this approach is that the contact listener itself is general-purpose enough to be used as it is in many projects. If you are less experienced with C++, having boilerplate code like this is always helpful.

Losing your ball

At this point, we would expect our ball to be lost when it reaches the bottom edge of the screen. But instead, it will simply bounce off because we have not defined any custom behavior for when the ball and the fixture at the bottom of the screen collide. If you recall, when we defined the edges, we kept a variable, `bottomGutter`, for this purpose.

We will be handling our collisions in our `update` method, directly after the `for` loop from earlier, where we controlled the ball's speed.

Filename: `BRPlayfieldLayer.mm`

```
std::vector<b2Body *>toDestroy;
std::vector<BRContact>::iterator pos;
for (pos = contactListener->_contacts.begin();
     pos != contactListener->_contacts.end(); pos++) {
  BRContact contact = *pos;

    // Get the bodies involved in this contact
    b2Body *bodyA = contact.fixtureA->GetBody();
    b2Body *bodyB = contact.fixtureB->GetBody();

    // Get the sprites attached to these bodies
    PhysicsSprite *spriteA =
                (PhysicsSprite*)bodyA->GetUserData();
    PhysicsSprite *spriteB =
                (PhysicsSprite*)bodyB->GetUserData();

    // Look for lost ball (off the bottom)
    if (spriteA.tag == kBall &&
        contact.fixtureB ==bottomGutter) {
```

```
            if (std::find(toDestroy.begin(),
                        toDestroy.end(), bodyA) ==
                        toDestroy.end()) {
                toDestroy.push_back(bodyA);
            }
    }
    // Look for lost ball (off the bottom)
    else if (contact.fixtureA == bottomGutter &&
                spriteB.tag == kBall) {
        if (std::find(toDestroy.begin(),
                        toDestroy.end(), bodyB) ==
                        toDestroy.end()) {
            toDestroy.push_back(bodyB);
        }
    }
}
```

In this code block we are mostly using C++ structures, but the concepts are straightforward. We begin by defining two vectors, which are a form of dynamic array. The `toDestroy` vector will house any objects that need to be destroyed. The vector `pos` is an iterator which, as the name suggests, is used to iterate over data elements. We then enter a `for` loop, which iterates over the contents of the `_contacts` variable that was populated in the contact listener. Inside the loop, we use the variable `contact` to represent the current contact/collision from `_contacts` that we are evaluating.

As the contact contains the fixtures that are contacting one another, we use the `GetBody()` function of the fixtures to get the two bodies involved, naming them `bodyA` and `bodyB`. We will need to get the tags from the attached `CCSprite` objects, so we also create `spriteA` and `spriteB` to represent the sprites associated with those bodies.

For now, we only have one type of collision that we need to address: the ball with the `bottomGutter` fixture. We identify the ball based on the sprite's tag of `kBall`, and we can identify the `bottomGutter` fixture because we stored a reference when it was created. To determine if we had a collision, we simply have to evaluate both objects to determine if one is a ball and other is the `bottomGutter` fixture. You will see from the code that we evaluate the collision twice, once comparing the "A" object to the ball and the "B" to the fixture, and then we evaluate again, with "A" and "B" swapped. We do this because the contact listener does not provide the fixtures "A" and "B" in any particular order. The ball might be "A" this time, and "B" the next time. The only way to reliably evaluate this is to have two checks for each collision in this manner. (You could always create a helper function to evaluate both of these ways for you, but it only results in slightly more compact code, but not necessarily any better performance.)

In both cases, if we identified a collision between the ball and the `bottomGutter`, then the offending body is added to the `toDestroy` vector. The additional `if` statement wrapped around it is checking to make sure this body is not already in the `toDestroy` vector, because we won't be able to destroy the same body twice.

Destruction

Now we have identified the objects to be destroyed, but we haven't actually destroyed anything. Just as with Objective-C, you should not attempt to remove objects from an array while iterating through it, and C++ vectors are no exception. As such, after we have evaluated all of our collisions, we add one more block of code at the bottom of the `update` method.

Filename: `BRPlayfieldLayer.mm`

```
// Destroy any bodies & sprites we need to get rid of
std::vector<b2Body *>::iterator pos2;
for(pos2 = toDestroy.begin(); pos2 != toDestroy.end();
                                        ++pos2) {
    b2Body *body = *pos2;
    if (body->GetUserData() != NULL) {
        PhysicsSprite *sprite =
                (PhysicsSprite*)body->GetUserData();
        [self spriteDestroy:sprite];
    }
    world->DestroyBody(body);
}
```

We use a similar iterator to loop through the `toDestroy` vector. We retrieve each body, check if it has a sprite attached to it (in `userData`), and call the `spriteDestroy` method if it does. Then we instruct the world to destroy the body of this object. The `spriteDestroy` method is used for all of the sprite destructions in our game. An abbreviated form of it looks as follows:

Filename: `BRPlayfieldLayer.mm`

```
-(void) spriteDestroy:(PhysicsSprite*)sprite {
    switch (sprite.tag) {
        case kBall:
            [[SimpleAudioEngine sharedEngine]
                            playEffect:SND_LOSEBALL];
            [sprite removeFromParentAndCleanup:YES];
            [self loseLife];
            break;
    }
}
```

We use the sprite tags here so that we can have custom destruction behavior for each type of object. We could have embedded this in the update method, but it will get pretty long by the end of this game. Separating the destruction code also keeps our Objective-C and C++ a little better separated in the code.

Paddling around

Now we have our basic game world, we have walls, and a ball that will drop off of the bottom of the screen. We need to turn our attention to the only piece of the game the user directly controls: the paddle. Let's look at how we build it:

Filename: BRPlayfieldLayer.mm

```
-(void) buildPaddleAtStartingPosition:(CGPoint)startPos {
    // Create the paddle
    paddle = [PhysicsSprite spriteWithSpriteFrameName:
                                        @"paddle.png"];
    paddle.position = startPos;
    paddle.tag = kPaddle;
    [bricksheet addChild: paddle];

    // Create paddle body
    b2BodyDef paddleBodyDef;
    paddleBodyDef.type = b2_dynamicBody;
    paddleBodyDef.position.Set(startPos.x/PTM_RATIO,
                            startPos.y/PTM_RATIO);
    paddleBodyDef.userData = paddle;
    paddleBody = world->CreateBody(&paddleBodyDef);

    // Connect the body to the sprite
    [paddle setPhysicsBody:paddleBody];

    // Build normal size fixure
    [self buildPaddleFixtureNormal];

    // Restrict paddle along the x axis
    b2PrismaticJointDef jointDef;
    b2Vec2 worldAxis(1.0f, 0.0f);
    jointDef.collideConnected = true;
    jointDef.Initialize(paddleBody, wallBody,
            paddleBody->GetWorldCenter(), worldAxis);
    world->CreateJoint(&jointDef);
}
```

Much of this is the same as when we built the ball. We create the `PhysicsSprite` first. Then we define the body at the same position, and attach the sprite to the body. You will notice that instead of building the fixture here, we call another method to define the fixture. This is because we will be using different fixtures for the paddle later, when we explore power-ups. We will get to the details of the fixture building in just a moment.

One new item that we need to build is a prismatic joint for the paddle, which connects the `paddleBody` to the `wallBody`. A prismatic joint allows a body to travel along a specific axis only. In our case, we define the `worldAxis` as constraining the movement along the x axis only, based on the coordinates we defined. One important flag we set for the paddle is `collideConnected` to `true`. This allows collisions to be detected between bodies connected by the joint. Since we are creating a joint between the paddle and the `wallBody`, we need to set this to allow the paddle to collide with the side walls. Without this established, the paddle will pass through the sides of the playfield and leave the game. Just as with other Box2D elements, we create the joint by passing the `CreateJoint` request to the world itself.

Paddle fixture

We will be implementing some power-ups later that will allow the paddle size to be changed. Because of this, we need the ability to change the paddle size. As we discussed earlier, the fixture handles the geometry and the physical properties of the body, so we have moved this fixture definition to its own method:

Filename: `BRPlayfieldLayer.mm`

```
-(void) buildPaddleFixtureNormal {
    // Define the paddle shape
    b2PolygonShape paddleShape;
    int num = 8;
    b2Vec2 verts[] = {
        b2Vec2(31.5f / PTM_RATIO, -7.5f / PTM_RATIO),
        b2Vec2(31.5f / PTM_RATIO, -0.5f / PTM_RATIO),
        b2Vec2(30.5f / PTM_RATIO, 0.5f / PTM_RATIO),
        b2Vec2(22.5f / PTM_RATIO, 6.5f / PTM_RATIO),
        b2Vec2(-24.5f / PTM_RATIO, 6.5f / PTM_RATIO),
        b2Vec2(-31.5f / PTM_RATIO, 1.5f / PTM_RATIO),
        b2Vec2(-32.5f / PTM_RATIO, 0.5f / PTM_RATIO),
        b2Vec2(-32.5f / PTM_RATIO, -7.5f / PTM_RATIO),
    };
    paddleShape.Set(verts, num);

    // Build the fixture
```

```
[self buildPaddleFixtureWithShape:paddleShape
            andSpriteFrameName:@"paddle.png"];
}
```

To build a normal paddle, we first define the `b2PolygonShape` that matches the paddle. Because we have created a paddle that is not a simple shape (circle or square), we have to define all of the points that define the boundary of the shape. It is important to remember that these coordinates are in points, not pixels. If you are only using non-Retina displays, this makes no difference. Since our project includes both Retina and non-Retina assets, these coordinates must be defined based on the non-Retina sprite. There are many tools to help you define what these points should be, but you can also use most graphics editing programs to identify the points that define the "corners" of the shape. It is important to define the points of the polygon in a counter-clockwise order. If you define them in the other direction, the program will crash, usually when Box2D is calculating the area of the shape.

 Box2D defaults to a maximum of eight vertices to define a shape. If you need more than that, you can easily change the setting in the `b2Settings.h` file. This maximum is defined as `b2_maxPolygonVertices`.

After the shape has been defined, we call out another method to actually build the fixture.

Filename: `BRPlayfieldLayer.mm`

```
-(void) buildPaddleFixtureWithShape:(b2PolygonShape)shape
                andSpriteFrameName:(NSString*)frameName {
    if (paddleFixture != nil) {
        paddleBody->DestroyFixture(paddleFixture);
    }

    // Create the paddle shape definition and add it to the body
    b2FixtureDef paddleShapeDef;
    paddleShapeDef.shape = &shape;
    paddleShapeDef.density = 50.0f;
    paddleShapeDef.friction = 0.0f;
    paddleShapeDef.restitution = 0.0f;
    paddleFixture = paddleBody->CreateFixture(&paddleShapeDef);

    // Swap the sprite image to the normal paddle
    [paddle setDisplayFrame:[[CCSpriteFrameCache
                        sharedSpriteFrameCache]
                        spriteFrameByName:frameName]];
}
```

We start this method with a check to make sure we don't already have a `paddleFixture` object defined. If we do, we destroy it.

Most of the fixture definition follows the same pattern we used in the ball definition. We set the `density`, `friction`, and `restitution`, and we attach the shape to the fixture and the fixture to the body. You will notice that we set the `shape` to the variable shape that we passed to this method. The final line of this method is redundant and unnecessary the first time we build the paddle. We call `setDisplayFrame` to change the sprite frame attached to the paddle. This will come in handy when we add the power-ups later.

Touching the paddle

To interact with the paddle, we need to create a new type of joint: the mouse joint. The mouse joint tries to make the body move toward the target set for it. In our case, the target will be our touched point. This will allow us to drag the paddle around while it is still a part of the Box2D world.

One approach for using the mouse joint is to detect touches on the paddle itself, and allow the player to move it directly. We will take an alternate approach, and detect any touches in the bottom portion of the screen as the target for the mouse joint. Naturally, we will begin with the `ccTouchesBegan` method:

Filename: `BRPlayfieldLayer.mm`

```
-(void)ccTouchesBegan:(NSSet *)touches
                withEvent:(UIEvent *)event {
  if (mouseJoint != NULL) return;

  UITouch *myTouch = [touches anyObject];
  CGPoint location = [myTouch locationInView:[myTouch view]];
  location = [[CCDirector sharedDirector]
                            convertToGL:location];
  b2Vec2 locationWorld = b2Vec2(location.x/PTM_RATIO,
                            location.y/PTM_RATIO);

  // We want any touches in the bottom part of the
  // screen to control the paddle
  if (location.y < 150) {
    b2MouseJointDef md;
    md.bodyA = wallBody;
    md.bodyB = paddleBody;
    md.target = locationWorld;
    md.collideConnected = true;
```

```
        md.maxForce = 1000.0f * paddleBody->GetMass();

        mouseJoint = (b2MouseJoint *)world->CreateJoint(&md);
        paddleBody->SetAwake(true);
    }
}
```

We begin by checking if there is already a mouseJoint defined. If there is, that means there is already one touch "in play", and we don't want to interfere with the current touch.

The next section uses fairly standard conversions from the touch to the OpenGL coordinates. However, here we also define the locationWorld b2Vec2, which is the Box2D version of the location variable.

We then check for a touch in the bottom portion of the screen. If the touch is there, we create a new mouse joint, and attach it to the wallBody and the paddleBody. The attachment to the wallBody is basically an anchor, since a joint must connect two bodies. Only the paddleBody will be moved by this joint. We set the maxForce variable to 1,000 times the mass of the paddle, so the player's movements completely override any other forces that may be trying to influence the paddle. We create the joint, and then make sure the paddle is awake (in case it was sitting idle long enough to sleep).

Now that we have the mouse joint instantiated, we need to make the mouse joint track the user's movements:

Filename: BRPlayfieldLayer.mm

```
- (void)ccTouchesMoved:(NSSet *)touches
                    withEvent:(UIEvent *)event {

    if (mouseJoint == NULL) return;

    if (isGameOver) return;

    UITouch *myTouch = [touches anyObject];
    CGPoint location = [myTouch locationInView:[myTouch view]];
    location = [[CCDirector sharedDirector]
                convertToGL:location];
    b2Vec2 locationWorld = b2Vec2(location.x/PTM_RATIO,
                                  location.y/PTM_RATIO);

    mouseJoint->SetTarget(locationWorld);
}
```

The `ccTouchesMoved` method is almost trivial. We determine the current location of the touch, and we set that as the new target for the mouse joint. That's all it takes to move the paddle around. There is one loose end, however. The final step of the touch handling is to handle the cancel and end events.

Filename: `BRPlayfieldLayer.mm`

```
-(void)ccTouchesCancelled:(NSSet *)touches
                withEvent:(UIEvent *)event {
  if(mouseJoint) {
    world->DestroyJoint(mouseJoint);
    mouseJoint = NULL;
  }
}

-(void)ccTouchesEnded:(NSSet *)touches
            withEvent:(UIEvent *)event {
    if (mouseJoint) {
        world->DestroyJoint(mouseJoint);
        mouseJoint = NULL;
    }
}
```

As you can see, both of these methods are identical. Because the touch handler is only concerned with moving around the paddle with the mouse joint, all we need to do to end (or cancel) the touch is to destroy the mouse joint. Now that we have completed the touch handler, the game now has enough components to move the paddle around and bounce the ball. Box2D will handle all of the collisions between the ball and paddle, without our code needing to do any collision handling of our own.

Storing player data

One of the challenges with a multi-level game is keeping the player's information between levels. There are two common approaches. One is to pass the player data (usually as a player object) from one scene to the next via the scene `init` methods. (We used this approach in the snake game in *Chapter 4, Give a Snake a Snack*.) The other is to use a Singleton.

A Singleton is a design pattern for a class of which there is only one instance allowed. Cocos2D is built on a foundation of Singletons like `CCDirector`, `CCSpriteFrameCache`, and so on. Pretty much anything where you reference a "sharedSomething" (for example, `[CCDirector sharedManager]`) is a Singleton. By design, there is a maximum of one "living" version of a Singleton class at any given time.

We will be using a Singleton class to handle our game variables currentLevel, currentLives, and currentScore. Let's take a look:

Filename: BRGameHandler.mm

```
static BRGameHandler *gameHandler = nil;

@implementation BRGameHandler

@synthesize currentLevel;
@synthesize currentScore;
@synthesize currentLives;
@synthesize playfieldLayer;

+ (id)sharedManager
{
    // Use Grand Central Dispatch to create it
    static dispatch_once_t pred;
    dispatch_once(&pred, ^{
        gameHandler = [[super allocWithZone:NULL] init];
    });
    return gameHandler;
}

- (id)retain {
  return self;
}

- (unsigned)retainCount {
  return NSUIntegerMax;
}

-(oneway void)release {
  //do nothing - the singleton is not allowed to release
}

- (id)autorelease {
  return self;
}
```

These are the general Singleton methods we will use. There are several methods that are not directly called in our game, but this is general enough to be used in many projects (other than the `@synthesize` statements). The `sharedManager` class method will check if there is a `gameHandler` already instantiated. If there is, it returns the existing instance. If not, it creates one. We are using **Grand Central Dispatch (GCD)** in the `sharedManager` method. It is beyond our scope here to go into detail on GCD, but this method is extremely lightweight and fast, compared to more traditional designs. (If you want to know more, check your favorite search engine for "Grand Central Dispatch Singleton" for further reading.) The first time you call `[BRGameHandler sharedManager]`, it will be created. This Singleton class will remain available for the life of the game, so you can rely on it to hold any variables you need to persist through your game.

Next we look at the game-specific methods we include in our Singleton:

Filename: `BRGameHandler.mm`

```
-(id) init {
    if (self == [super init]) {
        [self resetGame];
    }
    return self;
}

-(void) resetGame {
    // Start with the defaults
    currentLevel = 1;
    currentLives = 3;
    currentScore = 0;
}

-(void) addToScore:(NSInteger)newPoints {
    currentScore = currentScore + newPoints;
}

-(void) loseLife {
    currentLives--;
}
```

We have a couple of helper methods here to make our main code simpler.
The first time we instantiate the class, it will call resetGame to set the currentLevel,
currentLives, and currentScore variables to their starting values. As the Singleton
instance will not be released, we put the variable initializations in the resetGame
method. In this way, a single call to that method will fully reset the Singleton to
a "fresh" state for a new game. The addToScore and loseLife methods are for
convenience, so we don't have to "bother" our main playfield class with calculating
what the new values should be when we score points or lose a life.

Displaying player data

We now have a place to store the player data, but we will also need a way to display
this for the user. For this game, we are following "best practices" by separating
the **Heads-Up Display (HUD)** layer from the main playfield layer. The HUD is a
standard layer, with a background box, a place for the score, and a place for lives
remaining. One item to be pointed out is that in the HUD interface, we have
defined the following variable:

```
BRGameHandler *gh;
```

And in the init method of the HUD implementation, we have the paired line:

```
gh = [BRGameHandler sharedManager];
```

From this point on in this class, any time we want to reference our BRGameHandler
Singleton, we only have to use the variable gh. (Note: we also have this same variable
defined in the BRPlayfieldLayer class.)

Filename: BRHUD.mm

```
-(void) addToScore:(NSInteger)newPoints {
    [gh addToScore:newPoints];

    NSString *currScore = [NSString
            stringWithFormat:@"%i", [gh currentScore]];

    [scoreDisplay setString:currScore];
}
```

The HUD acts as a "bridge" between the playfield layer and the game handler for
scoring purposes. In the addToScore method, we first call out to the game handler
to add points to the current score, and then the HUD calls the setString method on
the scoreDisplay label to update the displayed score. By using a method like this,
the playfield layer only has to pass one message to the HUD, and it takes care of
the rest.

We want to get a little fancier with the display of lives remaining, and use `CCSprite` images of a ball for each life remaining, and we want a nice animation in the HUD when the player loses a life.

Filename: BRHUD.mm

```
-(void) createLifeImages {
    for (int i = 1; i <= gh.currentLives; i++) {
        CCSprite *lifeToken = [CCSprite
                spriteWithSpriteFrameName:@"ball.png"];
        [lifeToken setPosition:ccp(20 + (20 * i), 446)];
        [self addChild:lifeToken z:10];
        [livesArray addObject:lifeToken];
    }
}
```

Because we don't want to create a variable for each of the player's "life sprites", we instead opt to use an array to keep those sprites, called `livesArray`. When we call the `createLifeImages` method, it will generate the correct number of sprites, and space them out nicely in the display. It also stores them in the array.

Filename: BRHUD.mm

```
-(void) loseLife {
    // Remove a life from the GameHandler variable
    [gh loseLife];

    CCSprite *lifeToRemove = [livesArray lastObject];

    CCScaleBy *scaleLife = [CCScaleBy actionWithDuration:0.5
                                      scale:2.0];
    CCFadeOut *fadeLife = [CCFadeOut actionWithDuration:0.5];
    CCSpawn *scaleAndFade = [CCSpawn actionOne:scaleLife
                                   two:fadeLife];
    CCCallFuncND *destroyLife = [CCCallFuncND
                        actionWithTarget:self
                        selector:@selector(destroyLife:)
                        data:lifeToRemove];
    CCSequence *seq = [CCSequence actions:scaleAndFade,
                       destroyLife, nil];
    [lifeToRemove runAction:seq];

    [livesArray removeLastObject];
}

-(void) destroyLife:(CCSprite*)lifeToRemove {
    [lifeToRemove removeFromParentAndCleanup:YES];
}
```

When the player loses a life, we handle it in the same way we handled the score updates. We send the message to the game handler (which will subtract one from the `currentLives` variable). Our next step is to add a reference to the last sprite in the array with the `lifeToRemove` variable. After a little animation, we use `CCCallFuncND` to trigger the `destroyLife:` method, passing the `CCSprite` instance of the "life sprite" we want to remove from the game. That method simply removes it and frees up that memory. At the end of the `loseLife` method, we remove the sprite from the `livesArray`.

By encapsulating these updates in the HUD, we don't have to clutter up our playfield with methods that don't have anything to do with the core gameplay. If we were to radically alter the appearance and general behavior of the HUD (assuming that `addToScore:` and `loseLife` were still present), the gameplay layer code would not change at all. This design also means that we could use a completely different playfield class with this same HUD. That is the flexibility that we strive for in our coding.

Building bricks

We are missing one vital piece from our game: bricks to break. We want our game to be flexible enough that we will be able to define new levels without diving too deep into our source code, so we will be storing our levels as a **property list (plist)**.

For our game, we want to have unlimited play, so we will define a set number of brick patterns, and the game will loop through these in order. When you reach the end, it will go back to the first pattern and repeat the cycle.

We define the patterns in the plist as an array with the name in the format P#, so the patterns would be named P1, P2, P3, and so on. Inside each array are the strings representing each row of bricks. The rows begin at the bottom, so **Item 0** is the lowest row of bricks, and **Item 1** would be above it, and so on.

If we were to build a level editor for our game, we would be more likely to build a more robust plist structure. Because we are hand coding the level design, the easiest way to organize the data is in strings. For each row of each pattern, we define a string of 13 digits, each digit representing a brick. (Our screen size will only hold 13 bricks wide.) We will represent the bricks based on the numbering in their file names (`brick1.png`, `brick2.png`, and so on) as well as a zero, representing no brick in that position.

Let's take a look at one pattern from the plist, and how it will be displayed:

In this example showing pattern **P2**, **Item 0** is the bottom-most row of the final grid of bricks, shown to the right. You can see how it translates: brick number 3 is green, 4 is grey, 5 is orange, and so on. As long as we keep in mind the "bottom first" nature of the pattern, it becomes very easy to "see" the patterns in the numbers.

Loading a plist

So now we have a plist of pattern data, how do we load it? We have chosen to use an NSDictionary as the data structure that we want to hold the plist data once loaded. We add a plist loader into our BRGameHandler because it is a more general method, so we have it centralized if we decide we need to load a plist for some other part of the game.

Filename: BRGameHandler.mm

```
-(id) readPlist:(NSString*) fileName {
  NSData *plistData;
  NSString *error;
  NSPropertyListFormat format;
  id plist;

    // Assumes filename is part of the main bundle
  NSString *localizedPath = [[NSBundle mainBundle]
          pathForResource:fileName ofType:@"plist"];
  plistData = [NSData dataWithContentsOfFile:localizedPath];

  plist = [NSPropertyListSerialization
          propertyListFromData:plistData
          mutabilityOption:NSPropertyListImmutable
          format:&format errorDescription:&error];

  if (!plist) {
    NSLog(@"Error reading plist '%s', error '%s'",
        [localizedPath UTF8String], [error UTF8String]);
  }
  return plist;
}
```

This code is written with a couple of assumptions. One is that the passed filename will be without an extension (that is, we pass "patterns" if the filename is `patterns.plist`). The other assumption is that the plist file is in the main app bundle. You will notice that this method returns a value of type `id`. Since it was built as a general-purpose loader, we need one additional helper method to easily get the `NSDictionary` we desire for our data.

Filename: `BRGameHandler.mm`

```
-(NSDictionary*)getDictionaryFromPlist:(NSString*)fileName {
    return (NSDictionary*)[self readPlist:fileName];
}
```

This simply passes the filename to the `readPlist` method, and casts the returned value as an `NSDictionary`. (We can also use the same `readPlist` method to return an `NSArray`, using the same casting approach.)

Picking a pattern

Now that we know how to load the pattern data, let's take a look at the code from the `init` method of the `BRPlayfieldLayer` where we load the patterns, and decide which pattern to use:

Filename: `BRPlayfieldLayer.mm` (inside `init` method)

```
// Load the level patterns
patternDefs = [NSDictionary dictionaryWithDictionary:
[gh getDictionaryFromPlist:@"patterns"]];

// Load the brick pattern
NSInteger uniquePatterns = 4;
NSInteger newPattern =( [gh currentLevel] -1)
                                    % uniquePatterns;
[self buildBricksWithPattern:newPattern];
```

We load all of the pattern definitions into `patternDefs` using the `dictionaryFromDictionary` method. We then identify how many total patterns we have defined in the file. If we add new patterns to the plist, this is the only element of the actual code that needs to be modified.

The `newPattern` calculation uses a modulo operation to give us an endless repeating sequence of patterns. (We subtract one from the current level number because we start with Pattern P0 for Level 1.)

Now we move to the method that interprets the pattern data:

Filename: BRPlayfieldLayer.mm

```
-(void) buildBricksWithPattern:(NSInteger)patternNum {
    // Load in the desired pattern
    NSString *pattID = [NSString stringWithFormat:
                        @"P%i",patternNum];
    NSArray *tmpPattern = [patternDefs objectForKey:pattID];

    // We start at row 1
    NSInteger rowNum = 1;

    // Build each row of bricks
    for (NSString *aRow in tmpPattern) {
        [self buildBricksForRow:rowNum withString:aRow];
        rowNum++;
    }
}
```

Here we hold the array for the currently chosen pattern in the variable tmpPattern. Since each pattern is an array of strings, we then iterate through the tmpPattern array, and for each string in the array, we call the method to build the next row of bricks with this data:

Filename: BRPlayfieldLayer.mm

```
-(void) buildBricksForRow:(NSInteger)rowNum
                withString:(NSString*)brickString {
    for(int i = 0; i < [brickString length]; i++) {
        // Create brick and add it to the layer
        NSRange rng = NSMakeRange(i, 1);
        NSInteger newID = [[brickString
              substringWithRange:rng] integerValue];

        if (newID > 0) {
            NSString *newBrickName = [NSString
                stringWithFormat:@"brick%i.png", newID];

            PhysicsSprite *brick = [PhysicsSprite
                spriteWithSpriteFrameName:newBrickName];
            CGPoint startPos = [self positionForBrick:brick
                forRow:rowNum andColumn:i];

            brick.position = startPos;
```

```
        brick.tag = kBrick;
        [bricksheet addChild:brick z:10];

        // Create brick body
        b2BodyDef brickBodyDef;
        brickBodyDef.type = b2_dynamicBody;
        brickBodyDef.position.Set(startPos.x/PTM_RATIO,
                                  startPos.y/PTM_RATIO);
        brickBodyDef.userData = brick;
        b2Body *brickBody =
                world->CreateBody(&brickBodyDef);

        [brick setPhysicsBody:brickBody];

        // Create brick shape
        b2PolygonShape brickShape;
        brickShape.SetAsBox(
            brick.contentSize.width/PTM_RATIO/2,
            brick.contentSize.height/PTM_RATIO/2);

        //Create shape definition, add to body
        b2FixtureDef brickShapeDef;
        brickShapeDef.shape = &brickShape;
        brickShapeDef.density = 200.0;
        brickShapeDef.friction = 0.0;
        brickShapeDef.restitution = 1.0f;
        brickBody->CreateFixture(&brickShapeDef);
        }
    }
}
```

Because we are building an entire row of bricks, we approach this build method a little differently:

- We are passed the row number and the string representing this row of bricks

- We iterate through all of the characters of the string, one at a time

- We call NSMakeRange to substring only one character at a time, and convert that character to an integer value

- If the value is zero, there is no brick in that position, and no further action is taken for this position

If we need a brick here, we then proceed to build them in the same manner as the other objects. We build a sprite, body, shape, and fixture, and attach them together. When we define the shape of the fixture we use the SetAsBox function, so we can simply provide half the width of the sprite and half the height of the sprite, and Box2D builds the shape.

Breaking bricks, for real

Now we have all the core elements of the game defined, we need to add collision handling for the ball hitting the bricks. If we were to stop here, the ball would hit the bricks, and the bricks would go flying off from the force of the impact. We really want the brick to be destroyed, so we will revisit the update method we described earlier in the *Losing Your Ball* section. Immediately after the if...else statement in the update method, we add a couple of clauses:

Filename: `BRPlayfieldLayer.mm` (inside `init` method)

```
else if (spriteA != NULL && spriteB != NULL) {
  // Sprite A = ball, Sprite B = Block
  if (spriteA.tag == kBall && spriteB.tag == kBrick) {
   if (std::find(toDestroy.begin(), toDestroy.end(),
       bodyB) == toDestroy.end()) {
        toDestroy.push_back(bodyB);
    }
   }
  // Sprite B = block, Sprite A = ball
  else if (spriteA.tag == kBrick && spriteB.tag == kBall) {
    if (std::find(toDestroy.begin(), toDestroy.end(),
      bodyA) == toDestroy.end()) {
        toDestroy.push_back(bodyA);
    }
   }
 }
```

The outer clause makes sure we have sprites for both bodies involved in the contact. We then check the tag value for both sprites. If one is the brick and the other is the ball, then we add the brick to the toDestroy vector. As you recall, this is exactly how we handled the ball versus bottomGutter collisions earlier. The only primary difference is that we are comparing two sprites this time, and we are destroying the brick, not the ball.

Because we are using one common path of destruction for objects, we don't have to add anything else to the update method to make this process work. We only need to add a new case statement in the spriteDestroy method. Let's look at that method again:

Filename: `BRPlayfieldLayer.mm`

```
-(void) spriteDestroy:(PhysicsSprite*)sprite {
    switch (sprite.tag) {
        case kBrick:
            [[SimpleAudioEngine sharedEngine]
```

```
                              playEffect:SND_BRICK];
                 [self checkForRandomPowerupFromPosition:
                              sprite.position];
                 [sprite removeFromParentAndCleanup:YES];
                 [self addToScore:1];
                 break;
             case kBall:
                 [[SimpleAudioEngine sharedEngine]
                              playEffect:SND_LOSEBALL];
                 [sprite removeFromParentAndCleanup:YES];
                 [self loseLife];
                 break;
        }
    }
```

As you may remember, we actually destroy the Box2D body itself at the end of the update method, so we clean up the sprites here and take care of any additional housekeeping items, such as incrementing the score, playing sound effects, and so forth.

We have included one method in the case kBrick section that leads us to our next (and final) topic for this game: implementing power-ups.

Power-ups, good and bad

The idea of power-ups is core to the modern brick breaking experience. For our game, we will be implementing three types of power-ups: paddle expanding, paddle contracting, and multiball. As we just saw, when a brick is destroyed another method gets called to handle the power-ups.

Filename: BRPlayfieldLayer.mm

```
-(void) checkForRandomPowerupFromPosition:(CGPoint)brickPos {
    NSInteger rnd = arc4random() % 100;

    if (rnd < 25) {  // 25 % CHANCE
        [self buildPowerupAtPosition:brickPos];
    }
}
```

In this method we randomize a number. If it is below 25 percent, we call another method to actually build a power-up. It is important to point out that in the spriteDestroy method, we must call this method before we removeFromParentAndCleanup because we will need to use the position of the brick that is being destroyed here. This allows the power-up to drop from "inside" the brick that was just destroyed.

As we follow this code path, we now reach the point where we have decided to generate a power-up. This is another Box2D-enabled body, so let's review the build method for the power-ups:

Filename: `BRPlayfieldLayer.mm`

```
-(void) buildPowerupAtPosition:(CGPoint)startPos {
    NSInteger powerupType = arc4random() % 3;
    NSString *powerupImageName;
    NSInteger newTag;

    switch (powerupType) {
        case 1:
            powerupImageName = @"powerup_contract.png";
            newTag = kPowerupContract;
            break;
        case 2:
            powerupImageName = @"powerup_multi.png";
            newTag = kPowerupMultiball;
            break;
        default:
            powerupImageName = @"powerup_expand.png";
            newTag = kPowerupExpand;
            break;
    }

    // Create sprite and add it to layer
    PhysicsSprite *powerup = [PhysicsSprite
            spriteWithSpriteFrameName:powerupImageName];
    powerup.position = startPos;
    powerup.tag = newTag;
    [bricksheet addChild:powerup z:50];

    // Create body
    b2BodyDef powerupBodyDef;
    powerupBodyDef.type = b2_dynamicBody;
    powerupBodyDef.position.Set(startPos.x/PTM_RATIO,
                            startPos.y/PTM_RATIO);
    powerupBodyDef.userData = powerup;
    b2Body *powerupBody = world->CreateBody(&powerupBodyDef);

    // Connect the body to the sprite
    [powerup setPhysicsBody:powerupBody];

    // Define the fixture shape
```

```
b2PolygonShape powerupShape;
int num = 8;
b2Vec2 verts[] = {
    b2Vec2(-5.6f / PTM_RATIO, 4.3f / PTM_RATIO),
    b2Vec2(-5.6f / PTM_RATIO, -4.6f / PTM_RATIO),
    b2Vec2(-4.3f / PTM_RATIO, -5.8f / PTM_RATIO),
    b2Vec2(4.5f / PTM_RATIO, -5.8f / PTM_RATIO),
    b2Vec2(5.5f / PTM_RATIO, -4.8f / PTM_RATIO),
    b2Vec2(5.5f / PTM_RATIO, 4.4f / PTM_RATIO),
    b2Vec2(4.5f / PTM_RATIO, 5.6f / PTM_RATIO),
    b2Vec2(-4.7f / PTM_RATIO, 5.6f / PTM_RATIO)
};
powerupShape.Set(verts, num);

//Create shape definition and add to body
b2FixtureDef powerupShapeDef;
powerupShapeDef.shape = &powerupShape;
powerupShapeDef.isSensor = YES;
powerupBody->CreateFixture(&powerupShapeDef);

b2Vec2 force = b2Vec2(0,-3);
powerupBody->ApplyLinearImpulse(force,
              powerupBodyDef.position);
}
```

When we call this method, we only have gotten as far as knowing we need to
generate a power-up, but we have not yet identified which of the three available
power-ups we will generate. To that end, we use arc4random() to randomly choose
which of the power-ups we want to use. The only difference in this build method is
different values for the sprite file name and for the sprite's tag property.

For mathematical purists, none of the randomizing approaches used in
this book are "true randomness". There will be some small imbalance in
the frequency of numbers generated. However, this is just a game, so less
than perfect randomness is perfectly acceptable.

We continue to build the body, shape, and fixture much the same as we did for the
paddle body, including defining the polygon shape by its eight points. We could
have also gotten by with using a box shape instead, but we wanted to get "pixel-
perfect" with the rounded corners on the power-up blocks.

The fixture is a little different, however. We don't set the `density`, `friction`, or `restitution` for this fixture. Instead, we use a new property, `isSensor`. A sensor is a fixture that can take part in collisions, but doesn't actually cause things to impact it. A sensor can pass through another body without any hit-and-bounce-off actions. However, we can detect when a sensor and another fixture come in contact with each other. In our case, the power-ups will be picked up by the paddle, but they shouldn't bounce around and/or get hit by the ball or paddle.

We finish off the building of the power-up by applying a downward linear impulse on the body, so it will drop straight down. This simulates the effect of gravity, even though we have zero gravity for our world.

Picking up power-ups

Now we need to handle the collisions between the power-ups and the paddle. We have most of the pieces we need to make this happen already. Back in the `update` method, we add a few more checks directly after the brick versus ball checks. We need three more pairs of checks between the paddle and each type of power-up. (We only include the first pair for example – the other two are identical, just change the `tag` checked for the power-ups.)

Filename: `BRPlayfieldLayer.mm` (inside `update` method)

```
else if (spriteA.tag == kPowerupContract &&
        spriteB.tag == kPaddle) {
  if (std::find(toDestroy.begin(),toDestroy.end(),
          bodyA) == toDestroy.end()) {
     toDestroy.push_back(bodyA);
  }
}
else if (spriteA.tag == kPaddle &&
        spriteB.tag == kPowerupContract) {
  if (std::find(toDestroy.begin(), toDestroy.end(),
          bodyB) == toDestroy.end()) {
     toDestroy.push_back(bodyB);
  }
}
```

This is almost a direct copy-and-paste from the prior collision checking. Once again, when a power-up is "picked up", we simply add it to the `toDestroy` vector. As you have probably guessed, we handle the rest of the power-up triggering in the `spriteDestroy` method. In that method, we add three more case statements.

Filename: `BRPlayfieldLayer.mm` (inside `spriteDestroy` method)

```
case kPowerupContract:
  [sprite removeFromParentAndCleanup:YES];
  [self buildPaddleFixtureShort];
  paddleTimer = 10; // Set the timer to 10 seconds
  isPaddleDeformed = YES;
  break;
case kPowerupExpand:
  [sprite removeFromParentAndCleanup:YES];
  [self buildPaddleFixtureLong];
  paddleTimer = 10; // Set the timer to 10 seconds
  isPaddleDeformed = YES;
  break;
case kPowerupMultiball:
  [sprite removeFromParentAndCleanup:YES];
  shouldStartMultiball = YES;
  break;
```

For the contract and expand power-ups, we remove the sprite and then call to build a new fixture. The `paddleTimer` and `isPaddleDeformed` variables will be used to control when the paddle goes back to normal size.

For the multiball, there is a little more substance to it, so here we simply set the flag `shouldStartMultiball` to YES, so we can deal with it on the next `update` loop.

Paddle deformation

As you recall when we first build the paddle, we build the fixture itself in a separate method, `buildPaddleFixtureNormal`. When the player catches a contract or expand power-up, we simply need to destroy the existing fixture and build a new one. Let's look at the expansion:

Filename: `BRPlayfieldLayer.mm`

```
-(void) buildPaddleFixtureLong {
    // Define the paddle shape
    b2PolygonShape paddleShape;
    int num = 6;
    b2Vec2 verts[] = {
        b2Vec2(64.0f / PTM_RATIO, -7.5f / PTM_RATIO),
        b2Vec2(64.0f / PTM_RATIO, -0.5f / PTM_RATIO),
        b2Vec2(45.0f / PTM_RATIO, 6.5f / PTM_RATIO),
        b2Vec2(-48.0f / PTM_RATIO, 6.5f / PTM_RATIO),
```

```
            b2Vec2(-65.0f / PTM_RATIO, 0.5f / PTM_RATIO),
            b2Vec2(-65.0f / PTM_RATIO, -7.5f / PTM_RATIO)
        };
        paddleShape.Set(verts, num);

        // Build the fixture
        [self buildPaddleFixtureWithShape:paddleShape
                    andSpriteFrameName:@"paddle_wide.png"];
    }
```

Here we see why we divided the paddle fixture building into two methods. We can leverage all of the setup done by the `buildPaddleFixtureWithShape:` `andSpriteFrameName:` method we built earlier. The major differences are that we set a different `spriteFrameName`, and we define the `verts[]` with the coordinates that match the `paddle_wide.png` sprite's geometry.

The method `buildPaddleFixtureShort` follows the same design, using the display frame `paddle_short.png` and an alternate set of `verts[]` values. All the other code is identical to the "long" method.

Restoring the paddle

Now that we have either expanded or contracted the paddle, how do we go back to normal? We have set a 10 second timer value in the `spriteDestroy` method, but we need to actually do something with it. At the top of the `update` method, we add one simple `if` clause, as follows:

Filename: `BRPlayfieldLayer.mm` (inside `update` method)

```
    if (isPaddleDeformed) {
        paddleTimer = paddleTimer - dt;
        if (paddleTimer <= 0) {
            paddleTimer = 0;
            isPaddleDeformed = NO;
            [self buildPaddleFixtureNormal];
        }
    }
```

We only enter this clause if the `isPaddleDeformed` variable is set to `YES`. We subtract the current delta from the `paddleTimer`, and then check if our time has run out. If it has run out, we set `isPaddleDeformed` to `NO`, and call to the `buildPaddleFixtureNormal` method to restore our original paddle sprite and fixture. Thus, we are back to normal gameplay.

Multiball

Earlier we saw that the collision with the multiball power-up only sets the `shouldStartMultiball` variable to YES, and does not take any further action. Instead, we put the actual trigger at the end of the update method.

Filename: `BRPlayfieldLayer.mm` (inside `update` method)

```
if (shouldStartMultiball) {
    [self startMultiball];
    shouldStartMultiball = NO;
}
```

Why not simply call `startMutiball` directly? Because multiball involves the creation of new bodies, we want to make sure that the creation of those bodies does not happen while we are iterating through the world bodies (which we do at the top of the `update` method). To avoid this conflict, it is much safer to set triggers as we have done, and take action on them in a portion of the `update` method where you can be certain to be "in the clear".

Filename: `BRPlayfieldLayer.mm`

```
-(void) startMultiball {
    // Prevent triggering a multiball when the ball is lost
    if (!isBallInPlay) {
        return;
    }
    CGPoint startPos;
    for(b2Body *b = world->GetBodyList(); b;b=b->GetNext()) {
    if (b->GetUserData() != NULL) {
            // Get the sprite for this body
      CCSprite *sprite = (CCSprite *)b->GetUserData();

            if (sprite.tag == kBall) {
                startPos = sprite.position;

                // Build 2 new balls at the same position
                [self buildBallAtStartingPosition:startPos
                    withInitialImpulse:b2Vec2(0.2,1.5)];
                [self buildBallAtStartingPosition:startPos
                    withInitialImpulse:b2Vec2(-0.2,1.5)];

                multiballCounter = multiballCounter + 2;

                // We break out to avoid chain reactions
```

```
            break;
        }
    }
  }
}
```

The core of this method iterates over the bodies in the world, and looks for a sprite that has the tag `kBall`. It then calls the same `buildBall` method we used for the "normal" ball, and creates two new balls at the same position, but gives them a different impulse. This set of impulses gives a "popcorn" effect, so the two new balls go slightly up and to each side of the original ball.

We also have some extra code to prevent "bad behavior". The check of the `isBallInPlay` variable is to prevent a situation where the player catches a multiball right as the only ball in play is destroyed. This can cause a crash, if the sprite and body are destroyed at the same time the multiball is trying to interact with it.

We also force a break after one ball has been "multiballed". If we were to allow the iterator to continue evaluating other bodies, there is a strong possibility (depending on timing) that the two newly created balls would also be "multiballed" (that is, creating two new balls for each of them), and then those balls would also be "multiballed", and so on. The screen would instantly fill up with dozens of balls, and the game is unplayable.

Finally, we also keep track of how many "extra" balls we have in play, with the `multiballCounter` variable. This is important, so we don't accidentally trigger losing a life when the player still has balls in play.

Losing lives with multiball

Having more than one ball in play at a time makes detecting a lost ball a little more involved. Let's take a look at the final `loseLife` method:

Filename: `BRPlayfieldLayer.mm`

```
-(void) loseLife {
    if (multiballCounter > 0) {
        multiballCounter--;
    } else {
        isBallInPlay = NO;

        [hudLayer loseLife];
        // Do we need another ball?
        if ([gh currentLives] > 0) {
            [self scheduleOnce:@selector(newBall) delay:1.0];
```

```
        } else {
            // Game over
            [self prepareForGameOver];
        }
    }
}
```

We start by evaluating the `multiballCounter` variable. If there are any multiballs in play, we will subtract from that variable first, and the player's lives are not affected. If there is no multiball, then we call the HUD to lose a life. As you recall, this updates the HUD as well as updating the `currentLives` variable in the `BRGameHandler` class. Because of this, we can then evaluate the `[gh currentLives]` variable to determine the new number of lives for the player. If there are lives left, we create a new ball, and continue on. Otherwise, we begin the Game Over sequence.

Summary

We have covered a lot of (physics enabled) ground here. We have discussed the basics of Box2D, and we have built a pretty good brick breaker. We have focused on the core mechanics of the physics world, and how to translate between the Box2D and cocos2d positioning (using the `PTM_RATIO`). We have learned how to implement power-ups that affect the physics of the Box2D world during gameplay, and learned how to use a contact listener, and how to decide which collisions cause destruction.

In the next chapter, we will explore head-to-head action gaming with two players on the same device as well as our first two device game. Let's roll!

6
Cycles of Light

In this chapter, we will be shifting gears and developing a multiplayer iPad game. This game will include both two players on the same iPad as well as using Bluetooth connectivity with GameKit for a real head-to-head battle.

In this chapter, we cover the following:

- CCSprite movement without using actions
- Dynamic sprite stretching
- Efficient reuse of images
- Drawing with CCRenderTexture
- Using glScissor to clip drawing areas
- GameKit PeerPicker
- Bluetooth connectivity
- Sending and Receiving data

The game is…

In this chapter, we will be making a tribute to the "Light Cycles of TRON" game from the golden era of arcades. Each player has a bike driven in an enclosed game field. The bike has a fixed speed, and can only turn at right angles. The bike leaves a wall as a trail behind it. It is fatal to run into the walls created by the bikes. It is also fatal to run into the outside walls. To put our own spin on the game, our "bikes" will be light bulbs, each with their own "glow" of the appropriate color.

This is a two-player only game. Two players can play on the same iPad (positioned at opposite ends), or via a Bluetooth connection between two iPads. The game will be fully playable between Retina and non-Retina iPads at the same time.

Our finished game will look like the following screenshot:

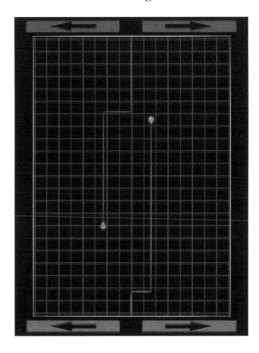

Design review

We will begin by discussing the approach that we will use for the design. One of our core design decisions for this game is to use as few graphic files as possible, without sacrificing the look and feel of the game. If you look at the source graphics, we only have four images: a white button with a right arrow on it, a light bulb, a white "bulb glow" image, and a white square image 1 x 1 point in size. From those images, we will drive the entire game.

Structurally, we want separate classes for the bike and the button. The bike will handle all of its own movement, and the button class will send messages directly to the bike it is controlling, so there is very little direct interaction with the game layer itself. The walls will be generated from the white square graphic, using on-the-fly scaling to stretch the walls behind the bike. All walls will be stored inside the game layer, since there is substantial need to share the walls between the bikes.

We will also use a separate layer for the "grid" graphics behind the playfield, because it truly is visual "fluff" with no interaction with the actual game field. This grid will have some visual effects, so it will never be static. This grid will be generated completely by the code, using the CCRenderTexture class to draw it when the game initializes.

Let's build a bike

We want to start with the basic element of the game, the `CLBike` class. We will look at this class in detail here, but first we want to see the `CLDefinitions.h` file.

Filename: CLDefinitions.h

```
// Audio definitions
#define SND_BUTTON @"button.caf"
#define SND_TURN @"bike_turn.caf"

// Graphics definitions
#define IMG_BIKE @"lightbulb.png"
#define IMG_GLOW @"glow.png"
#define IMG_BUTTON @"rightarrow.png"
#define IMG_SPECK @"whitespeck.png"

typedef enum {
    kBluePlayer,
    kRedPlayer
} PlayerID;

typedef enum {
    kNoChange, // NoChange only used in bluetooth games
    kUp,
    kRight,
    kLeft,
    kDown
} Direction;
```

Here we have a few definition for our graphic and sound assets. Centralizing the definitions makes it much easier to change your filenames in one place, rather than hunting through your code for all references.

We also create two `typedef enum` definitions. The `PlayerID` holds a value to make it easier to determine which player is being addressed. Likewise, we define `Direction` so we can use our directions without needing to keep notes to identify which number represents which direction. As we have mentioned before, these `typedef enum` are "integers in disguise", so we can pass these in as an integer if we ever need to (and we will later).

CLBike header

Now, we will look at the complete header for the CLBike class.

Filename: CLBike.h

```
#import <Foundation/Foundation.h>
#import "cocos2d.h"
#import "CLDefinitions.h"

@class CLPlayfieldLayer;

@interface CLBike : CCSprite {
    CGSize size; // Window size returned from CCDirector

    CLPlayfieldLayer *myPlayfield; // game layer

    PlayerID _thisPlayerID; // Player Number

    ccColor3B _wallColor; // Blue or green color

    float _bikeSpeed; // rate of travel for this bike
    Direction _bikeDirection; // facing which direction?

    CCSprite *glow; // The colored bulb glow sprite

    CCSprite *_currentWall; // Wall connected to bike
    CCSprite *_priorWall; // Wall created before current

    NSInteger wallWidth; // How wide the walls are

    BOOL isRemotePlayer; // Is this a non-local player?
    BOOL isCrashed; // Did this bike crash?
}

@property (nonatomic, assign) PlayerID thisPlayerID;
@property (nonatomic, assign) float bikeSpeed;
@property (nonatomic, assign) Direction bikeDirection;
@property (nonatomic, assign) ccColor3B wallColor;
@property (nonatomic, assign) BOOL isRemotePlayer;
@property (nonatomic, assign) BOOL isCrashed;
@property (nonatomic, retain) CCSprite *currentWall;
@property (nonatomic, retain) CCSprite *priorWall;

+(id) bikeForPlayer:(PlayerID)playerID
         PlayerNo:(NSInteger)playerNo
           onLayer:(CLPlayfieldLayer*)thisLayer
```

```
            isRemote:(BOOL)remotePlayer;

-(void) moveForDistance:(float)dist;
-(void) move;
-(void) turnRight;
-(void) turnLeft;
-(void) crash;

-(CGPoint) wallAnchorPoint;

@end
```

Most of these variables will be discussed during the explanation of the `CLBike.m` file, but there are a few items to touch on here. We keep a variable for `myPlayfield`, so the bike will be able to call methods from the main `CLPlayfieldLayer` class. You will notice that we do not `#import` that class, but instead use an `@class` line. As you may recall from *Chapter 3, Thumping Moles for Fun* and *Chapter 4, Give a Snake a Snack...*, this is a forward-declaration. It identifies that there will be a class by that name, but it doesn't know anything else about it in the header. The reason we use this is because the `CLPlayfieldLayer.m` file will import the `CLBike.h` header, so we would be stuck in a loop as the two classes try to import each other.

We also have a class "convenience" method here:

Filename: FileCLBike.h

```
+(id) bikeForPlayer:(PlayerID)playerID
         PlayerNo:(NSInteger)playerNo
          onLayer:(CLPlayfieldLayer*)thisLayer
         isRemote:(BOOL)remotePlayer;
```

Even though the `CLBike` class is a subclass of `CCSprite`, we have several other details of the class that we need to set up, so we have opted for this convenience method. We need to know the `playerID` (`kRedPlayer` or `kBluePlayer`), and the `playerNo` variable, which defines which "control position" the player is in. Player no. 1 is on the "home button" end of the iPad, and player no. 2 will play from the "top" of the iPad. We also pass the parent layer to the bike. The final argument is the Boolean variable `isRemote`, which identifies whether or not this bike will be controlled by someone who is not "local" to this iPad (that is during a Bluetooth game).

We also expose many variables and methods as properties in this class. This is because we want the other classes to be able to "ask" the bike for a lot of information. We also need to be able to completely control the bike from outside the class. If you recall from our design discussion, we want the control buttons to send messages directly to the bike, so we have to expose all of the control methods.

CLBike implementation

Now that we have a flavor for the CLBike header, we will move on to the implementation file. We will step through the core of the class here, and will revisit it later when we discuss playing over Bluetooth.

Filename: CLBike.m

```
#import "CLBike.h"
#import "CLPlayfieldLayer.h"
#import "SimpleAudioEngine.h"

@implementation CLBike

@synthesize thisPlayerID = _thisPlayerID;
@synthesize bikeSpeed = _bikeSpeed;
@synthesize bikeDirection = _bikeDirection;
@synthesize wallColor = _wallColor;
@synthesize currentWall = _currentWall;
@synthesize priorWall = _priorWall;
@synthesize isRemotePlayer;
@synthesize isCrashed;

+(id) bikeForPlayer:(PlayerID)playerID
        PlayerNo:(NSInteger)playerNo
         onLayer:(CLPlayfieldLayer*)thisLayer
        isRemote:(BOOL)remotePlayer
{
    return [[[self alloc] initForPlayer:playerID
                            PlayerNo:playerNo
                             onLayer:thisLayer
                            isRemote:remotePlayer]
        autorelease];
}
```

It is worth pointing out that we do have the #import "CLPlayfieldLayer.h" statement at the top of this file. This is the "pair" to the @class forward-declaration statement we used in the header. We need to use the #import line here because we will need the CLBike class to have access to the methods of the CLPlayfieldLayer class.

As we said earlier, we built a convenience method for creating a new bike. To adhere to the definition of a convenience method, we perform an alloc, an init, and mark the instantiated object as an autorelease object.

Filename: CLBike.m (initForPlayer, part 1)

```
-(id) initForPlayer:(PlayerID)playerID
          PlayerNo:(NSInteger)playerNo
            onLayer:(CLPlayfieldLayer*)thisLayer
           isRemote:(BOOL)remotePlayer {
    if(self = [super initWithSpriteFrameName:IMG_BIKE]) {
        myPlayfield = thisLayer;

        isRemotePlayer = remotePlayer;

        size = [[CCDirector sharedDirector] winSize];

        self.thisPlayerID = playerID;
        self.bikeSpeed = 3.0;
        self.bikeDirection = kUp;
        self.anchorPoint = ccp(0.5,0);
        self.scale = 0.25;
        self.isCrashed = NO;

        // Set the player's wall color
        switch (self.thisPlayerID) {
            case kRedPlayer:
                self.wallColor = ccc3(255, 75, 75);
                break;
            case kBluePlayer:
                self.wallColor = ccc3(75, 75, 255);
                break;
        }
```

Here we begin the initForPlayer: method. The "super" class of CLBike is
CCSprite, so we can call initWithSpriteFrameName: from the super class.
This takes care of the initialization of the standard CCSprite aspects of our class.
We only need to concern ourselves with the specialized CLBike initialization.

We keep the reference to the layer passed (in myPlayfield), the playerID
(in self.thisPlayerID), and the Boolean value of the remotePlayer variable
(in isRemotePlayer). The playerNo value is not stored in a variable, as it will
only be used while building the player's bike.

We set the default values for the bike to be facing up (kUp) with a bikeSpeed of 3.0,
and a scale of 0.25. We also set the anchorPoint to ccp(0.5, 0) which is a point
which is centered on the rear end of the bike.

Because we want to optimize our graphics, we will need to know what the player's color is. We don't want to set the sprite's color at all, because it would make the sprite look like a colored blob instead of a light bulb. Instead, we use `ccc3(r,g,b)` to build the colors we want, which are tinted slightly off pure red and pure blue, and then store them in the property `wallColor`.

Filename: `CLBike.m` (`initForPlayer`, part 2)

```
switch (playerNo) {
        case 1:
            // Starts at bottom of screen
            [self setPosition:ccp(size.width/2,64)];
            break;
        case 2:
            // Starts at top of screen
            [self setPosition:ccp(size.width/2,960)];
            self.bikeDirection = kDown;
            break;
    }

    [self rotateBike];

    glow = [CCSprite spriteWithSpriteFrameName:IMG_GLOW];
    [glow setAnchorPoint:[self anchorPoint]];
    [glow setPosition:ccp(34,26)];
    [glow setColor:self.wallColor];
    [self addChild:glow z:-1];

    // Bike's wall init here
    }
    return self;
}
```

Here we see the only code in the `CLBike` class that uses the `playerNo` value. If this is player 1, then the bike's starting position is centered toward the bottom of the screen. Player 2 is centered near the top of the screen, and their direction is changed to `kDown`. Once we have changed the bike's direction, we call the `rotateBike` method, which will correctly rotate the bike graphic (more on that method shortly).

We then add our "glow" graphic. This uses the solid white glow image, which we set to the color stored as the player's `wallColor`. We set the position as a little offset from the bike's position, to account for differences in the source image dimensions. We set the anchor point using the same `anchorPoint` value as the bike itself, and then we add the glow as a child of the bike (`self` in this class refers to the `CLBike` object), with a Z value of `-1`. This puts the glow behind the light bulb sprite. This lets us see the detail of the bulb, but also have the glowing effect visible through the transparent parts of the light bulb graphic.

The following screenshot shows the red bike, before and after we add the glow:

We will add some code to the end of this method later, but this will suffice for now.

Bike rotation

We have seen one method in this class that we haven't addressed yet, and it is simple enough to address now. After we position the bike, we call the rotateBike method.

Filename: CLBike.m

```
-(void) rotateBike {
    // Rotate the bike to match the direction
    switch (self.bikeDirection) {
        case kUp:
            self.rotation = 0;
            break;
        case kRight:
            self.rotation = 90;
            break;
        case kDown:
            self.rotation = 180;
            break;
        case kLeft:
            self.rotation = -90;
            break;
        default:
            break;
    }
}
```

We use a `switch` clause on the `self.bikeDirection` property. We then check which direction the bike is facing. Depending on the direction, we set the rotation for the sprite. The values chosen are simple right angles. So if the bike is facing in direction `kRight`, for example, we rotate the sprite to 90 degrees. If the bike is facing left, we rotate to -90 degrees. The movement will be controlled separately, so this graphic rotation is purely cosmetic. If we had chosen a symmetrical player graphic, we may not need to rotate at all.

Turning the bike

Rotating the bike graphics is all well and good, but we need to be able to change the actual direction in which the bike is travelling. We build two methods to control this: `turnLeft` and `turnRight`. We will look at the `turnRight` method here.

Filename: `CLBike.m`

```
-(void) turnRight {
    // Turn the bike to the right
    switch (self.bikeDirection) {
        case kUp:
            self.bikeDirection = kRight;
            break;
        case kRight:
            self.bikeDirection = kDown;
            break;
        case kDown:
            self.bikeDirection = kLeft;
            break;
        case kLeft:
            self.bikeDirection = kUp;
            break;
        default:
            break;
    }

    // Rotate the bike to the new direction
    [self rotateBike];

    // Play the turn sound
    [[SimpleAudioEngine sharedEngine] playEffect:SND_TURN];

    // Wall assignments

    // Remote game
}
```

When we call the `turnRight` method, we use a switch statement to determine the current `bikeDirection`. We then set the new `bikeDirection` that is appropriate for this turn. So, if you were going in the `kUp` direction and turned right, your new direction is `kRight`. If you were going `kRight`, the new direction is `kDown`. After the new direction has been set, we call to the `rotateBike` method we just discussed. We play a simple sound effect for the turn, and that's all we need to do at this point. We have placeholders for two additional pieces of code that we will add later (wall assignments and remote game).

The `turnLeft` method is nearly identical, except we obviously use a different set of new directions in the `switch` statement, so the bike will correctly turn to the left. There will be a slight difference in the remote game section that we will add later.

We could have compressed these two methods into one, with a conditional *if* statement for the parts of the code that differ. We have opted for reading clarity in this case, as the repeated code is really not that difficult to debug.

Building walls

Next, we will turn our attention to the creation of the game walls. There are two types of walls we need to address: walls created by a player's bike and the border walls around the playing grid. We will start by looking at how we can build our boundary walls.

Boundary walls

Before we look at the code, it is important to know two items that are set up in our `init` method of the `CLPlayfieldLayer` class. First, our `CCSpriteBatchNode` is in the variable `cyclesheet`. The second is that we have created an `NSMutableArray` called `bikeWalls` that will hold the `CCSprite` objects for all created walls (we will see this later, when we look at the `init` method in the `CLPlayfieldLayer` class). This array will be used in our collision detection, so we need to have our outer walls included in it.

Filename: `CLPlayfieldLayer.m`

```
-(void) createWallFrom:(CGPoint)orig to:(CGPoint)dest {
    CCSprite *aWall = [CCSprite
                      spriteWithSpriteFrameName:IMG_SPECK];
    [aWall setColor:ccYELLOW];
    [aWall setPosition:orig];
    [aWall setAnchorPoint:ccp(0,0)];
    [aWall setScaleX:ABS(orig.x - dest.x) + 3];
    [aWall setScaleY:ABS(orig.y - dest.y) + 3];
```

```
[cyclesheet addChild:aWall];

[bikeWalls addObject:aWall];
}
```

The first method we need is the ability to create a wall between two specified points, `orig` and `dest`, passed to it. If you recall from the beginning of the chapter, we said one of our goals with this game was to optimize the use of graphics. Here we see the first "real" use of that idea. We are using the image defined as `IMG_SPECK`, which is the file `whitespeck.png` in the sprite sheet. This is a 1 x 1 point white square image. We use this tiny image to create the wall sprite. We set the color to yellow, which works really well on a white sprite. Using `setColor` works in the opposite way to what most people expect. Instead of adding color to the sprite, it actually reduces the appropriate color registers to give the desired effect.

Setting a sprite to white (`ccWHITE`) actually sets the color to the original color. This dynamic is important to know if you are doing anything interesting with sprite colors. For example, if you set a sprite's color to blue and there is nothing in the blue register, the sprite could turn black. It is these unintended consequences that make it very appealing to use white sprites if your intention is to colorize them in-game.

Back to the code. We set the position of the sprite to the `orig` value we were passed, and we set the anchor point to the bottom-left corner. We do this to keep in check with the background we will be adding later. We then have a couple of odd lines for the `setScaleX` and `setScaleY`. Because we want to use this routine to draw all four walls, we won't know in which direction we are drawing. The formula in each of these lines does the same thing: Subtract the x (or y) values from each other. Take the absolute value (`ABS`) of the result. This will turn the negatives into positives. We then add 3 points, so we end up with a thick line (and avoid zero scale in the "thin" direction). This will take that simple 1 x 1 point graphic and stretch it out into a line the full length we requested, with a thickness of 3 points. This approach works well for horizontal or vertical lines, but will make a big rectangle if you use coordinates that are not straight lines. Our game uses only straight lines, so this will suit our needs perfectly.

We wrap up this method by adding the wall as a child of `cyclesheet`, and adding the created wall to the `bikeWalls` array. Now we have seen how to build a wall, we need another method to pass all of the coordinates we need to build the outer walls.

Filename: `CLPlayfieldLayer.m`

```
-(void) createOuterWalls {
    // Bottom
    [self createWallFrom:ccp(59,62) to:ccp(709,62)];
    // Top
    [self createWallFrom:ccp(59,962) to:ccp(709,962)];
    // Left
    [self createWallFrom:ccp(59,62) to:ccp(59,962)];
    // Right
    [self createWallFrom:ccp(709,62) to:ccp(709,962)];
}
```

We have decided that the desired offset from the left and right edges is 59 points. The offset from the top and bottom is 62 points. We call the `createWallFrom` method for each of the four boundary walls, and our work is done here.

Bike walls

Now we get to the real core of the cycles of light experience: the bike walls. Each bike will begin with a wall created behind it, and the walls will stretch until the bike turns. We start a new wall from that point.

Filename: `CLPlayfieldLayer.m`

```
-(CCSprite*) createWallFromBike:(CLBike*)thisBike {

    CCSprite *aWall = [CCSprite
                        spriteWithSpriteFrameName:IMG_SPECK];
    [aWall setColor:thisBike.wallColor];
    [aWall setAnchorPoint:[thisBike wallAnchorPoint]];
    [aWall setPosition:thisBike.position];

    [cyclesheet addChild:aWall];

    [bikeWalls addObject:aWall];

    return aWall;
}
```

This code is very similar to what we used for building the outer walls, with a few notable exceptions. When this method is called, the CLBike instance of the player's bike will be passed to it. We use this to get most of the parameters we need for the wall. We set the wall's color to the wallColor of the bike. We set the wall's position to the same position occupied by the bike. We also set the anchorPoint using a method called wallAnchorPoint that is part of the CLBike class (we'll look at that in just a moment).

We do not scale the wall sprite when it is created, so it is a single dot under the bike. We will handle the scaling of these walls from within the bike's movement code.

Like the other method, we still add the wall to the cyclesheet and to the bikeWalls array. However, we also return the wall to the caller. This is because the bike will need to know what wall is being created. Let's hop over to the CLBike class to see what's going on there.

Filename: CLBike.m

```
-(CGPoint) wallAnchorPoint {
    // Calculate the anchor point, based on direction
    switch (self.bikeDirection) {
        case kUp:
            return ccp(0.5,0);
            break;
        case kRight:
            return ccp(0,0.5);
            break;
        case kDown:
            return ccp(0.5,1);
            break;
        case kLeft:
            return ccp(1,0.5);
            break;
        default:
            return ccp(0.5,0.5);
            break;
    }
}
```

Here we have another method that uses the bikeDirection in a switch statement to determine a course of action. We set the anchor point to be at the center rear of the bike. So if the bike is currently going in direction kRight, then the anchor point should be set so x is equal to 0 (left edge) and y is equal to 0.5 (centered). We return the anchor point as a ccp() for all possible values of bikeDirection.

You will also notice that we return the value directly to the calling method. The only place where this method is called is from the createWallFromBike method we just reviewed. The reason we use the bike to determine the anchor point is that we want the wall to be attached to the rear end of the bike, no matter what direction it is heading. In this way, each time we create a bike, the wall is anchored correctly. If you're curious what it looks like when you incorrectly anchor a wall in the game, consider the following screenshot:

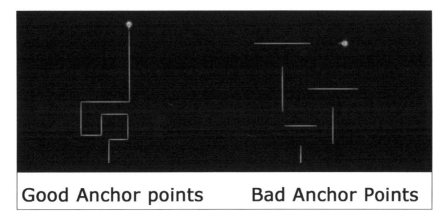

The same code was used in both of these images, except the wallAnchorPoint method was not used in the "Bad Anchor Points" example.

Bike integration

Now let's look at the code changes needed to integrate the walls into CLBike.

Filename: CLBike.m (initForPlayer end of method)

```
// Bike's wall init here
wallWidth = 5;

self.priorWall = nil;
self.currentWall = [myPlayfield
                    createWallFromBike:self];
```

Here we set a wallWidth to 5, and we set the priorWall to nil. Then we store the returned value of the createWallFromBike in the self.currentWall property. To avoid colliding with the prior wall when you turn, we need to be able to hold references to both the current wall and the wall just before it. Of course, here we are simply initializing the priorWall as nil for good measure.

We also need to insert identical code in both the `turnRight` and `turnLeft` methods of the `CLBike`.

Filename: `CLBike.m` (inside `turnRight` method)

```
// Wall assignments
self.priorWall = self.currentWall;
self.currentWall = [myPlayfield
                    createWallFromBike:self];
```

Both turn methods get identical "wall" code. This is the same as in the original `init` method, except here we first point the `priorWall` to the `currentWall` before we generate a new wall into the `currentWall` property. Because the `currentWall` property will first release the reference to the old wall before it creates a new one, this leaves the `priorWall` variable pointing to the previous wall, and the `currentWall` is now connected to the newly instantiated wall.

Bike movement

We will now move on to examine how we move the bike. Because the walls are central to the bike movement code, we left the movement until we understood the walls. The movement is broken down into two methods.

Filename: `CLBike.m`

```
-(void) move {
    // Move this bike (if local player)
    [self moveForDistance:self.bikeSpeed];

    // Remote game
}
```

This is the easy method. This looks a little silly now, but it will make more sense once we add the "remote game" functionality later. For now, this is just a pass-through to the `moveForDistance` method, passing the `bikeSpeed` parameter.

Filename: `CLBike.m`

```
-(void)moveForDistance:(float)dist {
    // Update bike position and scales the currentWall
    switch (self.bikeDirection) {
        case kUp:
            [self setPosition:ccp(self.position.x,
                                  self.position.y +
                                  dist)];
```

```
            [self.currentWall setScaleY:
             ABS(self.currentWall.position.y -
                  self.position.y)];

            [self.currentWall setScaleX:wallWidth];

          break;
        case kDown:
            [self setPosition:ccp(self.position.x,
                                  self.position.y -
                                  dist)];

            [self.currentWall setScaleY:
             ABS(self.currentWall.position.y
                  - self.position.y)];

            [self.currentWall setScaleX:wallWidth];

          break;
        case kLeft:
            [self setPosition:ccp(self.position.x -
                                  dist,
                                  self.position.y)];

            [self.currentWall setScaleX:
             ABS(self.currentWall.position.x
                  - self.position.x)];

            [self.currentWall setScaleY:wallWidth];

          break;
        case kRight:
            [self setPosition:ccp(self.position.x +
                                  dist,
                                  self.position.y)];

            [self.currentWall setScaleX:
             ABS(self.currentWall.position.x
                  - self.position.x)];

            [self.currentWall setScaleY:wallWidth];

          break;
        default:
          break;
      }
  }
```

We again use the common `switch` statement on the `bikeDirection`. For each direction the bike is travelling, we first set the new position for the bike. This position is adding (or subtracting) the value of `dist` (the `bikeSpeed` we passed in) to the appropriate x or y position. For example, if the bike is moving in the `kUp` direction, we add `dist` to the y position. To move down, we subtract `dist` from the y value.

The next two lines of code in each case are adjusting the `scaleX` and `scaleY` of the `currentWall`. If the bike is travelling in a y direction (up or down), we set the `scaleX` to the value of `wallWidth`. If the bike is travelling in an x direction (left or right), we set the `scaleY` to the value of `wallWidth`.

For the scale in the direction the bike is travelling, we take the absolute value (`ABS`) of the `currentWall` position minus the bike's current position. This will effectively stretch the wall from its origin to the bike with every move. This is exactly the same type of wall stretching we used when we created the outer walls, except this is dynamically resizing the wall every time the bike moves.

That's all it takes to make the bike move, and for the walls to grow appropriately.

Control buttons

Now that the bike and walls are fleshed out, we turn our attention to the control buttons. As we have mentioned before, we are optimizing our graphics, so we actually only have a single black and white button to use for all the control buttons. Let's look at the class header first.

Filename: CLButton.h

```
#import <Foundation/Foundation.h>
#import "cocos2d.h"
#import "CLDefinitions.h"
#import "CLBike.h"

@interface CLButton : CCSprite <CCTargetedTouchDelegate> {
    BOOL isLeft; // Is this a left turn button?
    CLBike *parentBike; // Bike the button controls
    CLPlayfieldLayer *myPlayfield; // main game layer
}

+(id) buttonForBike:(CLBike*)thisBike
        asPlayerNo:(NSInteger)playerNo
            isLeft:(BOOL)isLeftButton
           onLayer:(CLPlayfieldLayer*)thisLayer;

@end
```

Here we have kept references to both `myPlayfield` and the `parentBike`. The variable `myPlayfield` references the main playfield layer of our game. The `parentBike` is the bike that will be controlled by this button. The Boolean variable `isLeft` is used to determine if this is a left turn button. If this is set to NO, it is a right turn button.

We also have a convenience method to establish the class, which accepts values on behalf of these three variables, as well as a `playerNo` variable. The buttons need to know this for the same reason that we used it in the `CLBike` class; the buttons need to know on which end of the iPad they should be drawn.

Filename: CLButton.m

```
#import "CLButton.h"
#import "CLDefinitions.h"
#import "CLPlayfieldLayer.h"

@implementation CLButton

#pragma mark Initialization
+(id) buttonForBike:(CLBike*)thisBike
        asPlayerNo:(NSInteger)playerNo
            isLeft:(BOOL)isLeftButton
           onLayer:(CLPlayfieldLayer*)thisLayer {
    return [[[self alloc] initForBike:thisBike
                           asPlayerNo:playerNo
                               isLeft:isLeftButton
                              onLayer:thisLayer]
               autorelease];
}
```

Here we see the beginning of the implementation. We flesh out the class method, which follows the convenience method of building an autoreleased object.

Filename: CLButton.m

```
-(id) initForBike:(CLBike*)thisBike
      asPlayerNo:(NSInteger)playerNo
          isLeft:(BOOL)isLeftButton
         onLayer:(CLPlayfieldLayer*)thisLayer {
    if( self = [super initWithSpriteFrameName:IMG_BUTTON]) {

        // Store whether this is a left button
        isLeft = isLeftButton;

        // Keep track of the parent bike
```

```
        parentBike = thisBike;

        // Keep track of the parent layer
        myPlayfield = thisLayer;

        // Set the tint of the button
        [self setColor:parentBike.wallColor];

        // Base values for positioning
        float newY = 30;
        float newX = [[CCDirector sharedDirector]
                        winSize].width / 4;

        // Selective logic to position the buttons
        switch (playerNo) {
            case 1:
                if (isLeft) {
                    // Flip the image so it points left
                    [self setFlipX:YES];
                } else {
                    // Move it to the right
                    newX *= 3;
                }
                break;
            case 2:
                // Player 2 is upside down at the top
                newY = 994;

                // Flip the buttons to face player
                [self setFlipY:YES];

                if (isLeft) {
                    // Move it to the right
                    newX *= 3;
                } else {
                    // Flip the image so it points left
                    [self setFlipX:YES];
                }
                break;
        }

        [self setPosition:ccp(newX, newY)];

    }
    return self;
}
```

In the `initForBike` method, we begin by setting the three variables we saw in the header to their passed values. We then call `setColor` and tint the (formerly white) button to the `wallColor` of the `parentBike`. So now we will have a red or blue button, reflecting the player it controls.

We set "base" values of the `newX` to be ¼ of the screen width, and `newY` to be 30. We then have a switch statement using the `playerNo` variable to handle the placement of the buttons. For player 1, we check if this is the left button (the `isLeft` Boolean). If it is, we flip the button on its X axis. This is because our source graphic has the arrow pointing to the right. If it is the right button, we multiply the `newX` value by 3, so we are ¾ of the way across the screen.

For player 2, the logic is a little different, because we need to create the buttons at the top of the iPad, and completely backwards, compared to player 1. We reset the `newY` value to 994 (1024 – 30). We also flip the buttons on the Y axis, so they will be facing the player. If the button is the left button, we need multiply the `newX` by 3 to move it to ¾ of the way across the screen. This will put it on the left, relative to the player. If it is the right button, we flip it on the X axis. Notice the `flipX` and `newX` are exactly opposite to the way we handled player 1. Finally, we set the position to `newX`, `newY`.

Touching buttons

As you might imagine, we need a touch handler for the buttons.

Filename: `CLButton.m`

```
- (BOOL) ccTouchBegan:(UITouch *)touch withEvent:(UIEvent *)event {
    // Prevent touches if the layer not accepting touches
    if (myPlayfield.isTouchBlocked) {
        return NO;
    }

    CGPoint loc = [touch locationInView:[touch view]];
    CGPoint convLoc = [[CCDirector sharedDirector]
                    convertToGL:loc];

    // Create an expanded hit box for this class
    CGRect hitRect = CGRectInset(self.boundingBox, 0, -50.0);

    // If touched, send a turn msg to the parent bike
    if (CGRectContainsPoint(hitRect, convLoc)) {
        if (isLeft) {
            [self flashButton];
            [parentBike turnLeft];
```

```
        } else {
            [self flashButton];
            [parentBike turnRight];
        }
    }

    return YES;
}
```

We begin by making sure that myPlayfield does not have the isTouchBlocked Boolean set to YES. This is used during the game over routine to prevent rapid touching of the screen from exiting the game screen too fast. Here, we don't want to accept any touches on the buttons if the game is in this state.

We then convert the touch to OpenGL coordinates so we can determine what we touched. Now we define the hitRect, using something called CGRectInset. CGRectInset is used for transforming a CGRect. In this case, we are altering the bounding box for our evaluation. CGRectInset takes three arguments: a CGRect, the x inset, and the y inset. Using positive values will shrink the CGRect. Negative values will expand the CGRect. In our case, we are expanding the y value to effectively double the hit zone for the button. We do this because during testing, we determined that the button graphics, while visually satisfying, were a little too small to hit effectively during an exciting game. Rather than make huge buttons, we opted to simply expand the hit box.

We then check to see if the hitRect contains the touched location. If it does, we then send either the turnLeft or turnRight message to the parentBike.

Flashing with blocks

We also call to flashButton to give visual feedback to the users.

Filename: CLButton.m

```
-(void) flashButton {
    // Tint to the original white color
    CCTintTo *tintA = [CCTintTo actionWithDuration:0.1
                                                red:255
                                              green:255
                                               blue:255];
    // Tint back to the original color
    CCCallBlock *tintB = [CCCallBlock actionWithBlock:
                ^{[self setColor:parentBike.wallColor];}];
```

```
        // Run these two actions in sequence
        [self runAction:[CCSequence actions: tintA,
                        tintB, nil]];
    }
```

Here is the code for the `flashButton` method. We use the `CCTintTo` action to set the button to its original white color, and immediately set it back, using a `CCCallBlock` action. As we haven't really talked about blocks before, now is a good time.

A block is a self-contained chunk of code that can save a lot of "extra" code, and can use variables internally. Our example here is extremely simple, but the syntax might seem foreign. A block is wrapped in a structure like the following:

```
    ^{
    [self dosomething];
     }
```

There's a lot that can be done with blocks, but here it really saves us from building another method simply to make one call to `setColor`. (We could have built a separate method, and called it with `CCCallFunc` if we didn't want to use a block).

It is worth noting that blocks are only available in iOS 4.0 or higher, so code meant for older devices cannot use them. To learn about using blocks, we suggest consulting Apple's documentation on the topic at: `http://developer.apple.com/library/ios/#documentation/cocoa/Conceptual/Blocks/Articles/00_Introduction.html`

Finishing the buttons

We would be remiss if we didn't also include the `onEnter` and `onExit` methods for the `CLButton` class.

Filename: `CLButton.m`

```
    -(void)onEnter
    {
        [[[CCDirector sharedDirector] touchDispatcher]
         addTargetedDelegate:self
         priority:0
         swallowsTouches:NO];

        [super onEnter];
    }
```

```
- (void) onExit
{
    parentBike = nil;
    myPlayfield = nil;

    [[[CCDirector sharedDirector] touchDispatcher]
     removeDelegate:self];

    [super onExit];
}
```

We register a delegate with the touch dispatcher in the onEnter method, and we remove that delegate in the onExit method. We also set both the parentBike and myPlayfield to nil. It is always important to clean up after yourself. If we had failed to remove the delegate, this object would never be deallocated, and would leak.

Building the background grid

If we were to leave the background as it is, the game would look rather dull, with a black background. One option would be to simply drop in a background graphic to enhance the look. That would work, but we want to do something more dynamic to give the game some life. We will begin by using CCRenderTexture to build a sprite with a grid pattern on it.

A CCRenderTexture can be thought of as a second "blank sheet of paper" on which we can draw primitive shapes (like lines), draw sprites upon, and generally do anything visual on it. The power of the CCRenderTexture is that you can then use the resulting image as a sprite. One of the primary benefits for our project is that we can draw our grid on it once, and use it. If we were to put the ccDrawLine calls into our main layer's draw method, it would be drawing them from scratch with every refresh. In our case, we are drawing the lines once, and then using the resulting textured sprite without the additional overhead of redrawing the lines.

Let's look at the init method first.

Filename: CLRenderGrid.m

```
-(id) init {
    if(self = [super init]) {

        CGSize size = [[CCDirector sharedDirector] winSize];

        // create a blank render texture
```

```
firstGrid = [[CCRenderTexture alloc]
    initWithWidth:700 height:950
    pixelFormat:kCCTexture2DPixelFormat_RGBA8888];

// Draw the first grid in a render texture
[self drawGrid];

[[firstGrid sprite] setAnchorPoint:ccp(0.5,0.5)];
[[firstGrid sprite] setPosition:ccp(size.width/2,
                          size.height/2)];
[[firstGrid sprite] setOpacity:50];

// Override the default blend
[[firstGrid sprite] setBlendFunc:
    (ccBlendFunc){GL_SRC_ALPHA,
    GL_ONE_MINUS_SRC_ALPHA}];

[self addChild:firstGrid];


// Second grid

// Start grids moving

}
return self;
}
```

We begin by creating `firstGrid` as a `CCRenderTexture` with the dimensions 700 x 950. This is slightly larger than will be visible, but we want to be able to move it around later without seeing the edges. We will skip the `drawGrid` method call for now. We set the anchor point to the center and position the `firstGrid` sprite in the center of the layer. It is important to note that to access the sprite properties of the `CCRenderTexture`, you must specify `[firstGrid sprite]` to get to them. The `CCRenderTexture` itself does not have these properties. We also set our opacity to `50`, so the resulting sprite will be semi-transparent.

The next call, `setBlendFunc`, is not often seen in tutorials or code samples. The values set here force the sprite to use the "normal" sprite blending function. By default, a `CCRenderTexture` uses the blend function `GL_ONE`, `GL_ONE_MINUS_SRC_ALPHA`, which effectively negates any opacity settings used. A tutorial on OpenGL blending functions is beyond the scope of this discussion. For further reading on the topic, a good starting point is: http://www.khronos.org/opengles/sdk/docs/man/xhtml/glBlendFunc.xml

We wrap this up by adding the `firstGrid` to the layer. We have two placeholders for code we will add later.

Drawing the grid

Now we will see how we draw to the render texture.

Filename: CLRenderGrid.m

```
-(void) drawGrid {
    // Start drawing on the Render Texture
    [firstGrid begin];

    glLineWidth( 3.0f * CC_CONTENT_SCALE_FACTOR() );
    ccDrawColor4F(1, 1, 1, 1);

    float left = 0;
    float right = firstGrid.sprite.textureRect.size.width;
    float top = firstGrid.sprite.textureRect.size.height;
    float bottom = 0;
    float gridSize = 40;

    // Draw the vertical lines
    for (float x = left; x <= right; x+=gridSize) {
        ccDrawLine(ccp(x, bottom), ccp(x, top));
    }

    // Draw the horizontal lines
    for (float y = bottom; y <= top; y+=gridSize) {
        ccDrawLine(ccp(left, y), ccp(right, y));
    }

    // Done drawing on the Render Texture
    [firstGrid end];

}
```

To begin drawing on the render texture, we make the call to `begin`. To stop drawing, we call `end`. Everything in the middle is direct OpenGL drawing commands. We set the `glLineWidth` parameter to set the drawing pen size to 3 points wide. Whenever you are diving into drawing with OpenGL, you must keep in mind it does not have any direct knowledge of the points versus pixels scaling that cocos2d converts for you. Everything is in pixels only. So, to draw a line 3 points wide, we multiply the desired point size by the `CC_CONTENT_SCALE_FACTOR()`, which will be 1 for non-Retina devices, and 2 for Retina devices. This will give us the desired effect of a 3 point wide line, regardless of the display capabilities of the device. By using this scale factor "helper", it also means the code will not fail if we find ourselves using a device with a scale factor of 3 (though it doesn't exist, yet). We then set the drawing color using `ccDrawColor4F()`. The values of 1,1,1, and 1 translate to r, g, b, and a values, with all fully "on". This is an opaque white color.

We set floats to help us keep our code readable. We set the left and bottom to `0`, since we want to fill the render texture's space with our drawing. Likewise, we set the right and top to the total width and height (respectively) of the render texture's canvas. By "asking" the `firstGrid.sprite` for the size of the texture, it means we can change the size of the render texture in the `init` method without adjusting this code at all. We also set the grid size to `40` pixels wide. This is a fairly arbitrary number. Smaller numbers create a tighter grid, larger numbers have more open space.

We then use a `for` statement to draw the vertical lines. We loop through the x values from left to right, based on the floats we set earlier. One callout here is that we are not using the typical `x++` as the incrementor. Instead, we are using `x+=gridSize` as the incrementor. This controls the size of the "step" between the iterations. Using this means that the first iteration will use a value of 0, the second will be 40, then 80, and so forth. This will be perfectly placed for each line. We use the `ccDrawLine` function to draw a line from the bottom of the screen to the top with a constant value of x. This line is drawn every step of the loop, so it will fill the render texture with the vertical lines we need, at a 40 pixel spacing.

We then do exactly the same thing for the horizontal lines. This time we iterate through values of y, and draw from the left to the right at a constant y value. By the end, we have a perfectly drawn square grid.

In the interest of good memory management, we must remember that we have alloc'd the `firstGrid`, so we need to dealloc it appropriately.

Filename: `CLRenderGrid.m`

```
-(void) dealloc {
    [firstGrid release];

    [super dealloc];
}
```

It is important to always release whatever you have retained.

The second grid

We actually want to have two grids to give more visual fluff. We could draw the grid onto another render texture, but that seems a bit silly, since we already have drawn it the way we want it. Instead, we will clone the texture into a new sprite. Insert the following code at the "second grid" placeholder.

Filename: `CLRenderTexture.m` (inside `init` method)

```
// Second grid
// Clone the grid as a separate sprite
secondGrid = [CCSprite spriteWithTexture:
            [[firstGrid sprite] texture]];
[secondGrid setAnchorPoint:ccp(0.5,0.5)];
[secondGrid setPosition:ccp(size.width/2,
                            size.height/2)];
[secondGrid setOpacity:60];
[secondGrid setColor:ccWHITE];
[self addChild:secondGrid];
```

This is very similar to the settings we used for the `firstGrid`, except when we instantiate the sprite, we use `spriteWithTexture`, and pass it the texture of the sprite contained in the `firstGrid` object. This allows us to have a second sprite exactly like the render texture's sprite, but it will only behave as a sprite. This means we will not be able to draw more on the `secondGrid` (sprite only), but we could draw more on the `firstGrid` (CCRenderTexture).

Moving grids

Now we have two identical grids on top of each other. What we want is to set them both into continuous motion, preferably something we can start and forget about. We will be using `CCRepeatForever` actions to make it happen.

Filename: `CLRenderGrid.m`

```objc
-(void) moveFirstGrid {
    // Set up actions to shift the grid around
    CCMoveBy *left = [CCMoveBy actionWithDuration:1.0
                              position:ccp(-10,-10)];
    CCMoveBy *right = [CCMoveBy actionWithDuration:1.0
                               position:ccp(20,20)];
    CCMoveBy *back = [CCMoveBy actionWithDuration:1.0
                              position:ccp(-10,-10)];


    CCTintBy *tintA = [CCTintBy actionWithDuration:8.0
                                red:255 green:255 blue:0];
    CCTintBy *tintB = [CCTintBy actionWithDuration:4.0
                                red:0 green:255 blue:255];


    CCRepeatForever *repeater = [CCRepeatForever
            actionWithAction:[CCSequence actions:
                             left,
                             right,
                             back, nil]];
    CCRepeatForever *repeater2 = [CCRepeatForever
                                   actionWithAction:
                                   [CCSequence actions:
                                    tintA, tintB, nil]];


    [[firstGrid sprite] runAction:repeater];
    [[firstGrid sprite] runAction:repeater2];
}
```

Here we set up two "sets" of actions. The first set moves the grid around in a perfectly repeating pattern (after all three actions are run, the coordinates are back to where you started). The second set of actions uses the `TintBy` action to alter the colors in a slow fading pattern. Looking at the durations, it is a full 12 seconds for a complete cycle of this set of tints. We then wrap both of these sets of actions into a `CCSequence` inside a `CCRepeatForever` action. Because the two sets of actions affect different aspects of the sprite, they can be run simultaneously. We run these both on the `firstGrid` sprite.

We do nearly the same thing on the second grid, although we move the grid in the other diagonal direction, and we tint from black to white, in an 11 second cycle. We run this on the `secondGrid`. (Consult the code bundle for this book to see the movement code for the `secondGrid` sprite.)

To tie it all together, we insert the following lines into the `init` method at the "start grids moving" placeholder.

Filename: `CLRenderGrid.m` (inside `init` method)

```
// Start grids moving
[self moveFirstGrid];
[self moveSecondGrid];
```

The glScissor

We have one problem remaining. The grid is larger than the part of the screen we want to draw it in. Ideally, we want the grid to move around, but only be visible inside the yellow outer walls. Using the OpenGL `glScissor` is exactly what we need. Like its name suggests, the `glScissor` is used to clip an image from being visible. Here, we want to trim the visible graphics for this entire layer at the yellow line.

The following screenshot shows a before and after comparison:

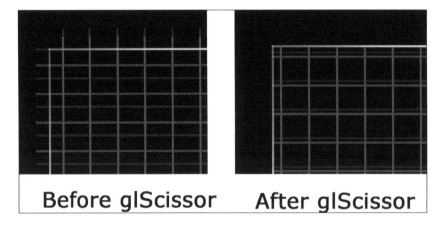

As you may have noticed, the `CLRenderGrid` is a subclass of `CCLayer`, so we have the same coordinate space for the layer that we do for the main grid. We can easily use `glScissor` to fix the problem.

Filename: `CLRenderGrid.m`

```
-(void) visit {
    // We use the glScissor to clip the edges
    // So we can shift stuff around in here, but not
    // go outside our boundaries
    glEnable(GL_SCISSOR_TEST);
```

```
glScissor(59 * CC_CONTENT_SCALE_FACTOR(),
          62 * CC_CONTENT_SCALE_FACTOR(),
          650 * CC_CONTENT_SCALE_FACTOR(),
          900 * CC_CONTENT_SCALE_FACTOR());
    [super visit];
    glDisable(GL_SCISSOR_TEST);
}
```

Here we use the same coordinates we used for drawing the outer walls in the main playfield layer. As we said earlier, OpenGL is not aware of the scale of the device, so we multiply each value by the CC_CONTENT_SCALE_FACTOR(). This will give the same clipping boundaries in Retina and non-Retina devices.

The playfield

We have assembled most of the "external" components, so it is time to turn our attention to the CLPlayfieldLayer class itself. Let's dive into the class instantiation and init methods first.

Filename: CLPlayfieldLayer.m

```
+(id) gameWithRemoteGame:(BOOL)isRemoteGame {
    return [[[self alloc] initWithRemoteGame:isRemoteGame]
autorelease];
}


-(id) initWithRemoteGame:(BOOL)isRemoteGame {
    if(self = [super init]) {

        size = [[CCDirector sharedDirector] winSize];

        // Load the spritesheet
        [[CCSpriteFrameCache sharedSpriteFrameCache]
           addSpriteFramesWithFile:@"cyclesheet.plist"];
        cyclesheet = [CCSpriteBatchNode
           batchNodeWithFile:@"cyclesheet.png"];

        // Add the batch node to the layer
        [self addChild:cyclesheet z:1];

        bikeWalls = [[NSMutableArray alloc] init];
        remoteGame = isRemoteGame;
        isGameOver = NO;
        isTouchBlocked = NO;
```

```
// Build the background grid
CCNode *grid = [CLRenderGrid node];
[self addChild:grid z:-1];

// Build the outer walls
[self createOuterWalls];

    }
    return self;
}
```

We use another convenience method here, this time only accepting one parameter, isRemoteGame. For a local only game this will be NO, and YES if it is a Bluetooth game.

The initWithRemoteGame method is fairly basic. We set up our cyclesheet batch node, establish the bikeWalls array, and set a few Boolean values. We also add our CLRenderGrid as a child with a Z order of -1, to keep it behind the rest of the game. Then we add our outer walls, and that's it.

We put the actual bike building calls in the onEnterTransitionDidFinish method. We do this because if we choose to use a transition to enter the scene, we don't want the game starting up before the transition is complete.

Filename: CLPlayfieldLayer.m

```
-(void) onEnterTransitionDidFinish {
    if (remoteGame) {
        // Remote Game
        [self findPeer:self];
    } else {
        // Initial Player Setup
        [self generateRedAsPlayerNo:1 isRemote:NO];
        [self generateBlueAsPlayerNo:2 isRemote:NO];
        [self scheduleUpdate];
    }
    [super onEnterTransitionDidFinish];
}
```

We have left a small piece of the remote game code here, so you can see the difference in how we set up the start of the game. For a local game only, we set up both players, and schedule the update. We will look at the "generate" methods next.

Generating the bikes

Adding the player bikes and buttons to the playfield is trivial here, since we have done most of the work in the CLBike and CLButton classes. We use nearly identical methods for the red and blue bikes, so we will only include one here.

Filename: CLPlayfieldLayer.m

```
-(void) generateRedAsPlayerNo:(NSInteger)playerNo
                   isRemote:(BOOL)remotePlayer {
    // Generate the red player's bike
    redBike = [CLBike bikeForPlayer:kRedPlayer
                          PlayerNo:playerNo
                           onLayer:self
                          isRemote:remotePlayer];
    [cyclesheet addChild:redBike];

    // Only create buttons for the local player
    if (remotePlayer == NO) {

        CLButton *right = [CLButton
                           buttonForBike:redBike
                           asPlayerNo:playerNo
                           isLeft:NO
                           onLayer:self];
        [cyclesheet addChild:right];

        CLButton *left = [CLButton
                          buttonForBike:redBike
                          asPlayerNo:playerNo
                          isLeft:YES
                          onLayer:self];
        [cyclesheet addChild:left];
    }
}
```

Here we instantiate a new redBike, specifying that it belongs to kRedPlayer, and we add it to the sheet. We then check if this is a remotePlayer. If it is not, then we also build the right and left buttons for the player. (Remote players do not need to have buttons drawn for this device). You will notice that we do not retain a reference to the buttons we create. The buttons need to know about the layer (as we saw earlier), and they need to know about the bike they are controlling, but the layer doesn't need to do anything special with the buttons except to add them as children of the layer. They are self-sufficient, so we can build them and ignore them here.

The `generateBlueAsPlayerNo:isRemote:` method is nearly identical, except the initial bike creation is instantiated as `blueBike`, with `kBluePlayer` as the parameter. As we discussed in the `CLBike` class earlier, we could probably collapse this into a single method, but separate methods like this are easier to follow.

Collision handling

When it comes to collision handling, we have already put all of the pieces into place to make collisions easy to check for. We have all walls in the game stored in the `bikeWalls` array. Each bike keeps track of both the `currentWall` and `priorWall` objects created by that bike. This is all we need to do to check for all possible collisions.

Filename: `CLPlayfieldLayer.m`

```
-(void) checkForCollisions {
    for (CCSprite *aWall in bikeWalls) {
        // Compare wall to blue bike
        if (CGRectIntersectsRect([aWall boundingBox],
                                 [blueBike boundingBox])
            && aWall != blueBike.currentWall
            && aWall != blueBike.priorWall) {
                [self crashForBike:blueBike];
            break;
        }
        //Compare wall to red bike
        if (CGRectIntersectsRect([aWall boundingBox],
                                 [redBike boundingBox])
            && aWall != redBike.currentWall
            && aWall != redBike.priorWall) {
                [self crashForBike:redBike];
            break;
        }


    }
}
```

When we check for collisions, we iterate through all the wall sprites in the `bikeWalls` array. We first check for the `blueBike`. If its `boundingBox` intersects with the wall and the wall is not the `currentWall` or `priorWall` of the `blueBike`, then that bike crashed. We do the same check for the `redBike`, this time making sure it is not the `currentWall` or `priorWall` of the `redBike`. The question is probably coming to mind: why two walls for each bike? Isn't tracking the `currentWall` object enough?

When a bike turns, it turns at an abrupt right angle. The ending of the `priorWall` is at exactly the same point as the origin of the new `currentWall`. For a single update cycle, the bike is on this exact point. If we don't track the `priorWall`, then the bike will crash on that point. As there is no way the bike can correctly crash into the `priorWall`, we can safely ignore any collisions with it.

Making it move

We use a very simple `update` method, which actually passes most of the control to the bikes themselves.

Filename: `CLPlayfieldLayer.m`

```
-(void) update:(ccTime)dt {
    // We only use the move method if this is a local
    // player.  We move the opponent via the data
    // connection
    if (![redBike isRemotePlayer]) {
        [redBike move];
    }

    if (![blueBike isRemotePlayer]) {
        [blueBike move];
    }

    [self checkForCollisions];
}
```

If the player is not a remote player, we tell the bike to move, using the `move` method we saw earlier. (In case you're wondering, we will handle the remote player's moves more explicitly). We then check for collisions after every move.

Crashing bikes

Now we will look at what happens when a bike crashes. We want a little visual flair, so we will put the actual "crash" code in the `CLBike` class, but the core handler is in the `CLPlayfieldLayer` class, because the entire game needs to know about the crash, not just the bike.

Filename: `CLPlayfieldLayer.m`

```
-(void) crashForBike:(CLBike*)thisBike {
    [self unscheduleUpdate];

    // The bike crash sequence
```

```
        [thisBike crash];

        // Prevent all touches for now
        isTouchBlocked = YES;

        // Identify game over
        isGameOver = YES;

        // Game over sequence
        [self displayGameOver];
    }
```

We unscheduled the `update` method, told the bike that it crashed, and set a couple of Boolean values. We used the `isTouchesBlocked` variable to prevent the player from rapidly mashing buttons and exiting the game without seeing the results. Players need a little time to enjoy their victory, or ponder their defeat. We will not cover the `displayGameOver` method in the book. Please consult the source code for that method. (It is a fairly basic "Red Player Wins!" label, not much more than that.)

Filename: `CLBike.m`

```
-(void) crash {
    self.isCrashed = YES;

    [glow removeFromParentAndCleanup:NO];

    CCScaleTo *scale = [CCScaleTo actionWithDuration:0.5
                                               scale:2];
    CCFadeOut *fade = [CCFadeOut actionWithDuration:1.0];

    [self runAction:[CCSequence actions:scale, fade, nil]];
}
```

Here we see the `crash` method. We remove the glow image, scale the sprite up to be really big, and then quickly fade it out. We also set the `isCrashed` variable to YES, which is used in the `displayGameOver` method to determine who won and who lost.

Bluetooth multiplayer

We now have a complete two-player game on the same iPad. Now we will turn our attention to using GameKit to create a local Bluetooth game between two iPads. A word of caution to begin this discussion: this does not work correctly on the simulator, so you must have two iPads (any generation will do) in order to test this code.

To get the game prepared for using GameKit, we need to make sure the `GameKit.framework` is included in our project. You can check this by selecting your target project, and selecting the "Build Phases" heading. Then, expand the **Link Binary With Libraries** tab, and see if it is listed. If it is not, click on the **+** button at the bottom of the section, and select `GameKit.framework`.

In Xcode, it looks like the following screenshot:

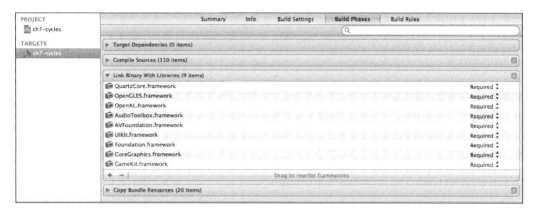

We also need to make a couple of additions to the `CLPlayfieldLayer.h` file to include the GameKit.

Filename: `CLPlayfieldLayer.h` (partial)

```
#import <GameKit/GameKit.h>

@interface CLPlayfieldLayer : CCLayer <GKPeerPickerControllerDelegate,
GKSessionDelegate> {
```

As you can see, we have imported GameKit with the "framework style" angle brackets, and we have declared two delegate types for our `CLPlayfieldLayer` class. This will let us receive the callbacks from GameKit.

We also need a few specific variables in the header.

Filename: `CLPlayfieldLayer.h` (partial):

```
 // GameKit specific variables
GKPeerPickerController *gkPicker; // Peer Picker
GKSession *gkSession; // The session
NSString *gamePeerId; // Identifier from peer
NSInteger playerNumber; // To assign bike colors
GKPeerConnectionState currentState;
```

The first three are needed by GameKit itself, and the `playerNumber` is a variable that we will be using to handle the issue of which player gets which color bike. The `currentState` is our own variable that we will be using to handle refused connections.

Peer Picker

We will be using the default Peer Picker that comes as part of GameKit. This is a full GUI interface for finding players and making the connection between the devices. This GUI is called the **Peer Picker**. There are quite a few callbacks that are needed, so don't be put off by the amount of code we are about to see. Most of it is boilerplate and can be re-used with little, if any, modifications in other projects.

Filename: CLPlayfieldLayer.m

```
-(void) findPeer:(id)sender {
    //Initialize and show the picker
    gkPicker = [[GKPeerPickerController alloc] init];
    gkPicker.delegate = self;
    gkPicker.connectionTypesMask =
                GKPeerPickerConnectionTypeNearby;
    [gkPicker show];

    playerNumber = 1;
}
```

We begin by creating the `GKPeerPickerController`, setting its delegate, and specifying the connection mask. The `connectionTypesMask` property controls what types of connections are considered when looking for a game. The value we have specified, `GKPeerPickerConnectionTypeNearby`, limits the Peer Picker to local Bluetooth connections only. We also set the starting `playerNumber` to be 1. For the purposes of this game, player no. 1 is the red player, and player no. 2 is the blue player.

Filename: CLPlayfieldLayer.m

```
-(GKSession*) peerPickerController:(GKPeerPickerController*)picker
sessionForConnectionType:(GKPeerPickerConnectionType)type {
    gkSession = [[GKSession alloc]
            initWithSessionID:@"Ch6_Cycles"
            displayName:nil
            sessionMode:GKSessionModePeer];
            gkSession.delegate = self;
            return gkSession;
}
```

Here we establish the GKSession for the connection. We limit the available connections even further by specifying the SessionID. In our case, it is "Ch6_Cycles", which is the way our game identifies itself. This SessionID must match between the devices, or they will not be able to "see" each other. This does mean that both players must have the game running at the same time in order to attempt to connect with each other.

We also set the sessionMode to be GKSessionModePeer. There are three types of sessions: client, server, and peer. A **peer** is essentially a client and server at the same time. This means it can initiate connections to a server (or another peer), or it can receive connections from a client (or another peer). In most cases, you would want to set this to peer, so you can send and receive connection requests.

Filename: CLPlayfieldLayer.m

```
-(void) peerPickerController:(GKPeerPickerController*)picker
            didConnectPeer:(NSString*)peerID
                toSession:(GKSession*)currSession {
    // Dismiss the peerPicker
    [gkSession setDataReceiveHandler:self
                        withContext:NULL];
    [gkPicker dismiss];
    gkPicker.delegate = nil;
    [gkPicker autorelease];

    //Set the other player's ID
    gamePeerId = peerID;
}
```

This callback will be called when a connection to a peer is made. It will configure the gkSession that was created in the previous method to identify the receiver of the data (self, in our case). We also dismiss the gkPicker, since we are done picking our opponent. Finally, we store the peerID in the gamePeerId variable. This peerID is how the devices identify themselves. We store this because we will need it when we want to send messages to the other player.

Filename: CLPlayfieldLayer.m

```
-(void) peerPickerControllerDidCancel: (GKPeerPickerController*)picker
{
    //User cancelled.  Release the delegate.
    picker.delegate = nil;
    [picker autorelease];

    // If there is a session, cancel it
    if(gkSession != nil) {
```

```
            [self invalidateSession:gkSession];
            gkSession = nil;
        }


        // Return to the main menu
        [self returnToMainMenu];
    }
```

The final callback we need for the Peer Picker is the `peerPickerControllerDidCancel` method. This is called if, at any point while the Peer Picker was active, the user clicked on **Cancel**. In this method, we release the delegate and invalidate (get rid of) the session that was created. The `invalidateSession` method will be covered shortly. We also added our own behavior, the call to the `returnToMainMenu` method.

Filename: `CLPlayfieldLayer.m`

```
    -(void) returnToMainMenu {
        // If there is a GameKit Session, invalidate it
        if(gkSession != nil) {
            [self invalidateSession:gkSession];
            gkSession = nil;
        }

        [[CCDirector sharedDirector]
                replaceScene:[CLMenuScene node]];
    }
```

The `returnToMainMenu` method checks to see if we have a `gkSession`, and will invalidate the session if needed. We then call the `replaceScene` method to go back to the menu scene.

The following screenshot gives an example of what the Peer Picker GUI looks like:

Session callbacks

Now we will look at the session delegate callback methods. These callbacks will be triggered based on the current state of the gkSession we created with the Peer Picker. There are a few smaller methods that we will examine first.

Filename: CLPlayfieldLayer.m

```
-(void) session:(GKSession*)session
didReceiveConnectionRequestFromPeer:(NSString*)peerI {
    //We are player 2 (blue)
    playerNumber = 2;
}
```

This method is called when the game receives a connection request from a peer. This means that the other player is taking the role of client, and the current device is being asked to take the role of the server. We made the design decision that the client is always red, and the server is always blue. Since this request makes us the server, we change the playerNumber variable to 2 to identify this device as the blue player. Since this method will only be called by one of the two devices, we can be certain the other player is red.

Filename: CLPlayfieldLayer.m

```
-(void) session:(GKSession*)session
    connectionWithPeerFailed:(NSString*)peerID
                withError:(NSError*)error {
    // Connection Failed
    [gkPicker dismiss];
    gkPicker.delegate = nil;
    [gkPicker autorelease];

    [self returnToMainMenu];
}

-(void) session:(GKSession*)session
            didFailWithError:(NSError*)error {
    // Connection Failed
    [gkPicker dismiss];
    gkPicker.delegate = nil;
    [gkPicker autorelease];

    [self returnToMainMenu];
}
```

These two methods are called when there is a connection error. There's nothing we can do, so we have both methods dismiss the Peer Picker, and return the player to the main menu.

Filename: `CLPlayfieldLayer.m`

```
-(void) invalidateSession:(GKSession*)session {
    if(session != nil) {
        [session disconnectFromAllPeers];
        session.available = NO;
        [session setDataReceiveHandler: nil
                            withContext: NULL];
        session.delegate = nil;
        [session autorelease];
        session = nil;
    }
}
```

This method is called when we need to abandon the session. As we saw earlier, this will be called when the user cancels out of the Peer Picker. If the session exists, it disconnects from all peers, marks itself unavailable, removes all delegates, and gets rid of the session.

Filename: `CLPlayfieldLayer.m`

```
-(void) session:(GKSession*)session peer:(NSString*)peerID
        didChangeState:(GKPeerConnectionState)state {
    if (currentState == GKPeerStateConnecting &&
        state != GKPeerStateConnected) {
        // Reset the player number
        playerNumber = 1;
    } else if(state == GKPeerStateConnected){
        //We have now connected to a peer
        if (playerNumber == 2) {
            // We are the server, blue player
            [self generateRedAsPlayerNo:2 isRemote:YES];
            [self generateBlueAsPlayerNo:1 isRemote:NO];
        } else {
            // We are the client, red player
            [self generateRedAsPlayerNo:1 isRemote:NO];
            [self generateBlueAsPlayerNo:2 isRemote:YES];
        }
        // Start the game
        [self scheduleUpdate];
```

```
    } else if(state == GKPeerStateDisconnected) {
        // We were disconnected
        [self unscheduleUpdate];
        // User alert
        NSString *msg = [NSString stringWithFormat:
                            @"Lost device %@.",
                        [session displayNameForPeer:peerID]];
        UIAlertView *alert = [[UIAlertView alloc]
                            initWithTitle:@"Lost Connection"
                            message:msg delegate:self
                            cancelButtonTitle:@"Game Aborted"
                            otherButtonTitles:nil];
        [alert show];
        [alert release];

        [self returnToMainMenu];
    }
    // Keep the current state
    currentState = state;
}
```

This method is called whenever the session's state changes. We begin by checking for one specific condition. When PeerPicker receives a request, the device that would be the server will be presented with the option to accept or decline the connection. We need to identify if the user pressed the "Decline" button. We check to see if the currentState (which is set at the bottom of this method, now holding the value from the last call to this method) is GKPeerStateConnecting, and the new state (the state variable) is not GKPeerStateConnected, then we reset the playerNumber. Why do we do this? When the connection request is first received, the session:d idReceiveConnectionRequestFromPeer: method was called. As we saw earlier, that sets the playerNumber to 2. As there is no callback received when the "Decline" button is pressed in the PeerPicker, this is the only way we can trap this situation, so we can "undo" the playerNumber being set to 2. Why do we care? If we do not have this trap in place, here is a scenario that can happen:

- Device 1 requests connection to Device 2. (Device 2 is now PlayerNumber 2)

- Device 2 declines the connection.

- Device 2 requests connection to Device 1. (Device 1 is now PlayerNumber 2)

- Device 1 accepts the connection.

- Game starts, and both players are BLUE, and think their opponent is RED.

By trapping the "Decline" condition, we can avoid this undesirable situation.

There are two standard states we need to handle: GKPeerStateConnected and GKPeerStateDisconnected. If the game is connected, we check which playerNumber we are. If this is playerNumber 2 (server) we set up the bikes correctly for this side of the game. The remote player is red, starting at the top of the device (remember, that is what the AsPlayerNo:2 represents), and we specify that this is a remote player, which means there will be no control buttons created. The local player is blue, in position 1 (bottom of iPad), with control buttons created.

If this is playerNumber 1 (client) then we do everything backwards. The local player is red with buttons, the remote player is blue, without buttons.

We then schedule the update method, and the game is on!

If the state is changed to GKPeerStateDisconnected, we unschedule the update (in case the game was running when disconnected), and we create a UIAlert object to inform the player that they lost their connection.

Sending messages

So we have a connection. Now what? We need to be able to send messages to the remote device, and accept messages from the remote device. We have determined we only need to send two types of data: move distance and turn direction. We will never send "real" data for both at the same time, so we will need to parse out the messages and take appropriate action. Let's look at the data sending method first.

Filename: CLPlayfieldLayer.m

```
-(void) sendDataWithDirection:(Direction)dir
                orDistance:(float)dist {

    //Pack data
    NSMutableData *dataToSend = [[NSMutableData alloc] init];
    NSKeyedArchiver *archiver = [[NSKeyedArchiver alloc]
            initForWritingWithMutableData:dataToSend];

    [archiver encodeInt:dir forKey:@"direction"];
    [archiver encodeFloat:dist forKey:@"distance"];

    [archiver finishEncoding];

    // Send the data, reliably
        [gkSession sendData:dataToSend toPeers:
        [NSArray arrayWithObject:gamePeerId]
            withDataMode:GKSendDataReliable
```

```
                                  error:nil];

        [archiver release];
        [dataToSend release];
    }
```

Here we pass the turn direction, `dir`, and the distance travelled, `dist`. We create an `NSMutableData` object and wrap that in an `NSKeyedArchiver`. We encode both variables with explicitly named keys, and we send the data via the `gkSession`. In the `sendData` method, you see that we are using the `gamePeerId` we stored earlier, and we are also sending the data in a mode called `GKSendDataReliable`. When you send data, you can either send it reliably or unreliably. The difference is that reliable packets must arrive and be processed in order. Unreliable data gives no guarantee of when it will be delivered, nor in which order the messages will be received and processed. Since we definitely need our data to arrive in order, on time, we send this reliably.

Receiving data

Now let's see how to receive and process the data when we receive it.

Filename: `CLPlayfieldLayer.m`

```
-(void) receiveData:(NSData*)data fromPeer:(NSString*)peer
          inSession:(GKSession*)session context:(void*)context {

    NSKeyedUnarchiver *unarchiver = [[NSKeyedUnarchiver
                  alloc] initForReadingWithData:data];

    Direction dir = [unarchiver
                    decodeIntForKey:@"direction"];
    NSInteger dist = [unarchiver
                    decodeFloatForKey:@"distance"];

    // Determine which bike to use, hold in whichBike
    CLBike *whichBike = ((playerNumber == 1)? blueBike:
                    redBike);

    // Process the data
    if (dir == kNoChange) {
        // This was a move forward packet
        [whichBike moveForDistance:dist];
    } else if (dir == kLeft) {
        // This is a turn left packet
```

```
            [whichBike turnLeft];
        } else if (dir == kRight) {
            // This is a turn right packet
            [whichBike turnRight];
        }
    }
}
```

When we receive data, we create an NSKeyedUnarchiver to interface with the data received. We decode both variables, and store them in local variables dir and dist (we use the same names in both methods to avoid confusion). We then check to see which player is local to this device. If the local player is number 1, then the messages we are receiving must be for the blue bike. Otherwise, they would be the red bike. We create whichBike, which will point to whichever bike we have determined should be moved. Then, we check to see if the direction is kNoChange. If it is, then this is a movement packet, so we call to the moveForDistance method for whichBike, and pass it the value of dist. This will explicitly move the remote player's bike on the local game. We then check to see if the direction was kLeft or kRight. For each, we call to the bike's turnLeft or turnRight method, as needed.

Upgrading our bikes

The receiveData method we just reviewed will handle everything we need in how to handle moving the remote bike on the local device. Now we need to upgrade our CLBike class to be able to send the appropriate messages to the remote device.

Filename: CLBike.m

```
-(void) sendPacketForMove:(float)distance {
    // We only send a packet if we are playing a remote
    // game, and this bike is the LOCAL player
    if (myPlayfield.remoteGame && self.isRemotePlayer == NO) {
        [myPlayfield sendDataWithDirection:kNoChange
                            orDistance:distance];
    }
}
```

In this method, we check to make sure we are playing a remote game, and that this bike does not belong to a remote player. If both of these conditions pass, we call to the sendData method in the CLPlayfieldLayer, and pass it the distance argument. We also pass the direction as kNoChange, so we know there is no turn included in this message. So what calls this method? In the move method of the CLBike class, we left a placeholder "remote game". Let's fill that in now.

Filename: `CLBike.m`

```
-(void) move {
    // Move this bike (if local player)
    [self moveForDistance:self.bikeSpeed];

    // Remote game
    [self sendPacketForMove:self.bikeSpeed];
}
```

As you recall from the `update` method in the `CLPlayfieldLayer` class, we only call `move` if the bike is a local player. So the local player's bike will move itself (locally) and then send the message for the other device to move this bike on the other device. This is the reason we separated the `move` method from the `moveForDistance` method. The remote player's moves are processed directly through the `moveForDistance` method, so we will not re-send the remote player's moves back to this player's device.

We follow a similar approach for the turn commands. First we build a similar send method for turns.

Filename: `CLBike.m`

```
-(void) sendPacketForTurn:(Direction)turnDir {
    // We only send a packet if we are playing a remote
    // game, and this bike is the LOCAL player
    if (myPlayfield.remoteGame && self.isRemotePlayer == NO) {
        [myPlayfield sendDataWithDirection:turnDir
                                 orDistance:0];
    }
}
```

Just as we did with the `sendPacketForMove` method earlier, we make sure this is a remote game and that the bike does not belong to a remote player. We then send the `turnDir` argument with a `distance` of `0`. As we saw with the `receiveData` method, the turns will be processed first, so it actually doesn't matter what value we send for distance, but it is a good idea to fill in default values to avoid unintended consequences of unexpected data.

To call this method, we insert code into the end of the `turnRight` and `turnLeft` methods we discussed earlier. In both methods, we insert the new code at the "Remote game" placeholder.

Filename: `CLBike.m` (`turnRight`)

```
// Remote game
[self sendPacketForTurn:kRight];
```

Filename: `CLBike.m` (`turnLeft`):

```
// Remote game
[self sendPacketForTurn:kLeft];
```

Now, every time the player turns, we call to the `sendPacketForTurn` method, and if this is a local player, we will send the appropriate message to the remote device.

Why send moves?

A natural question on a game like this is why do we send the move, if it is a predetermined, constant rate? The primary reason we do this is to avoid game glitches if a message was to get delayed.

Imagine a game where red is the local player, and blue is the remote player. We have implemented the game so we are only sending turns, not move forward messages. So on each update, the local device moves both players forward a distance of 5 points. Blue turns, but the message is delayed slightly, so it is received two update cycles late. On the local (red player) game, blue has moved forward 10 points, then turned. On the remote (blue player) game, the blue player has turned, then moved forward 10. This means the two devices have a different image of the game board, and we cannot bring them back into sync. So blue might appear to crash into a wall on the red player's iPad, but is actually still alive and playing on their different version of the game board. The only way to avoid this sort of board mutation on this type of game is to do as we have and explicitly send every movement to the other player. This way we can guarantee that the game board as seen by either player is exactly the same.

Summary

In this chapter, we implemented our first iPad game, our first simultaneous two-player game, and our first two-player Bluetooth game. We spent some time learning about how we can optimize our images to make a lot out of very few graphic assets. We also saw how we can create a simple animated background using `CCRenderTexture`, and used `glScissor` to cut that moving image to fit a non-moving screen area.

We covered the basics of a GameKit two player game, and hopefully we had some fun along the way. There is a lot to learn about optimization for networked games, and we have so far only scratched the surface with what is possible. There is also a whole world of other connectivity and lag issues you will face when you branch out to include Internet-based multiplayer games. If you are interested in exploring that, I advise you to read up on Apple's documentation and use your favorite search engine to find other resources, as network communication code is a specialty unto itself.

In the next chapter, we will revisit Box2D to build an old school top-down pool game. We will implement a rules system as well as experiment with different control mechanics. Rack 'em up, and let's start the next chapter!

7

Playing Pool, Old School

In this chapter we will be developing another project using the Box2D physics engine. Our emphasis in this chapter will be on how to easily implement multiple control methods, as well as alternate rule sets.

In this chapter, we will cover:

- Using sensors
- Implementing multiple control schemes
- Designing a rules engine

The game is…

Our game in this chapter is an old-school, top-down pool game. While our goal is to have suitably realistic movements, our emphasis will be on a fun arcade-style game. The main reason for this is it is impossible to accurately simulate the physics of a physical pool table without using a full 3D environment. Since we are working in 2D, we will not have features such as backspin, putting "English" on the ball, and so forth. We will also be using "bar room" variations on the games we implement. We have made this choice because there are literally hundreds of variations of each established game, so we are opting for "more fun" rather than "official rules". The game will be a pass-and-play two player game.

Overall design

To make a 2D pool game, there are really only a few objects we will need to render on the screen. The table will be made of the side rails and the pockets. The rest of the table, as far as we are concerned, is just graphic fluff. Of course, we will need to build the 15 numbered pool balls and the cue ball. We will also need a cue stick, which we will create as a sprite but it will not be a body in the Box2D physics simulation. Why not? If we were to create the pool cue as a physics-enabled body, then we would have to consider the "unintended hits" of the pool cue running into other (non-cue ball) balls on the table. While this might happen on a real table, it is generally undesirable. Instead, we will use the pool cue as a visual "marker" of the planned shot, with the distance from the ball acting as our measure of the strength of the shot. Most of the interactions on the pool table will be handled by the Box2D simulation itself, so that will be the easy part.

We will focus more on the control mechanisms and the rules engine in this chapter. We will adopt two different touch-based control mechanisms, and we will build a rules engine that can play "bar style" Eight Ball as well as Nine Ball. As we said in the introduction, we are using "bar rules" as a baseline approach. Feel free to extend the rules engine however you see fit to play pool your way.

Building the table

Our first task at hand is to build the pool table. We will start by looking at our definitions, because we will be using these extensively throughout this chapter:

Filename: `OPDefinitions.h`

```
// Audio definitions
#define SND_BUTTON @"button.caf"

// Box2D definition
#define PTM_RATIO 32

// Define the pocket's tag
#define kPocket 500

typedef enum {
    kBallNone = -1,
    kBallCue = 0,
    kBallOne,
    kBallTwo,
```

```
        kBallThree,
        kBallFour,
        kBallFive,
        kBallSix,
        kBallSeven,
        kBallEight,
        kBallNine,
        kBallTen,
        kBallEleven,
        kBallTwelve,
        kBallThirteen,
        kBallFourteen,
        kBallFifteen
    } BallID;

    typedef enum {
        kRackTriangle = 50,
        kRackDiamond,
        kRackFailed
    } RackLayoutType;


    typedef enum {
        kStripes = 100,
        kSolids,
        kOrdered,
        kStripesVsSolids,
        kNone
    } GameMode;
```

You should be familiar with `typedef enum` statements by now. We create the `BallID` type to represent the numbered balls for simplicity. To be able to easily convert from `NSInteger` values to `BallID` values, we set the numbered balls to equal the number on the balls. The cue is zero, and we also keep a reference for `kBallNone` as `-1` so we can cover our bases (useful when detecting a table scratch). We define two types of `RackLayoutType`, diamond and triangle. We also set our `GameMode` to be stripes, solids, ordered, or stripes versus solids. We use this last value to identify the game before anyone has pocketed any stripes or solids (also known as the table being "open"). We also have the `#define` statement to define the `kPocket` as `500`. We will use this in our collision detection to determine when a ball hits a pocket. Finally, there is also the `PTM_RATIO`, which you should be familiar with from *Chapter 5, Brick Breaking Balls with Box2D*, which defines the Points-To-Meters ratio.

The Box2D world

With any Box2D simulation, we need to define a world for the bodies to inhabit. (If you need to brush up on the Box2D world and the structures inside it, please go back and re-read the *Box2D: a primer* section in *Chapter 5, Brick Breaking Balls with Box2D*.)

Filename: `OPPlayfieldLayer.mm`

```
-(void) initWorld
{
  b2Vec2 gravity;
  gravity.Set(0.0f, 0.0f);
  world = new b2World(gravity);

  // Do we want to let bodies sleep?
  world->SetAllowSleeping(true);
  world->SetContinuousPhysics(true);

    // Create contact listener
    contactListener = new OPContactListener();
    world->SetContactListener(contactListener);
}
```

As we did in *Chapter 5*, we define our world with zero gravity, since we do not want any downward force on our environment. We allow bodies to sleep, and we allow the continuous physics to run, which will increase the accuracy of the simulation. Finally, we establish a contact listener. For this game, we use a nearly identical contact listener to the one in *Chapter 5, Brick Breaking Balls with Box2D*. The only difference is we have changed the naming convention from BR... to OP... for all the elements in it. We will not repeat the code here, so please feel free to refer to that chapter or to the source code bundle for this chapter.

Building the rails

The rails are one of the most interacted elements on the pool table, so we will build them first. Since the physical properties of all six rails are the same, we will build a single method to create a rail and pass parameters to that method to create each rail. We'll look at the "core code" first:

Filename: `OPPlayfieldLayer.mm`

```
-(void) createRailWithImage:(NSString*)img atPos:(CGPoint)pos
withVerts:(b2Vec2*)verts {
    // Create the rail
    PhysicsSprite *rail = [PhysicsSprite
```

```
                    spriteWithSpriteFrameName:img];
    [rail setPosition:pos];
    [poolsheet addChild: rail];

    // Create rail body
    b2BodyDef railBodyDef;
    railBodyDef.type = b2_staticBody;
    railBodyDef.position.Set(pos.x/PTM_RATIO,
                             pos.y/PTM_RATIO);
    railBodyDef.userData = rail;
    b2Body *railBody = world->CreateBody(&railBodyDef);

    // Store the body in the sprite
    [rail setPhysicsBody:railBody];

    // Build the fixture
    b2PolygonShape railShape;
    int num = 4;

    railShape.Set(verts, num);

    // Create the shape definition and add it to the body
    b2FixtureDef railShapeDef;
    railShapeDef.shape = &railShape;
    railShapeDef.density = 50.0f;
    railShapeDef.friction = 0.3f;
    railShapeDef.restitution = 0.5f;
    railBody->CreateFixture(&railShapeDef);
}
```

This method takes three arguments: the name of the sprite image, the position for the sprite and body, and an array of verts to define the shape of the rail. The rails are defined using the PhysicsSprite class, which we also saw in *Chapter 5*, *Brick Breaking Balls with Box2D*. A PhysicsSprite object, as you may recall, is like a normal CCSprite, except it holds a reference to the body attached to it. Cocos2d will automatically keep the sprite's position and rotation in sync with the underlying Box2D body.

For the rails, we build the sprite using the passed image name, and then build the associated body. After the body is built, we attach the body to the sprite with the setPhysicsBody method. Next, we define the shape for the rail. Because the rails are very simple shapes, we know that we only need four verts to define each rail. When we define the fixture, we set a pretty high density of 50.0f, a moderate friction of 0.3f, and an in-the-middle value for restitution of 0.5f. These have been tweaked during play testing to give a good "bounciness" to the rails that feels more like a real table.

Now we can look at how we call this method to define the six rails for the table:

Filename: `OPPlayfieldLayer.mm`

```
-(void) createRails {
    // Top left rail
    CGPoint railPos1 = ccp(58,338);
    b2Vec2 vert1[] = {
        b2Vec2(5.5f / PTM_RATIO, -84.0f / PTM_RATIO),
        b2Vec2(4.5f / PTM_RATIO, 80.0f / PTM_RATIO),
        b2Vec2(-5.5f / PTM_RATIO, 87.0f / PTM_RATIO),
        b2Vec2(-5.5f / PTM_RATIO, -87.0f / PTM_RATIO)
    };
    [self createRailWithImage:@"rail1.png" atPos:railPos1
withVerts:vert1];

    // Bottom left rail
    CGPoint railPos2 = ccp(58,142);
    b2Vec2 vert2[] = {
        b2Vec2(5.5f / PTM_RATIO, 84.5f / PTM_RATIO),
        b2Vec2(-5.5f / PTM_RATIO, 86.5f / PTM_RATIO),
        b2Vec2(-5.5f / PTM_RATIO, -86.5f / PTM_RATIO),
        b2Vec2(5.5f / PTM_RATIO, -78.5f / PTM_RATIO)
    };
    [self createRailWithImage:@"rail2.png" atPos:railPos2
withVerts:vert2];

    // Bottom rail
    CGPoint railPos3 = ccp(160,44);
    b2Vec2 vert3[] = {
        b2Vec2(-88.5f / PTM_RATIO, -5.5f / PTM_RATIO),
        b2Vec2(88.5f / PTM_RATIO, -5.5f / PTM_RATIO),
        b2Vec2(81.5f / PTM_RATIO, 5.5f / PTM_RATIO),
        b2Vec2(-81.5f / PTM_RATIO, 5.5f / PTM_RATIO)
    };
    [self createRailWithImage:@"rail3.png" atPos:railPos3
withVerts:vert3];

    // Bottom right rail
    CGPoint railPos4 = ccp(262,142);
    b2Vec2 vert4[] = {
        b2Vec2(5.5f / PTM_RATIO, -86.0f / PTM_RATIO),
        b2Vec2(5.5f / PTM_RATIO, 86.0f / PTM_RATIO),
        b2Vec2(-5.5f / PTM_RATIO, 85.0f / PTM_RATIO),
        b2Vec2(-5.5f / PTM_RATIO, -78.0f / PTM_RATIO)
    };
    [self createRailWithImage:@"rail4.png" atPos:railPos4
withVerts:vert4];

    // Top right rail
```

```
    CGPoint railPos5 = ccp(262,338);
    b2Vec2 vert5[] = {
        b2Vec2(5.5f / PTM_RATIO, 86.5f / PTM_RATIO),
        b2Vec2(-5.5f / PTM_RATIO, 78.5f / PTM_RATIO),
        b2Vec2(-5.5f / PTM_RATIO, -85.5f / PTM_RATIO),
        b2Vec2(5.5f / PTM_RATIO, -86.5f / PTM_RATIO)
    };
    [self createRailWithImage:@"rail5.png" atPos:railPos5
withVerts:vert5];

    // Top rail
    CGPoint railPos6 = ccp(160,436);
    b2Vec2 vert6[] = {
        b2Vec2(89.0f / PTM_RATIO, 6.0f / PTM_RATIO),
        b2Vec2(-89.0f / PTM_RATIO, 6.0f / PTM_RATIO),
        b2Vec2(-82.0f / PTM_RATIO, -5.0f / PTM_RATIO),
        b2Vec2(81.0f / PTM_RATIO, -5.0f / PTM_RATIO)
    };
    [self createRailWithImage:@"rail6.png" atPos:railPos6
withVerts:vert6];
}
```

This looks like a lot of code to begin with, but it is the same pattern repeated six times to accommodate each rail.

For each rail, we define the position based on the center point of the sprite, as we are using the default centered anchor point for the rails. We then define the array of four `verts` that define the four sides of each rail. You will notice that they are not square, as we need the tapered ends around the pockets to make a smoother "mouth" for each pocket. Finally, we call the `createRailWithImage` method we just reviewed. We now have our rails, which look like this:

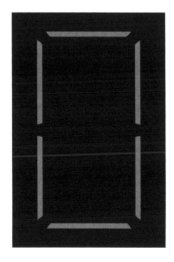

Building pockets

Now that we have our rails built, we need to add the only other "interactive" elements of the table itself, the pockets. We will also use a similar two-method approach to build them, as the only difference in the pockets is their location.

Filename: `OPPlayfieldLayer.mm`

```
-(void) createPocketAtPos:(CGPoint)pos {
    // Create sprite and add it to layer
    CCSprite *pocket = [CCSprite
            spriteWithSpriteFrameName:@"whitespeck.png"];
    pocket.position = pos;
    pocket.tag = kPocket;
    [pocket setColor:ccBLACK];
    [self addChild:pocket z:0];

    // Create a pocket body
    b2BodyDef pocketBodyDef;
    pocketBodyDef.type = b2_dynamicBody;
    pocketBodyDef.position.Set(pos.x/PTM_RATIO,
                            pos.y/PTM_RATIO);
    pocketBodyDef.userData = pocket;
    b2Body *pocketBody = world->CreateBody(&pocketBodyDef);

    //Create a circle shape
    b2CircleShape circle;
    circle.m_radius = 7.0/PTM_RATIO;

    //Create fixture definition and add to body
    b2FixtureDef pocketFixtureDef;
    pocketFixtureDef.shape = &circle;
    pocketFixtureDef.isSensor = YES;

    pocketBody->CreateFixture(&pocketFixtureDef);
}
```

Here we follow the same basic formula we used for the rails. We build a sprite, body, shape, and fixture. Even though we don't technically need a sprite for the pocket, we will use our trusty `whitespeck.png` that we used heavily in *Chapter 6, Cycles of Light*. In this case, we color it black, so that it disappears into the pocket. (For debugging, it is also helpful to change it to a brighter color, so that you can see where the pockets are.) So why use it at all? We like using a sprite here because it allows us to add a tag, `kPocket`, to the sprite. This makes the collisions a little simpler, as we will be able to use sprite tags for all objects whose collisions we care about (pockets and balls only).

You may notice that, unlike the rails, we don't need this to be "physics enabled", so the pocket sprites are using normal `CCSprite` classes instead of `PhysicsSprite` classes. When we define the shape for the pocket, we use a circle with a radius of `7.0`. This is because we need a larger target to detect a ball in pocket. We made these circles a little smaller than the actual physical size of the pockets on the table, because we want to allow balls to hang on the edge of the pocket, just as they do on a real table.

Finally, when we define the `pocketFixtureDef`, you will notice we did not use any of the usual values such as `density`, `friction`, or `restitution`. This is because we do not want the pockets to participate in the "bouncing around" of the physics simulation. Instead, we simply set `isSensor` to `YES`. A sensor is a physics object that registers in the collision handler, but does not actually have any physical "presence" in the world. We will register a contact when something touches the sensor, but other objects will be able to pass through the sensor.

Now we can look at the second method used to drive the creation of the pocket sensors:

Filename: `OPPlayfieldLayer.mm`

```
-(void) createPockets {
    // Left top pocket
    [self createPocketAtPos:ccp(57,437)];

    // Left middle pocket
    [self createPocketAtPos:ccp(52,240)];

    // Left bottom pocket
    [self createPocketAtPos:ccp(57,43)];

    // Right top pocket
    [self createPocketAtPos:ccp(265,437)];

    // Right middle pocket
    [self createPocketAtPos:ccp(272,240)];

    // Right bottom pocket
    [self createPocketAtPos:ccp(265,43)];
}
```

Compared to the extra code we needed to build the rails in their second method, this one is really simple. We have six pockets, so we simply call the previous method and pass it the coordinates for the pocket, and we're done.

Creating the cue stick

The cue stick is purely cosmetic. We will be controlling the "hitting" of the cue ball programmatically, and the cue stick is used as an aiming point of reference only. Nevertheless, without a cue stick, the game wouldn't "feel" like pool. The cue stick will be on the screen only during aiming, and will be faded out when we make the shot. Because the cue stick is deeply connected with the way the controls are built, we will save the discussion on how the cue stick will be used for later in the chapter. For now, let's take a look at how we build it:

Filename: `OPPlayfieldLayer.mm`

```
-(void) createPoolCue {
    poolcue = [CCSprite
        spriteWithSpriteFrameName:@"cue_stick.png"];
    [poolcue setAnchorPoint:ccp(0.5,1)];
    [poolcue setVisible:NO];
    [poolsheet addChild:poolcue z:50];
}
```

As it is primarily cosmetic, we use a normal `CCSprite`. We set the `anchorPoint` property to the tip of the cue (centered at the top). As we rotate the cue stick, this will allow it to pivot on its tip. We also set the visible property to `NO`, because the stick will only be made visible when needed.

Loading the rules

We won't be able to progress much farther without discussing the rules engine. Some of the configuration of the game, including what type of rack we use for the balls, is controlled by the rules. We will be using a separate "rules" class, `OPRulesBase`. Let's look at the complete header for this class first:

Filename: `OPRulesBase.h`

```
#import <Foundation/Foundation.h>
#import "cocos2d.h"
#import "OPDefinitions.h"

@interface OPRulesBase : CCNode {
    RackLayoutType rackStyle;
    BallID lastBall;
    BOOL orderedBalls;
    GameMode gameMode;
    BOOL replaceBalls;
```

```
    BOOL isBreak;
    GameMode player1Goal;
    GameMode player2Goal;
    BallID nextOrderedBall; // Number of next ball
    NSInteger currentPlayer;
    BOOL isTableScratch;
}

@property (nonatomic, assign) RackLayoutType rackStyle;
@property (nonatomic, assign) BallID lastBall;
@property (nonatomic, assign) BOOL orderedBalls;
@property (nonatomic, assign) GameMode gameMode;
@property (nonatomic, assign) BOOL replaceBalls;
@property (nonatomic, assign) NSInteger currentPlayer;
@property (nonatomic, assign) BOOL isTableScratch;
@property (nonatomic, assign) GameMode player1Goal;
@property (nonatomic, assign) GameMode player2Goal;
@property (nonatomic, assign) BallID nextOrderedBall;

-(id) initWithRulesForGame:(NSString*)gameName;
-(BOOL) isLegalFirstHit:(BallID)firstBall;
-(BOOL) didSinkValidBall:(NSArray*)ballArray;
-(BOOL) didSinkLastBall:(NSArray*)ballArray;
-(BOOL) didSinkCueBall:(NSArray*)ballArray;
-(BOOL) isValidLastBall:(NSArray*)ballsSunk
        withBallsOnTable:(NSArray*)ballsOnTable;
-(void) findNextOrderedBall:(NSArray*)tableBalls;

@end
```

The first five variables are all parameters we need to define the rules of the game. Because these will all be used from the OPPlayfieldLayer class, we must make them all properties as well. The other variables you see will be explained later in the discussion as we use them. The classes in this header give you a little bit of a "sneak preview" on how we will approach the full rules engine implementation later in the chapter. As you can see, most of the classes are "questioning" methods to "ask" the rules engine about the status of various conditions. These methods will vary based on the type of game, which is why these "question methods" are part of the rules engine.

As we move to the implementation file, we will begin by looking at the custom `init` method we will use for the rules:

Filename: `OPRulesBase.mm`

```
-(id) initWithRulesForGame:(NSString*)gameName {
    if(self = [super init]) {
        // Load the rules for the game chosen
        [self loadRulesWith:gameName];

        isTableScratch = NO;
        isBreak = YES;
    }
    return self;
}
```

This is a pretty simple `init` method that calls the `loadRulesWith:gameName` method, and sets a couple of starting values for the table variables (`isTableScratch` and `isBreak`). Before we get to the `loadRulesWith` method, there are other methods we need to review first:

Filename: `OPRulesBase.mm`

```
-(id) readPlist:(NSString*) fileName {
  NSData *plistData;
  NSString *error;
  NSPropertyListFormat format;
  id plist;

    // Assumes filename is part of the main bundle
  NSString *localizedPath = [[NSBundle mainBundle]
          pathForResource:fileName ofType:@"plist"];
  plistData = [NSData dataWithContentsOfFile:localizedPath];
  plist = [NSPropertyListSerialization
          propertyListFromData:plistData
          mutabilityOption:NSPropertyListImmutable
          format:&format errorDescription:&error];

  if (!plist) {
    NSLog(@"Error reading plist from file '%s', error '%s'",
          [localizedPath UTF8String], [error UTF8String]);
  }
  return plist;
}

-(NSDictionary*)getDictionaryFromPlist:(NSString*)fileName {
    return (NSDictionary*)[self readPlist:fileName];
}
```

The `readPlist` and `getDictionaryFromPlist` methods we have seen before, also in the *Brick breaker* section in *Chapter 5, Brick Breaking Balls with Box2D*. The `readPlist` method will load the named plist into memory, and return it as a general type id. The `getDictionaryFromPlist` method casts the result of `readPlist` as an `NSDictionary`, and returns it to the calling method. That's all it takes to get our plist into an `NSDictionary`.

Rules.plist

Before we go any further into the loader, we should see what the plist for our rules actually looks like. This is the plist itself:

Key	Type	Value
▼ Root	Dictionary	(2 items)
▼ Nine Ball	Dictionary	(5 items)
RackStyle	String	kRackDiamond
LastBall	String	9
OrderedBalls	Boolean	YES
GameMode	String	Ordered
ReplaceBalls	Boolean	YES
▼ Eight Ball	Dictionary	(5 items)
RackStyle	String	kRackTriangle
LastBall	String	8
OrderedBalls	Boolean	NO
GameMode	String	StripesVsSolids
ReplaceBalls	Boolean	YES

As you can see from the plist, the first level in the structure is the named game (**Eight Ball**, **Nine Ball**), and inside those Dictionaries are a set of Strings and Booleans that define the details of the game. Because we have chosen to represent the `RackStyle` and `GameMode` elements as strings, we will need to convert those into something more usable by the engine.

Now we have the pieces together to understand the `loadRulesWith` method.

Filename: `OPRulesBase.mm`

```
-(void) loadRulesWith:(NSString*)listKey {
    // Load the rules plist
    NSDictionary *ruleBook = [NSDictionary
                dictionaryWithDictionary:
                [self getDictionaryFromPlist:@"rules"]];
    NSDictionary *theseRules = [NSDictionary
                dictionaryWithDictionary:
                [ruleBook objectForKey:listKey]];
```

```
        self.rackStyle = [self convertRackType:
                  [theseRules objectForKey:@"RackStyle"]];
        self.lastBall = (BallID)[[theseRules
                  objectForKey:@"LastBall"] integerValue];
        self.orderedBalls = [[theseRules
                  objectForKey:@"OrderedBalls"] boolValue];
        self.gameMode = [self convertGameMode:[theseRules
                  objectForKey:@"GameMode"]];
        self.replaceBalls = [[theseRules
                  objectForKey:@"ReplaceBalls"] boolValue];

        player1Goal = gameMode;
        player2Goal = gameMode;

        if (self.gameMode == kOrdered) {
            nextOrderedBall = kBallOne;
        }

        currentPlayer = 1;
    }
```

We begin by loading in the `rules.plist` using the `getDictionaryFromPlist` method. We load the rules into the `ruleBook` dictionary, and then we create another dictionary, `theseRules`, which gets the named game dictionary from inside our `ruleBook` dictionary. From there, we begin populating our base rules properties from that "game level" dictionary. Because an `NSDictionary` stores objects only, we have to convert the values for several of the keys before we can insert them into the properties. For `LastBall`, we convert the object to the `integerValue` of the object (which is stored as an `NSNumber`). You will notice that we convert this to an integer, but then we cast it to a `BallID` type when we set the property's value. This is where the numeric representations we set in the `typedef enum` in the `OPDefinitions.h` file come in handy. Because, for example, `kBallNine` is internally represented as the integer 9, we can freely bridge across these data types. Had we used other values for the `typedef enum`, we would have been forced to do some more complex conversions, probably with an extended `switch` statement. Similarly, we get the `boolValue` of both the `OrderedBalls` and `ReplaceBalls` keys, so they will "fit" into our Boolean properties.

The other two rule properties need special consideration. Because we have chosen to store those as strings in the `rules.plist`, we have to do string comparison to convert them into the values our game wants to use. Let's look at the conversion methods now:

Filename: `OPRulesBase.mm`

```objc
- (RackLayoutType) convertRackType:(NSString*)rackStr {
    if ([rackStr isEqualToString:@"kRackDiamond"]) {
        return kRackDiamond;
    } else if ([rackStr isEqualToString:@"kRackTriangle"]) {
        return kRackTriangle;
    } else {
        NSLog(@"unknown rack type %@ in the plist.", rackStr);
    }
    return kRackFailed;
}


- (GameMode) convertGameMode:(NSString*)gameStr {
    if ([gameStr isEqualToString:@"Ordered"]) {
        return kOrdered;
    }
    else if ([gameStr isEqualToString:@"StripesVsSolids"]) {
        return kStripesVsSolids;
    }
    return kNone;
}
```

For both of these methods, we pass it the string that comes from the dictionary, and compare the strings to our defined values. We can then return the `typedef enum` values that correspond to the chosen options. We could have avoided this by storing the rack types and game modes as numbers in the plist, but that makes the human reading (and writing) of the plist less easy to understand. Because we only perform these comparisons when loading the rules, there is no performance drawback on using this slower approach.

In the final lines of the `loadRulesWith` method, we assign the current `gameMode` (that we just loaded) to the `player1Goal` and `player2Goal` properties. This identifies for the players what their goal in the game is going to be. Why is this at a player level? It really comes down to the inherent complexity in the game of Eight Ball, where one player will be shooting for stripes, and the other for solids. Before any balls are sunk, the table is "open", so all shots (except for the last ball) are legal. So, in this case, the starting game is "Stripes vs Solids" for both players, until the game progresses to the point where one is deemed to have a goal of "Stripes" and the other "Solids".

We also check if the `gameMode` is `kOrdered`. This means that balls will be sunk in numeric order. If this is the case, the `nextOrderedBall` variable is set to `kBallOne`. If the game is anything else, `nextOrderedBall` will be ignored. Finally, `currentPlayer` always starts as player 1.

Rack 'em up

Now that we know what type of game we will be playing, we have enough information to build the rack on the table. First we need to know how to build the balls.

Filename: `OPPlayfieldLayer.mm`

```
-(void) createBall:(BallID)ballID AtPos:(CGPoint)startPos {
    // Create the filename
    NSString *ballImg = [NSString
                    stringWithFormat:@"ball_%i.png",ballID];

    // Create sprite and add it to layer
    OPBall *ball = [OPBall spriteWithSpriteFrameName:ballImg];
    ball.position = startPos;
    ball.tag = ballID;
    [self addChild:ball z:10];

    // Create ball body
    b2BodyDef ballBodyDef;
    ballBodyDef.type = b2_dynamicBody;
    ballBodyDef.position.Set(startPos.x/PTM_RATIO,
                            startPos.y/PTM_RATIO);
    ballBodyDef.userData = ball;
    b2Body *ballBody = world->CreateBody(&ballBodyDef);

    // Store the body in the sprite
    [ball setPhysicsBody:ballBody];

    //Create a circle shape
    b2CircleShape circle;
    circle.m_radius = 7.5/PTM_RATIO;   // 7.5 point radius

    //Create fixture definition and add to body
    b2FixtureDef ballFixtureDef;
    ballFixtureDef.shape = &circle;
    ballFixtureDef.density = 1.0f;
    ballFixtureDef.friction = 0.5f;
    ballFixtureDef.restitution = 0.9f;

    ballBody->CreateFixture(&ballFixtureDef);
    ballBody->SetFixedRotation(false);
    ballBody->SetLinearDamping(0.7f);
    ballBody->SetAngularDamping(0.5f);
```

```
      ballBody->SetBullet(TRUE);

      if (ballID == kBallCue) {
          cueBallBody = ballBody;
      }
  }
```

This is similar to the builders we used to create the rails and pockets, with a few exceptions. We pass both the `BallID` and `startPos` variables to this method, so we know which ball to build, and where to build it. We use the class `OPBall`, which is a subclass of `PhysicsSprite`, to represent the balls. The `OPBall` class is a direct pass-through of the `PhysicsSprite`, with no added functionality. We do this because we gain the ability in the collision handler to use the `isMemberOfClass` method to determine if the object is a ball or not. If we designed the collision handler differently, we could have used `PhysicsSprite` for the balls instead.

For the rest of the ball instantiation, we follow the pattern of building a body, assigning it to the sprite, creating the fixture, and attaching it to the body. We use a `density` of `1.0f`, a `friction` of `0.5f`, and a `restitution` of `0.9f` to give a good "pool ball feel" to the fixtures. We then use a few additional members of the body object that we haven't really used before. We turn off `SetFixedRotation`, so the balls will be able to rotate, rather than remaining at their original rotation. We set the linear damping to `0.7f`, and the angular damping to `0.5f`. Together, these will help simulate the effect of the balls rolling on the table felt. This is the one place in this game where we are "faking" the physics world, because we are not actually creating a table top object. Linear damping will slow the ball's forward progress, and angular damping will help slow the ball's rotation. Together with the fixture's settings, these provide a fairly realistic feel for a pool table.

Building the rack

Now we can build the rack. Let's look at the code:

Filename: `OPPlayfieldLayer.mm`

```
  -(void) createRackWithLayout:(RackLayoutType)rack {
      // Define the standard ball positions
      CGPoint footSpot = ccp(160,335);
      CGPoint r1b1 = ccp(153,348);
      CGPoint r1b2 = ccp(167,348);
      CGPoint r2b1 = ccp(146,361);
      CGPoint r2b2 = ccp(160,361);
      CGPoint r2b3 = ccp(174,361);
      CGPoint r3b1 = ccp(139,374);
```

```
CGPoint r3b2 = ccp(153,374);
CGPoint r3b3 = ccp(167,374);
CGPoint r3b4 = ccp(181,374);
CGPoint r4b1 = ccp(132,388);
CGPoint r4b2 = ccp(146,388);
CGPoint r4b3 = ccp(160,388);
CGPoint r4b4 = ccp(174,388);
CGPoint r4b5 = ccp(188,388);

switch (rack) {
    case kRackTriangle:
        // Build a standard triangle rack
        [self createBall:kBallNine AtPos:footSpot];
        [self createBall:kBallSeven AtPos:r1b1];
        [self createBall:kBallTwelve AtPos:r1b2];
        [self createBall:kBallFifteen AtPos:r2b1];
        [self createBall:kBallEight AtPos:r2b2];
        [self createBall:kBallOne AtPos:r2b3];
        [self createBall:kBallSix AtPos:r3b1];
        [self createBall:kBallTen AtPos:r3b2];
        [self createBall:kBallThree AtPos:r3b3];
        [self createBall:kBallFourteen AtPos:r3b4];
        [self createBall:kBallEleven AtPos:r4b1];
        [self createBall:kBallTwo AtPos:r4b2];
        [self createBall:kBallThirteen AtPos:r4b3];
        [self createBall:kBallFour AtPos:r4b4];
        [self createBall:kBallFive AtPos:r4b5];
        break;
    case kRackDiamond:
        // Build a diamond rack
        [self createBall:kBallOne AtPos:footSpot];
        [self createBall:kBallFive AtPos:r1b1];
        [self createBall:kBallSeven AtPos:r1b2];
        [self createBall:kBallEight AtPos:r2b1];
        [self createBall:kBallNine AtPos:r2b2];
        [self createBall:kBallThree AtPos:r2b3];
        [self createBall:kBallTwo AtPos:r3b2];
        [self createBall:kBallSix AtPos:r3b3];
        [self createBall:kBallFour AtPos:r4b3];
        break;
    default:
        break;
    }
}
```

In this method, we first define the positions where the balls will be located. We use a shorthand notation for most of the `CGPoint` positions. The abbreviation means row and ball in row, so `r1b1` is the leftmost ball in the first row past the foot spot (the foot spot is the front "point" of the rack). We define all the positions first, and then check which rack we want. If we called for a triangle rack (as in Eight Ball), then we will fill in every position with a ball. If we need a triangle rack (used in Nine Ball), then we only use 9 of the 15 positions defined. The positions, you will notice, are actually a little too close together. This is intentional, because Box2D will nudge the balls a little bit so they all fit. The end result is that the balls are all touching, which is known as a "tight rack" in pool.

Player HUD

As we are building a two-player game, let's take a quick look at how we build the Heads-Up Display to provide feedback to the players:

Filename: `OPPlayfieldLayer.mm`

```
-(void) createPlayerScores {
    CCLabelTTF *player1 = [CCLabelTTF
                          labelWithString:@"P1"
                          fontName:@"Verdana"
                          fontSize:14];
    [player1 setPosition:ccp(20,460)];
    [self addChild:player1];

    CCLabelTTF *player2 = [CCLabelTTF
                          labelWithString:@"P2"
                          fontName:@"Verdana"
                          fontSize:14];
    [player2 setPosition:ccp(300,460)];
    [self addChild:player2];

    player1TargetLbl = [CCLabelTTF
                       labelWithString:@" "
                       fontName:@"Verdana" fontSize:8];
    [player1TargetLbl setPosition:ccp(20,440)];
    [self addChild:player1TargetLbl z:2];

    player2TargetLbl = [CCLabelTTF
                       labelWithString:@" "
                       fontName:@"Verdana" fontSize:8];
    [player2TargetLbl setPosition:ccp(300,440)];
    [self addChild:player2TargetLbl z:2];
```

```
markPlayer = [CCSprite spriteWithSpriteFrameName:
            @"whitespeck.png"];
[markPlayer setColor:ccGREEN];
[markPlayer setPosition:ccp(20,450)];
[markPlayer setScaleX:10 * CC_CONTENT_SCALE_FACTOR()];
[self addChild:markPlayer z:2];

// Update the display
if ([rules orderedBalls]) {
    CCLabelTTF *nextBallLbl = [CCLabelTTF
                        labelWithString:@"Next Ball"
                        fontName:@"Verdana"
                        fontSize:12];
    [nextBallLbl setPosition:ccp(122,470)];
    [self addChild:nextBallLbl z:100];
}
}
```

We build simple labels to identify player 1 and player 2, and we also create target labels, which we will use to identify "stripes" or "solids" for the player. We use our `whitespeck.png` image again, this time to make a nice green line that will identify which player's turn it is, using the `markPlayer` variable to hold that sprite. Finally, if we are playing a game with ordered balls, we also add the legend **Next Ball** at the top of the display. As we have discussed the goals a few times, let's see how they are identified for the players:

Filename: `OPPlayfieldLayer.mm`

```
-(void) updatePlayerGoals {
    // Update the stripes/solids display for the players
    if ([rules player1Goal] == kStripes) {
        [player1TargetLbl setString:@"Stripes"];
        [player2TargetLbl setString:@"Solids"];
    } else if ([rules player1Goal] == kSolids) {
        [player1TargetLbl setString:@"Solids"];
        [player2TargetLbl setString:@"Stripes"];
    }

    // Update the display
    if ([rules orderedBalls]) {
        // Update the ordered ball goals, if applicable
        [rules findNextOrderedBall:
                [self ballSpritesOnTable]];
        if (nextGoal != nil) {
            [nextGoal removeFromParentAndCleanup:YES];
```

```
        }
        // Create the filename
        NSString *ballImg = [NSString stringWithFormat:
                        @"ball_%i.png",
                        (BallID)[rules nextOrderedBall]];
        // Create sprite and add it to layer
        nextGoal = [CCSprite spriteWithSpriteFrameName:
                        ballImg];
        [nextGoal setPosition:ccp(160,470)];
        [self addChild:nextGoal];
    }
}
```

Referring back to our discussion in the rules about player goals, here we simply check each player's goal. Depending on if it has been set to stripes or solids, we update the appropriate target labels to display to the users what they are shooting for. Then we check if it is a game with ordered balls. If it is, we check with the rules engine to determine what the lowest numbered ball on the table is, and we add an image of that ball to the top of the display, next to the **Next Ball** label. You will notice we call the ballSpritesOnTable method, so we should go there now:

Filename: OPPlayfieldLayer.mm

```
-(NSArray*) ballSpritesOnTable {
    // Returns an array of all ball sprites on the table
    NSMutableArray *currentBalls = [[[NSMutableArray alloc]
                        initWithCapacity:16] autorelease];

    for(b2Body *b = world->GetBodyList(); b;b=b->GetNext()) {
        if (b->GetUserData() != nil) {
            OPBall *aBall = (OPBall*)b->GetUserData();
            if (aBall.tag < 100) {
                [currentBalls addObject:aBall];
            }
        }
    }
    return currentBalls;
}
```

Here we iterate through all the bodies in the Box2D world, and find those that have sprites attached. You will notice we check to make sure the tag is lower than 100. This is because the pockets also have sprites attached, but we set the #define for kPocket to be 500, so we don't accidentally add a pocket sprite to the array. With all balls accounted for, we return an NSArray to the calling method.

The only significant player method we have left is the active player change:

Filename: `OPPlayfieldLayer.mm`

```
-(void) playerChange {
    if ([rules currentPlayer] == 1) {
        [self displayMessage:@"Player 2's turn" userDismiss:NO];
        [rules setCurrentPlayer:2];
        [markPlayer setPosition:ccp(300,450)];
    } else {
        [self displayMessage:@"Player 1's turn" userDismiss:NO];
        [rules setCurrentPlayer:1];
        [markPlayer setPosition:ccp(20,450)];
    }
}
```

This is a short and sweet method. If it is currently player 1's turn, we change the `currentPlayer` to player 2, and vice versa. We move the `markPlayer` sprite to the appropriate side of the display (below the P1 or P2 labels), and we call the `displayMessage` method to give feedback to the players.

Displaying messages

Throughout the game, there are many times we need to present messages to the player. Rather than building the same basic message display repeatedly, we have consolidated that functionality in the `displayMessage` and `dismissMessage` methods.

Filename: `OPPlayfieldLayer.mm`

```
-(void) displayMessage:(NSString*)msg
            userDismiss:(BOOL)userDismiss {
    // If there is a current message, wait for it
    if (isDisplayingMsg) {
        CCDelayTime *del = [CCDelayTime
                            actionWithDuration:0.1];
        CCCallBlock *retry = [CCCallBlock
                            actionWithBlock:^{
          [self displayMessage:msg
                  userDismiss:userDismiss];
        }];
        [self runAction:[CCSequence actions:del,
                        retry, nil]];
        return;
    }
```

```
        isDisplayingMsg = YES;
        isUserDismissMsg = userDismiss;

        // Create the message label & display it
        message = [CCLabelTTF labelWithString:msg
                                     fontName:@"Verdana"
                                     fontSize:20];
        [message setPosition:ccp(size.width/2,
                                 size.height/2)];
        [self addChild:message z:20];

        // If userDismiss is NO, set a 2 second destruct
        if (userDismiss == NO) {
            CCDelayTime *wait = [CCDelayTime
                                 actionWithDuration:2.0f];
            CCCallFunc *dismiss = [CCCallFunc
                        actionWithTarget:self
                        selector:@selector(dismissMessage)];
            [self runAction:[CCSequence actions:wait,
                            dismiss, nil]];
        }
    }
```

In this method, we first check to make sure we are not already displaying a message. If we are (as indicated by the isDisplayingMsg Boolean variable), then we wait for 0.1 second and call it again with the same parameters. If there is no message displaying, we create a label with the requested message and display it on the screen. If the userDismiss is NO, then we set a 2 second timer and then call dismissMessage. If the userDismiss is YES, then the message will be displayed until the user touches the screen to dismiss it.

Filename: OPPlayfieldLayer.mm

```
-(void) dismissMessage {
    isDisplayingMsg = NO;
    [message removeFromParentAndCleanup:YES];
}
```

The dismissMessage method is simple. If we didn't need to have the user dismiss option, then we could have easily embedded this in a CCCallBlock action in the displayMessage method, but we wanted the extra flexibility here.

Collision handling

Before we get to the final stretch covering the controls and the rest of the rules engine, we now know enough about our game that we can implement the collision detection, which uses the same contact listener we used in *Chapter 5, Brick Breaking Balls with Box2D*. We will look at the update method in pieces, so we can discuss it along the way:

Filename: OPPlayfieldLayer.mm (update, part 1)

```
-(void) update: (ccTime) dt
{
  int32 velocityIterations = 30;
  int32 positionIterations = 30;

  // Instruct the world to perform a single step
  world->Step(dt, velocityIterations, positionIterations);

    // Evaluate all contacts
    std::vector<b2Body *>toDestroy;
  std::vector<OPContact>::iterator pos;
  for (pos = contactListener->_contacts.begin();
    pos != contactListener->_contacts.end(); pos++) {
    OPContact contact = *pos;

      // Get the bodies involved in this contact
    b2Body *bodyA = contact.fixtureA->GetBody();
    b2Body *bodyB = contact.fixtureB->GetBody();

      // Get the sprites attached to these bodies
      CCSprite *spriteA = (CCSprite*)bodyA->GetUserData();
      CCSprite *spriteB = (CCSprite*)bodyB->GetUserData();
```

The first important thing to see here is that we have really ramped up the number of iterations that the simulation uses in each step, to increase the accuracy of the simulation. As we only have a small number of bodies, it does not adversely affect performance.

We step the world forward and then, using C++ vectors, we iterate through all the contacts that have been collected by the contact listener. For each contact, we get the bodies and their related sprites, which we store in bodyA, bodyB, spriteA, and spriteB. We hold the sprites as CCSprite objects, because we can't be sure which subclass of CCSprite the object will be.

Filename: `OPPlayfieldLayer.mm` (update, part 2)

```
// Look for balls touching the pocket sensor
if ([spriteA isMemberOfClass:[OPBall class]] &&
    spriteB.tag == kPocket) {
    if (std::find(toDestroy.begin(),
                  toDestroy.end(),
                  bodyA) == toDestroy.end()) {
        toDestroy.push_back(bodyA);
    }
}
// Check the same collision with opposite A/B
else if (spriteA.tag == kPocket && [spriteB
            isMemberOfClass:[OPBall class]]) {
    if (std::find(toDestroy.begin(),
                  toDestroy.end(),
                  bodyB) == toDestroy.end()) {
        toDestroy.push_back(bodyB);
    }
}
if ([spriteA isMemberOfClass:[OPBall class]] &&
    [spriteB isMemberOfClass:[OPBall class]]) {
    // Two balls collided
    // Let's store the FIRST collision
    if ((spriteA.tag == kBallCue ||
         spriteB.tag == kBallCue) &&
        firstHit == kBallNone) {
        if (spriteA.tag == kBallCue) {
            firstHit = (BallID)spriteB.tag;
        } else {
            firstHit = (BallID)spriteA.tag;
        }
    }
}
}
```

In this section, we compare `spriteA` and `spriteB` to see if one of them is an `OPBall` object, and the other has a tag of `kPocket`. If this is true, then a ball has landed in a pocket, so we add the ball to the `toDestroy` vector to deal with later. As you probably recall from *Chapter 5, Brick Breaking Balls with Box2D*, we cannot guarantee in which order the bodies will be reported to us, so we have to check everything in both ways.

The next check is to determine if two balls collided with each other. If there are two balls, then we check to see if one of them is the cue ball. If it is, and this is the first contact of the cue ball with another ball since the cue ball was last hit, then we keep a reference to that tag in the variable firstHit. Why do we do this? Pool has a rule that requires you to hit your own ball first, before the cue ball touches any other balls. By storing the first ball touched in the firstHit variable, we will be able to properly track what the cue ball hit first. We will use this information later.

Filename: OPPlayfieldLayer.mm (update, part 3)

```
// Destroy any bodies & sprites we need to get rid of
std::vector<b2Body *>::iterator pos2;
for(pos2 = toDestroy.begin(); pos2 != toDestroy.end();
                                            ++pos2) {
    b2Body *body = *pos2;
    if (body->GetUserData() != NULL) {
        OPBall *sprite = (OPBall *) body->GetUserData();
        [self sinkBall:sprite];
    }
    world->DestroyBody(body);
}

if ([self isTableMoving]) {
    self.isTouchBlocked = YES;
} else {
    self.isTouchBlocked = NO;

    // Table is done.  Let's resolve the action.
    if (pendingTable) {
        [self checkTable];
        pendingTable = NO;
    }
}
}
```

In this final section of the update method, we proceed to destroy any bodies (balls) that were added to the toDestroy vector, and we send the corresponding sprites to the sinkBall method.

We then check if the table is moving, that is, are any balls still rolling. If there are, we block any user input (with the isTouchBlocked Boolean variable), and then we call the checkTable method to see what happened. We use the pendingTable variable to allow us to only check the status of the table when everything is at rest. We will set pendingTable to YES when we take a shot, and this section will wait until everything is settled, and then check the table once.

We will get to the `checkTable` method later, but for now let's look at the `sinkBall` and `isTableMoving` methods to see how they work:

Filename: `OPPlayfieldLayer.mm`

```
-(void) sinkBall:(OPBall*)thisBall {

    // Keep the ball in the temp array
    [ballsSunk addObject:thisBall];

    // Destroy The Sprite
    [thisBall removeFromParentAndCleanup:YES];
}
```

If we wanted to do something fancy with the balls that are sunk, this would be the place. For our game, we are quite content with simply having the balls added to the `ballsSunk` array and then remove the ball from the layer.

Filename: `OPPlayfieldLayer.mm`

```
-(BOOL) isTableMoving {
    for(b2Body *b = world->GetBodyList(); b;b=b->GetNext()) {
        // See if the body is still noticeably moving
        b2Vec2 vel = b->GetLinearVelocity();

        if (vel.Length() > 0.005f) {
            return YES;
        }
    }
    return NO;
}
```

To check if the table is moving, we could simply poll to see if all bodies are sleeping. The problem with this approach is that it takes a while for physics bodies to completely stop and go to sleep. Through testing, we determined that this was too long and boring. So instead, we check the velocity length of each body. If the value is greater than `0.005f`, then the ball is still noticeably moving. Below that speed, everything is crawling slowly enough for us to proceed with checking the table.

Building the control base

We are now to the point where we can build the controls for the player. As we said in the introduction, we will be building two control schemes. The first is what we call "one touch". This controller will track from the moment the touch is detected until it is released. While the touch is on the screen, we will update the cue stick to follow the touch, aiming at the cue ball. When the touch is ended (finger lifted) we will take the shot from the position of the cue stick, and the distance from the cue ball will determine the strength of the shot.

The second control scheme, which we call "two touch", will be similar in the way it tracks the shot, but it will not automatically take the shot when the touch is lifted. Instead, a button that says **Shoot!** will appear at the bottom of the screen, and touching that button will take the shot.

Both control schemes share some code, so we have created the OPControlBase class, which we will then subclass with OPControlOneTouch and OPControlTwoTouch to handle the specifics of those two control schemes. We will start by looking at the OPControlBase class:

Filename: OPControlBase.h

```
@class OPPlayfieldLayer;

@interface OPControlBase : CCLayer {
    OPPlayfieldLayer *mp; // Main playfield
    float shotLength; // Length of the stroke
    CGPoint plannedHit; // Where the cue will hit
    CCLabelTTF *shootButton; // Only used by 2 touch
    CGPoint aimAtPoint; // Point the cue will aim at
    CCSprite *cueBallInHand; // For placing the cue ball
}

@property (nonatomic, assign) OPPlayfieldLayer *mp;
@property (nonatomic, assign) float shotLength;
@property (nonatomic, assign) CGPoint plannedHit;
@property (nonatomic, assign) CGPoint aimAtPoint;

-(void) updateCueAimFromLoc:(CGPoint)convLoc;
-(void) hideCue;

@end
```

In the header we can see the variables we need to track for both control schemes. We will keep a reference to the main playfield layer, since we need to interact with it. We keep track of the `shotLength` variable (used as the strength), the `plannedHit` variable (the point we will hit from), and the `aimAtPoint` variable, which will be the cue ball's position. We also have the `cueBallInHand` sprite. This will be used when we are positioning the cue ball on the table, as we really don't need or want an actual physics object to ram into other balls as the player is moving the cue ball around.

Filename: `OPControlBase.mm`

```
-(void) updateCueAimFromLoc:(CGPoint)convLoc {
    // Position the cue at the cue ball
    CGPoint offset = ccpSub(aimAtPoint,convLoc);
    CGPoint approach = ccpNormalize(offset);

    // Move the cue into the right angle
    [mp.poolcue setPosition:ccpSub(aimAtPoint, offset)];
    [mp.poolcue setVisible:YES];
    [mp.poolcue setRotation:
     (-1 * CC_RADIANS_TO_DEGREES(
                         ccpToAngle(approach))) + 90];

    // Calculate the power of the hit
    shotLength = sqrtf((offset.x* offset.x) +
                    (offset.y*offset.y)) - 4.5;

    // We limit how far away the cue can be
    if (shotLength > 75 || shotLength < 4) {
        // We reject this hit
        [self hideCue];
        return;
    } else {
        // Calculate the planned hit
        float hitPower = shotLength / 6;
        plannedHit = ccp(hitPower * approach.x,
                    hitPower * approach.y);
        mp.isHitReady = YES;
        shootButton.visible = YES;
    }
}
```

This is the primary method that is shared between the two control schemes. The input parameter, `convLoc`, is the converted location from the touch handler, which we will pass here after the necessary conversions to OpenGL space. We determine the `offset` as a subtraction of the `aimAtPoint` position (the cue ball) from the `convLoc` position (touch location). We then use the `ccpNormalize` function to convert that `offset` into the smallest possible coordinates that still represent the angle desired. This will allow us to control the power of the hit ourselves, without having to compensate for the distance in our calculations.

Using the `mp` variable as a reference to the main playfield layer, we proceed to move the pool cue to the correct location, and we use the `ccpToAngle` function to convert the `approach` variable to something more useful. This creates a value in radians. We use `CC_RADIANS_TO_DEGREES()` to convert this to a degree-based angle, and add it to `90` (which we need to accommodate the rotation of our graphic for the cue stick), and multiply the whole thing by `-1`. This gives us the correct angle we need to make the cue stick point at the cue ball from the point we are currently touching.

We then calculate the `shotLength` value using some simple geometry. If the length is less than `4` (too close to the ball) or greater than `75` (too far away to be sensible), we reject the hit and hide the cue stick. Otherwise, we calculate the `hitPower` (the `shotLength` divided by `6`, to make it a more sensible power level), and we use that to determine the planned hit. This method does not actually make the shot. Rather, it updates the visuals and generates all the calculations we need to be ready to make the shot. The astute reader will also notice that we are setting the `shootButton` sprite to be visible. This is only in existence in our two touch control class, so in the case of the one touch control, this call will send a message to a `nil` object, which is completely ignored.

Filename: `OPControlBase.mm`

```
-(void) hideCue {
    // Hide the pool cue
    [mp.poolcue setPosition:CGPointZero];
    [mp.poolcue setVisible:NO];
    [mp.poolcue setOpacity:255];

    // There is not a valid hit
    // Reset all hit vars
    mp.isHitReady = NO;
    plannedHit = CGPointZero;
    shotLength = 0;

    // Hide the shoot button
    shootButton.visible = NO;
}
```

The `hideCue` method takes away the cue stick and resets all variables to baseline values because we don't have any shot to make. This is important to do here, because this will be called not only after the shot is made, but also when the shot is invalidated (stick too far away, and so on). We are again adjusting the `shootButton` sprite's visibility, if the button's sprite exists. If it doesn't exist, then this line is ignored automatically.

One-touch control

We will look at the one touch control first. The class `OPControlOneTouch` is a subclass of `OPControlBase`, but does not have any additional variables needed.

Filename: `OPControlOneTouch.mm`

```
-(BOOL) ccTouchBegan:(UITouch *)touch withEvent:(UIEvent *)event {
    // Reject touches for now
    if (mp.isTouchBlocked) {
        return NO;
    }
    if (mp.isUserDismissMsg) {
        [mp dismissMessage];
        [mp setIsUserDismissMsg:NO];
        return NO;
    }
    // The next touch returns to the menu
    if (mp.isGameOver) {
        [mp returnToMainMenu];
        return YES;
    }
    // Determine touch position
    CGPoint loc = [touch locationInView:[touch view]];
    CGPoint convLoc = [[CCDirector sharedDirector]
                    convertToGL:loc];
    // If there was a scratch, the cue is in hand
    if (mp.isBallInHand) {
        cueBallInHand = [CCSprite
            spriteWithSpriteFrameName:@"ball_0.png"];
        [cueBallInHand setPosition:convLoc];
        [mp addChild:cueBallInHand z:10];
        return YES;
    }
    // Check if the touch is on the table
    if (CGRectContainsPoint([[mp table] boundingBox],
            convLoc)) {
```

```
            // Store the point we are aiming at
            aimAtPoint = [mp getCueBallPos];

            // Update the cue position
            [self updateCueAimFromLoc:convLoc];
            return YES;
        }
        return NO;
    }
```

We begin the ccTouchBegan method by checking for a couple of special cases. If isTouchBlocked is YES on the main playfield, then we reject the touch. We then check for any user-dismissed messages, to see if we need to clear those messages. If the main playfield has the isGameOver flag set, then the next touch will return to the main menu. We now convert the touch location to the convLoc variable using the standard coordinate transforms. If the player should have the cue ball in hand (after a scratch), then the touch will create a new cueBallInHand sprite. Finally, if the touch is inside the table, then we set the aimAtPoint position to be the cue ball's position, and we call the updateCueAimFromLoc method we discussed earlier.

Filename: OPPControlOneTouch.mm

```
    -(void)ccTouchMoved:(UITouch *)touch withEvent:(UIEvent *)event {
        // Determine touch position
        CGPoint loc = [touch locationInView:[touch view]];
        CGPoint convLoc = [[CCDirector sharedDirector]
                            convertToGL:loc];
        // If there was a scratch, the cue is in hand
        if (mp.isBallInHand) {
            [cueBallInHand setPosition:convLoc];
            return;
        }
        [self updateCueAimFromLoc:convLoc];
    }
```

The ccTouchMoved method follows the same approach as the ccTouchBegan method. If the ball is in hand, then the touch movement will move the cueBallInHand sprite to the touched location, so the ball will follow the touch. If the ball is not in hand, then we again call updateCueAimFromLoc to update the cue stick.

Filename: OPControlTouchOne.mm

```
    -(void) ccTouchEnded:(UITouch *)touch withEvent:(UIEvent *)event {
        // If there was a scratch, the cue is in hand
        if (mp.isBallInHand) {
            [mp createBall:kBallCue AtPos:[cueBallInHand
```

```
                                            position]];
            [cueBallInHand removeFromParentAndCleanup:YES];
            mp.isBallInHand = NO;
        }
        // Only make the shot if it is in the legal range
        if (shotLength > 75 || shotLength < 4) {
            // Reject the shot
        }
        else {
            // Take the shot
            [mp makeTheShot];
        }
    }
}
```

The final method of our control is `ccTouchEnded`, which makes the shot when the touch is lifted. For this controller, we want this to cause the shot to be made. As in the previous two touch methods, we first check if the ball is in hand. If it is, then we call the main playfield to create a new "real" cue ball at that location, and discard the `CCSprite` we were using to represent it. Here we also check the `shotLength` value to make sure it is not too long, to avoid a shot being made with an invisible cue stick. (Without this check, the shot will still be made, whether you can see the stick or not!) Finally, we call to the main playfield to actually make the shot. Before we move on to see the two touch controls, let's go back to the main playfield and see what the `makeTheShot` method does:

Filename: `OPPlayfieldLayer.mm`

```
-(void) makeTheShot {
    // Reset the "first hit" var
    firstHit = kBallNone;

    // The controller tells us where to aim
    CGPoint aimPoint = [contr aimAtPoint];

    // Set up the pool cue animation
    CCMoveTo *move = [CCMoveTo actionWithDuration:0.05
                                    position:aimPoint];
    CCCallBlock *hitIt = [CCCallBlock actionWithBlock:^{
        // Get ready to hit the ball
        b2Vec2 impulse = b2Vec2(contr.plannedHit.x,
                            contr.plannedHit.y);
        b2Vec2 aim = b2Vec2(aimPoint.x / PTM_RATIO,
                        aimPoint.y / PTM_RATIO);
        // Hit it
        cueBallBody->ApplyLinearImpulse(impulse, aim);
```

```
        }];
        CCDelayTime *wait = [CCDelayTime actionWithDuration:0.1];
        CCFadeOut *fadeCue = [CCFadeOut actionWithDuration:0.4];
        CCCallBlock *checkTbl = [CCCallBlock actionWithBlock:^{
            pendingTable = YES;
        }];
        CCCallFunc *hideCue = [CCCallFunc actionWithTarget:contr
                                selector:@selector(hideCue)];
        [poolcue runAction:[CCSequence actions:move, hitIt,
                        wait, fadeCue, hideCue, checkTbl,  nil]];
    }
```

When we make the shot, we set our `aimPoint` to match the controller's `aimAtPoint` (that is, the cue ball). We create a sequence of actions to give the illusion of hitting the ball with the cue stick. First, we move the stick rapidly at the `aimPoint`, then we use a `CCCallBlock` action to apply a linear impulse on the ball, and then we fade the cue out. As we have seen before, the `CCCallBlock` action here is effectively used to avoid the need to build another method. Everything inside the `^{ }` will be executed when this block is called in the sequence. Here it simply sets the `pendingTable` variable to `YES`.

The linear impulse is set using the `plannedHit` variable from the control class, and it applies it directly at the center of the cue ball. (Yes, pool purists, we are aware of the effects of hitting the cue ball off-center. For this game, we have opted to not include any offset controls. It's arcade pool, not a true pool simulator, after all!) You will notice that we add an additional `CCDelayTime` action after we fade out the cue, and then set the `pendingTable` to `YES`. Why do we do this? We need the `pendingTable` variable set to `YES` so the `checkTable` in the `update` method will work correctly when the table comes to rest. However, if we set it as soon as this method is called, the table checking will happen before the shot is made, because the table will still technically be "at rest" for the first half second or so of the action. As we need the balls to be moving before we set this variable, embedding it into the action sequence seemed like a natural fit.

Two-touch control

Our second control method will use two touches, but much of the "plumbing" is very similar to the one touch controller. Let's take a look and then discuss:

Filename: `OPControlTwoTouch.mm`

```
-(id) init {
    if(self = [super init]) {
        shootButton = [CCLabelTTF labelWithString:@"Shoot!"
```

```
                    fontName:@"Verdana" fontSize:20];
        [shootButton setAnchorPoint:ccp(0.5,0)];
        [shootButton setPosition:ccp(160,0)];
        [shootButton setVisible:NO];
        [self addChild:shootButton z:10];
    }
    return self;
}
```

The first difference is that we are using our own `init` method for the two touch control. This `init`, as you can see, simply creates the **Shoot!** button, and positions it at the bottom center of the screen, and sets its `visible` property to NO. We could recreate it each time we need it, but that seems wasteful, so we build it once, and toggle the visible property when we need it.

The two touch control scheme in action looks as follows:

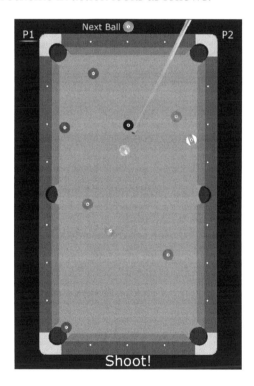

Filename: `OPControlTwoTouch.mm`

```objc
-(BOOL) ccTouchBegan:(UITouch *)touch withEvent:(UIEvent *)event {
    // Reject touches for now
    if (mp.isTouchBlocked) {
        return NO;
    }
    if (mp.isUserDismissMsg) {
        [mp dismissMessage];
        [mp setIsUserDismissMsg:NO];
        return YES;
    }
    // If game over splash is finished, next touch
    // returns to the menu
    if (mp.isGameOver) {
        [mp returnToMainMenu];
        return YES;
    }
    // Determine touch position
    CGPoint loc = [touch locationInView:[touch view]];
    CGPoint convLoc = [[CCDirector sharedDirector]
                    convertToGL:loc];
    // If there was a scratch, the cue is in hand
    if (mp.isBallInHand) {
        cueBallInHand = [CCSprite
            spriteWithSpriteFrameName:@"ball_0.png"];
        [cueBallInHand setPosition:convLoc];
        [mp addChild:cueBallInHand z:10];
        return YES;
    }
    // If we are tracking the aim
    aimAtPoint = [mp getCueBallPos];
    // Check if the Shoot Button was touched
    if (CGRectContainsPoint([shootButton boundingBox],
                convLoc)) {
        [mp makeTheShot];
        return YES;
    }
    // Check if the touch is on the table
    if (CGRectContainsPoint([[mp table] boundingBox],
                convLoc)) {
        // Update the cue position
        [self updateCueAimFromLoc:convLoc];
        return YES;
    }
    return NO;
}
```

In ccTouchBegan, we follow the same code structure up to and including the isBallInHand variable evaluation. It is after that point that we see the differences. We still set the aimAtPoint variable to the cue ball's position, but then we check to see if the shoot button was touched. If it was, then we call makeTheShot. If there was any other touch on the table, then we update the cue stick's position.

Filename: OPControlTwoTouch.mm

```
-(void)ccTouchMoved:(UITouch *)touch withEvent:(UIEvent *)event {
    // Determine touch position
    CGPoint loc = [touch locationInView:[touch view]];
    CGPoint convLoc = [[CCDirector sharedDirector]
                       convertToGL:loc];

    // If there was a scratch, the cue is in hand
    if (mp.isBallInHand) {
        [cueBallInHand setPosition:convLoc];
        return;
    }

    // If not ball in hand, control the cue
    [self updateCueAimFromLoc:convLoc];
}
```

This method is exactly the same as the one touch version of this method. It will track the touch, and keep updating the cue stick (and all the power and distance variables) as the touch moves.

Filename: OPControlTwoTouch.mm

```
-(void)ccTouchEnded:(UITouch *)touch withEvent:(UIEvent *)event {
    // If there was a scratch, the cue is in hand
    if (mp.isBallInHand) {
        [mp createBall:kBallCue AtPos:[cueBallInHand position]];
        [cueBallInHand removeFromParentAndCleanup:YES];
        mp.isBallInHand = NO;
    }
}
```

Because we are not causing any automatic shot to happen when you release your touch, the only handling we need in the ccTouchEnded method is the handling for the ballInHand situation.

That's all we need to do for both control schemes. Looking over the code, there are some similarities where it would be possible to refactor so that the two touch class is a subclass of the one touch class (or vice versa), but we wanted to keep the two separate to make it easier to add other control schemes later on without having too much tangled code.

The rules engine

We are nearing the end of our journey through the pool hall. There is still one gaping hole in our game: the logic of the rules engine and how we use it. Earlier, we saw how we load the rules into our OPRulesBase class, and we have done a little in the OPPlayfieldLayer class with using the player goals to update the player's display. We will dig into the rules engine with the smaller, simpler methods first.

Filename: OPRulesBase.mm

```
-(GameMode) getCurrentPlayerGoal {
    if (currentPlayer == 1) {
        return player1Goal;
    } else {
        return player2Goal;
    }
}
```

Because every rule in the game of pool will depend on which player is taking their turn (especially in the case of Eight Ball), this is our helper method to determine what the current player's goal really is. This will be used by several of the other methods in this class.

Filename: OPRulesBase.mm

```
-(BOOL) didSinkLastBall:(NSArray*)ballArray {
    for (OPBall *aBall in ballArray) {
        if (aBall.tag == lastBall) {
            return YES;
        }
    }
    // Last ball not sunk
    return NO;
}
```

This is the first of the "asking" methods we talked about earlier. We pass this method a `ballArray`, and "ask" if it contains the ball that was identified as the `lastBall` in the `rules.plist`. In Eight Ball, this is the ball numbered 8. In Nine Ball, this is the ball numbered 9. In other games of your own making, it could be anything. You might ask, what exactly is in the `ballArray`? When we call this method during the `checkTable` method (we'll see this soon), we will be passing the `ballsSunk` array to this method, so it knows what balls were sunk during this turn only.

Filename: `OPRulesBase.mm`

```
-(BOOL) didSinkCueBall:(NSArray*)ballArray {
    for (OPBall *aBall in ballArray) {
        if (aBall.tag == kBallCue) {
            return YES;
        }
    }
    // Cue ball not sunk
    return NO;
}
```

This is the same idea as the `didSinkLastBall` method, except this time we are strictly checking to see if the cue ball was sunk, which is a scratch. Now we can move on to the slightly larger, more complex methods.

Filename: `OPRulesBase.mm`

```
-(BOOL) isLegalFirstHit:(BallID)firstBall {
    // Reset the value
    isTableScratch = NO;

    if (firstBall == kBallNone) {
        // Table scratch if nothing touched
        isTableScratch = YES;
        return NO;
    }
    GameMode currGoal = [self getCurrentPlayerGoal];

    switch (currGoal) {
        case kStripesVsSolids:
            // lastBall cannot be hit first
            return firstBall != kBallEight;
        case kStripes:
            // Striped ball hit first to be legal.
            return firstBall > kBallEight;
        case kSolids:
```

```
            // Solid ball hit first to be legal.
            return firstBall < kBallEight;
        case kOrdered:
            if (firstBall == nextOrderedBall || isBreak) {
                // The correct next number was hit first,
                // Or this was the break shot
                isBreak = NO;
                return YES;
            }
            break;
        default:
            // No goal set, all balls are legal
            return NO;
            break;
    }
    return NO;
}
```

Here we pass this method the firstBall variable, which is the ball identified as the first ball hit in the update method we saw earlier. This is the first ball that the cue ball impacted. If the firstBall variable is set to the default kBallNone, it means the cue ball didn't hit any other balls, so this is a table scratch. If it is, we store that in the isTableScratch variable so we can use it later.

We then run through a switch statement on the goal for the current player. If the game is still kStripesVsSolids (so the table is open), then any ball except the ball numbered 8 is legal. If the goal is stripes, the ball number must be above 8. If the goal is solids, the ball number must be a lower number than the 8. Finally, if the game is ordered, then the first ball must be the nextOrderedBall *or* isBreak must be true (that is, it is the break shot, so anything is legal to hit first).

Filename: OPRulesBase.mm

```
-(BOOL) didSinkValidBall:(NSArray*)ballArray {
    GameMode currGoal = [self getCurrentPlayerGoal];

    for (OPBall *aBall in ballArray) {
        switch (currGoal) {
            case kStripes:
                // Striped ball dropped to be legal.
                return aBall.tag > kBallEight;
            case kSolids:
                // Solid ball dropped to be legal.
                return aBall.tag < kBallEight;
            case kOrdered:
```

```
                // The correct next number must be sunk.
                return aBall.tag == nextOrderedBall;
            case kStripesVsSolids:
                // lastBall cannot be hit first
                // everything else is valid
                if (aBall.tag == lastBall) {
                    return NO;
                } else {
                    return YES;
                }
                break;
            default:
                // No goal set, all balls are legal
                return NO;
                break;
        }
    }
    return NO;
}
```

The didSinkValidBall method is used to parse out whether the player sank a ball that was valid for them. We again receive the ballsSunk array as a parameter and iterate through all balls in the array. We go through a switch statement to determine what their current goal is, and go through a similar check to see if the ball was valid. Since we are iterating through the entire array of sunk balls, at least one ball sunk must be valid for the player, in order to return a YES to the calling method. The one major difference is that here we are also checking to see if the ball sunk has the same value as the lastBall variable. Unless we are trying to sink the last ball, that is not a valid play, so it will return NO.

Filename: OPRulesBase.mm

```
-(BOOL) isValidLastBall:(NSArray*)ballsSunk
        withBallsOnTable:(NSArray*)ballsOnTable {
    // Are all other balls for this player sunk already?
    GameMode currGoal = [self getCurrentPlayerGoal];

    switch (currGoal) {
        case kSolids:
            for (OPBall *aBall in ballsOnTable) {
                if (aBall.tag < lastBall) {
                    // Solids left on table.  Illegal.
                    return NO;
                }
            }
```

```
                return YES;
                break;
        case kStripes:
            for (OPBall *aBall in ballsOnTable) {
                if (aBall.tag > lastBall && aBall.tag < 100) {
                    // Solids left on table.  Illegal.
                    return NO;
                }
            }
            return YES;
            break;
        case kOrdered:
            for (OPBall *aBall in ballsOnTable) {
                if (aBall.tag != lastBall && aBall.tag < 100) {
                    // Balls left on table.  Illegal.
                    return NO;
                }
            }
            return YES;
            break;
        default:
            return NO;
            break;
    }
    return NO;
}
```

The last major method in this class is isValidLastBall:withBallsOnTable:.
This again follows a similar pattern to the other classes we have reviewed. In this
case, we are looking through the balls that are still on the table, rather than the
balls that were sunk. This will only be evaluated if the lastBall was sunk, so we
are more concerned with what's left on the table. If we are playing Eight Ball, for
example, and the current player is playing solids, then there must not be any ball
numbered lower than the lastBall left on the table. If we are playing an ordered
game, then all of the balls on the table must be sunk already.

There is only one small but very useful method left in the OPRulesBase class,
so let's look at it before we return to the playfield:

Filename: OPRulesBase.mm

```
-(void) findNextOrderedBall:(NSArray*)tableBalls {
    // Look for each ball, from lowest to highest
    for (int i = 1; i < 16; i++) {
        for (OPBall *aBall in tableBalls) {
```

```
        if (aBall.tag == i) {
            nextOrderedBall = (BallID)i;
            return;
        }
    }
}
}
```

When you're playing an ordered ball game, like Nine Ball, the player must always aim at the lowest numbered ball. Since balls can be sunk out of order, we can not simply increment the ball number as the next ball. Instead, we look for each ball, starting at number 1 and continuing to 15, and checking the `tableBalls` array to see what the lowest numbered ball on the table really is. When we find a ball, we set that value to the `nextOrderedBall` variable, and return control to the calling method.

Putting balls back

Before we move to the `checkTable` method to tie it all together, we have one more method in the playfield to see. As we have a rule defined as `ReplaceBalls`, we need a way to put illegally sunk balls back on the table. This is defined in the plist, so you can set this to your favorite rules. Playing "bar style", this is usually not an option, as coin-operated tables do not allow you to retrieve balls once they are sunk.

Filename: `OPPlayfieldLayer.m`

```
- (void)putBallsBackOnTable:(NSMutableArray*)ballArray {
    // We put the balls we need back on the table,
    // following racking positions, if the rules specify
    if ([rules replaceBalls]) {
        NSMutableArray *deleteArray =
                [[NSMutableArray alloc] init];

        // First we make sure the cue is NOT in the array
        for (OPBall *aBall in ballArray) {
            // If it is, we add it to the delete array
            if (aBall.tag == kBallCue) {
                [deleteArray addObject:aBall];
            }
        }

        // Delete any flagged balls from the array
        [ballArray removeObjectsInArray:deleteArray];
        [deleteArray release];
```

```
CGPoint footSpot = ccp(160,335);

CGPoint r1b1 = ccp(153,348);
CGPoint r1b2 = ccp(167,348);

CGPoint r2b1 = ccp(146,361);
CGPoint r2b2 = ccp(160,361);
CGPoint r2b3 = ccp(174,361);

for (int i = 0; i < [ballArray count]; i++) {
    OPBall *thisBall = [ballArray objectAtIndex:i];
    BallID newBall = (BallID)thisBall.tag;

    switch (i) {
        case 0:
            // foot spot
            [self createBall:newBall AtPos:footSpot];
            break;
        case 1:
            // r1b1
            [self createBall:newBall AtPos:r1b1];
            break;
        case 2:
            // r1b2
            [self createBall:newBall AtPos:r1b2];
            break;
        case 3:
            // r2b1
            [self createBall:newBall AtPos:r2b1];
            break;
        case 4:
            // r2b2
            [self createBall:newBall AtPos:r2b2];
            break;
        case 5:
            // r2b3
            [self createBall:newBall AtPos:r2b3];
            break;
        default:
            break;
    }
}
```

We receive the `sunkBalls` array as the parameter passed as `ballArray` to this method. If the rules specify `replaceBalls` = `YES`, then we first look through the balls to make sure the cue ball is not in the array. If it is, we delete it from the `ballArray`. We then iterate through all balls in the `ballArray`, and put them back on the table following the same positioning we used when we first built the rack. If they are too close to other balls on the table, they will be nudged out of the way by Box2D. We have made the decision that there is probably very little likelihood of there being six or more balls that need to be replaced at the same time, so we have capped this method to only replace the first six balls. Realistically, three is probably the highest number of balls we have ever seen that need to be replaced, and that is a rare occurrence.

Checking the table

We have finally reached the `checkTable` method. As you recall, this is called by the `update` method after the balls have come to rest after a shot. This is where the rest of the game interacts with the rules engine, so we will take this method in pieces.

Filename: `OPPlayfieldLayer.m` (`checkTable`, part 1)

```
-(void) checkTable {
    NSInteger currPlayer = [rules currentPlayer];

    BOOL isValidFirst = NO;
    BOOL isValidSink = NO;
    BOOL isLastBall = NO;
    BOOL isTableScratch = NO;
    BOOL isScratch = NO;
    BOOL replaceBalls = NO;
    BOOL isPlayerChange = NO;
    BOOL isValidLastBall = NO;
    BOOL playerLoses = NO;

    isValidFirst = [rules isLegalFirstHit:firstHit];
    isValidSink = [rules didSinkValidBall:ballsSunk];
    isTableScratch = [rules isTableScratch];
    isLastBall = [rules didSinkLastBall:ballsSunk];
    isScratch = [rules didSinkCueBall:ballsSunk];
    isValidLastBall = [rules isValidLastBall:ballsSunk
            withBallsOnTable:[self ballSpritesOnTable]];
```

We begin by setting up a lot of Boolean variables to hold the "answers" from the method calls to the rules engine. We then go through each of the conditions from the rules engine and populate the Boolean variables with the returned values from those methods.

Filename: `OPPlayfieldLayer.mm` (`checkTable`, part 2)

```
if (isLastBall) {
    if (isValidLastBall) {
        if (isScratch) {
            // Player loses
            playerLoses = YES;
        } else {
            // Player wins
            isGameOver = YES;
            [self gameOverWithWinner:
                [rules currentPlayer]];
            return;
        }
    } else {
        // player loses
        playerLoses = YES;
    }
}
if (playerLoses) {
    isGameOver = YES;
    [self displayMessage:@"Fail!" userDismiss:NO];
    [self gameOverWithLoser:[rules currentPlayer]];
    return;
}
```

The entirety of the `checkTable` method has to be specifically ordered to make sure that the highest priority events are handled first. The first check we make is to see if the `lastBall` was sunk. If it was, we then check `isValidLastBall` to see if this was a legal sinking of the `lastBall`. Then we further check to see if the player scratched at the same time. If it is a valid last ball and the player did not scratch, then the game is over – the current player wins. Otherwise, the player has sunk the `lastBall` too early in the game, and they have lost. If the player loses, we display a disparaging message, and end the game, declaring their opponent a winner.

Filename: `OPPlayfieldLayer.mm` (`checkTable`, part 3)

```
if (isScratch) {
    [self displayMessage:@"Scratched" userDismiss:NO];
    [self displayMessage:@"Place the cue ball"
```

```
            userDismiss:NO];
        replaceBalls = YES;
        isBallInHand = YES;
        isPlayerChange = YES;
    }
    else if (isTableScratch) {
        replaceBalls = YES;
        [self displayMessage:@"table scratch" userDismiss:NO];
        isPlayerChange = YES;
    }
    else if (isValidFirst == NO) {
        replaceBalls = YES;
        [self displayMessage:@"wrong first ball hit"
                userDismiss:NO];
        isPlayerChange = YES;
    }
```

If the player scratched (without the last ball being sunk), we let the player know they scratched, and the cue ball is now in hand for the other player. We also identify that we need to `replaceBalls` (if the option is set), and that we need to change players.

If the player did not scratch (cue ball in a pocket), but did table scratch (cue ball did not touch any other balls), then we simply change players. You will notice that this section is a chain of `if...else` statements, because these conditions are all mutually exclusive, and we don't need to check the remaining conditions if we have met an earlier one.

Next we check to see if the player did not hit a valid first ball (they hit an opponent's ball first), then we call `replaceBalls`, display a message, and indicate a player change.

Filename: `OPPlayfieldLayer.mm` (`checkTable`, part 4)

```
    else if (isValidSink) {
        if (currPlayer == 1) {
            [p1BallsSunk addObjectsFromArray:ballsSunk];

            // If there is nothing set, choose
            if ([rules player1Goal] == kStripesVsSolids) {
                OPBall *aBall = [p1BallsSunk objectAtIndex:0];
                if (aBall.tag < 8) {
                    [rules setPlayer1Goal:kSolids];
                    [rules setPlayer2Goal:kStripes];
                } else {
                    [rules setPlayer1Goal:kStripes];
```

```
                    [rules setPlayer2Goal:kSolids];
                }
            }
        }
        else {
            [p2BallsSunk addObjectsFromArray:ballsSunk];

            // If there is nothing set, choose
            if ([rules player2Goal] == kStripesVsSolids) {
                OPBall *aBall = [p2BallsSunk objectAtIndex:0];
                if (aBall.tag < 8) {
                    [rules setPlayer2Goal:kSolids];
                    [rules setPlayer1Goal:kStripes];
                } else {
                    [rules setPlayer2Goal:kStripes];
                    [rules setPlayer1Goal:kSolids];
                }
            }
        }
    } else {
        // Nothing dropped, but the hit was OK.
        // Change players
        isPlayerChange = YES;
    }

    // If we need to put balls back on the table
    if (replaceBalls) {
        [self putBallsBackOnTable:ballsSunk];
    }

    if (isPlayerChange) {
        [self playerChange];
    }

    // Clear the array for the next turn
    [ballsSunk removeAllObjects];

    // Update goal displays as needed
    [self updatePlayerGoals];
}
```

In this final section of code, if isValidSink is YES, then we add the balls sunk by the player to their own ballsSunk array, and if their goal is still kStripesVsSolids, then we look at the first ball sunk, and that determines whether they are stripes or solids.

If nothing of interest happened, we simply change players.

The remaining checks in this method are to handle the `isPlayerChange` and `replaceBalls` conditions we set earlier in the method, if needed. With that, the core gameplay is complete, and we're ready to play some pool!

The playfield init method

We have omitted some small areas of code, specifically those related to the main menu itself. We have built convenience methods to start the game with a specified rule set and a specified control scheme. (If you want to see these in detail, please refer to the code bundle for this chapter.) There's really nothing that we haven't done before in earlier chapters, but we will briefly go over the `initWithControl:andRules:` method of the `OPPlayfieldLayer` class, so you can see how we have structured the initialization of the game:

Filename: `OPPlayfieldLayer.mm`

```
-(id) initWithControl:(NSString*)controls andRules:(NSString*)
gameRules {
    if(self = [super init]) {
        size = [[CCDirector sharedDirector] winSize];

        // Load the spritesheet
        [[CCSpriteFrameCache sharedSpriteFrameCache]
            addSpriteFramesWithFile:@"poolsheet.plist"];
        poolsheet = [CCSpriteBatchNode
            batchNodeWithFile:@"poolsheet.png"];

        // Add the batch node to the layer
        [self addChild:poolsheet z:1];


        table = [CCSprite
            spriteWithSpriteFrameName:@"table.png"];
        [table setPosition:ccp(size.width/2, size.height/2)];
        [poolsheet addChild:table];

        isGameOver = NO;
        isTouchBlocked = NO;
        isHitReady = NO;
        firstHit = kBallNone;

        ballsSunk = [[NSMutableArray alloc] init];
        p1BallsSunk = [[NSMutableArray alloc] init];
        p2BallsSunk = [[NSMutableArray alloc] init];
```

```
// Start up the interface control structure
if ([controls isEqualToString:@"One Touch"]) {
    // Add the controls
    contr = [[OPControlOneTouch alloc] init];
} else if ([controls isEqualToString:@"Two Touch"]) {
    // Add the controls
    contr = [[OPControlTwoTouch alloc] init];
} else {
    [self displayMessage:@"Failed To Find Controls"
            userDismiss:YES];
}
contr.mp = self;
[self addChild:contr z:20];

// Load the rules
rules = [[OPRulesBase alloc]
        initWithRulesForGame:gameRules];

// Set up the Box2D world
[self initWorld];

// Build the table features
[self createRails];
[self createPockets];

[self createPoolCue];
[self createPlayerScores];

// Cue ball setup
[self displayMessage:@"Place the cue ball"
            userDismiss:NO];
isBallInHand = YES;

// Build the variable elements
[self createRackWithLayout:rules.rackStyle];

// Update goal displays
[self updatePlayerGoals];

// Schedule the update method
[self scheduleUpdate];
}
return self;
}
```

As you can see, we call our custom `init` method with `NSString` representations of the control and rule names. We do this for clarity's sake more than for compact programming. As we discussed in the review of the `rules.plist` design, we sometimes need to sacrifice some small amount of optimizations in favor of readable code. Isn't it easier to know that the rule set we want is "Eight Ball" rather than game number 1? If these were checks that were happening repeatedly throughout the game, we would never make this performance trade-off. However, in all cases where we have used these strings, the code is run once per game, so the microseconds it takes does not impact performance at all.

Summary

Well, we have covered a lot of code in this chapter. We have come back to Box2D after being away from it for a while, and we have built a pretty fun pool game. Along the way, we have explored alternate control schemes, how to make the same engine run with different game rules with a minimum of messy code in the core class, and hopefully learned a few new approaches to coding issues, too. Did we build a world-class pool simulator? Absolutely not. We built a fun game that you, the reader, can expand on and explore on your own. There are many ways you could expand on this game. Add new rules to play pool your way. We kept arrays of each player's sunken balls, but we never did anything interesting with them. (That was intentional.) Perhaps you could draw images of the balls from those arrays on the screen to show who sank which balls? The possibilities are there, and by now you should be ready to hack and slash at the code and make it your own.

In the next chapter we will be building a top-down shooter, using tile maps and onscreen joysticks. It also has a strange fruit versus vegetable theme, just for fun. See you there!

8
Shoot, Scroll, Shoot Again

In this chapter, we will be creating a game using tile maps and an on-screen joystick. We will explore how to use **Tiled**, the free tile map editor, as well as how to implement SneakyJoystick. As a stretch, we will also use some advanced pathfinding code to make slightly smarter enemies.

In this chapter, we cover the following:

- Tiled
- SneakyJoystick
- Tilt Controls
- Separating our game layers
- Semi-smart enemies

The game is…

In this chapter, we will be building a top-down scrolling shooter. It sounds simple, but we will be making it a little more challenging with on-screen joystick control, enemy AI, and some more sophisticated layer designs. Traditionally, this type of game is military-themed, with soldiers running around shooting each other. For our game, we have decided it is fruits versus vegetables battling in the desert. We don't really have a good backstory to explain this. However, if millions of mobile gamers accept that birds and pigs are mortal enemies, then you can certainly invent an equally improbable storyline to explain this odd pairing.

Design review

The design of this game is based on a decent sized tile map, 50 tiles wide and 50 tiles high. Our basic tile size (non-Retina) is 32 x 32 pixels. We will implement the tile map as a single scrolling layer, keeping our hero centered on the screen (except near the edges, but we'll get to that). The goal of the hero is to pick up three goal "signposts" scattered around the map. There will also be health power-ups on the map to restore the hero's health. We want to have two types of enemies. The first will move in a straight path toward the hero. The second type will be a little smarter. When they run into an impassable wall, we will use an `A* Pathfinding` algorithm to find a way around the wall, and then revert to the same straight line toward the hero logic. The player will be able to control the hero using either an on-screen joystick or tilt controls. With either method, there will be a fire button on-screen to shoot. We will break out our game into three layers for easier management: the map layer, the Heads-Up Display (HUD) layer, and the control layer. This will keep our code cleaner, and avoid the problem of having our controls scroll off-screen when the tile map moves. Shall we get started?

Tiled – a primer

Tiled is an open source tile map editor available at `http://mapeditor.org`. It is available for Mac, Windows, and Linux. As Tiled is an open source program, you can also download the source code if you want to see what is "under the hood". We are using Tiled version 0.8.1, which is the current version at the same time writing.

When you first load Tiled, you will create a new map. Go to **File** | **New** from the menu. In the **New Map** dialog box, configure your map like this:

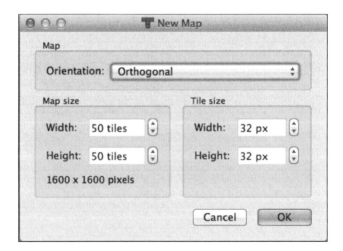

For our game, we will be building our map using non-Retina assets and will later "fake" a Retina sizing. Normally, you would be building the Retina version first, and then "shrink" the map for the non-Retina version. The same techniques work both ways, so we will leave it to you to decide. Anyway, most of these settings are self-explanatory, except perhaps the "Orientation". **Orthogonal** is a term most people are not familiar with. Basically, it means normal square grid, aligned to the x and y axes.

You will now be presented with a blank grid of squares. We need to have some tiles to use, so we use the menu option **Map | NewTileset...**, and are presented with the following dialog:

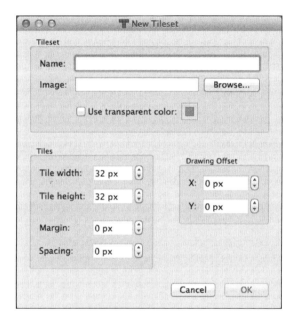

For our game, we will be using the tile map file `tmw_desert_spacing.png` that is bundled with the Tiled download under the folder `examples`. (This image is also included in the cocos2D downloadable as well, under `Resources/TileMaps`.)

We select this as our image in the dialog box, and then we need to adjust the parameters at the bottom of the window. Our tiles are 32 x 32, so we set those values for the **Tile width** and **Tile height**. If you look at the tile image, you will see that the tiles are not exactly touching. There are black boundaries that enforce the grid so you can see which tile is which easily. Because of this, we need to set the **Margin** to 1 and the **Spacing** to 1. You will know these settings are correct because in the **Tilesets** window (by default in the lower-right pane), you will see the tiles arranged nicely without any traces of the black gridlines between them. Tiled shows the tiles with white separators, which is fine.

Drawing the ground

To draw your map, you simply select the tile you want to use from the **Tilesets** pane, and draw on the grid. (If the **Tilesets** pane is not visible, you can turn it on under the **View** | **Tilesets** in the menu.)

One of the strengths of Tiled is that you can define multiple layers on a map. These layers are visible in the **Layers** pane, which is normally at the top left of the display. We start by drawing our basic ground layer, so we rename the default layer from **Tile Layer 1** to ground. Before we go any further, let's see part of our ground layer that we have drawn:

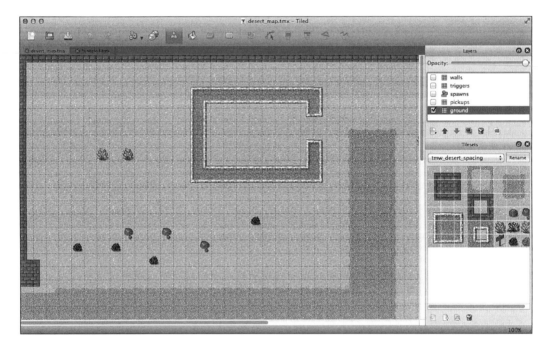

When we drew our ground layer, we avoided drawing anything that would be picked up from the map. In our game, we will be able to pick up health and our goals. The reason we avoid drawing those on the ground layer is that when we pick them up, the image will be removed from the map. If we had the pickups on the ground layer, we would have a blank spot in the map after we picked them up. Instead, we create a new layer, name it pickups, and draw the items we want to be picked up. The following screenshot shows the same area of the map, with the ground layer turned off, and only the pickups layer visible:

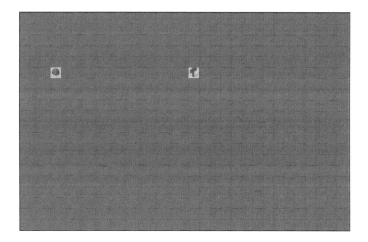

As you see, the goal marker (the signpost) will be inside the building, and the health (flowery cactus thing) will be near the top-left corner. Simply adding the graphics is not enough. We need to be able to add triggers to the map to be able to easily interpret the map. We will handle this by building what we refer to as "logic layers" into the map. These will not be seen by the user, but will be used to trigger events in the code.

Logic layers

To identify where tiles should have some logic associated with them, we need a new tileset. We have built another tileset called `tile_markers.png` that we need to load. This tileset is simply three semi-transparent boxes of different colors. When you load this, it is important to change the spacing and margin to 0 (we didn't use any grid lines in this PNG file.) Also, since we have transparency saved in the image file, make sure the **Use transparent color** box is *not* checked. If it is, then any transparency in the loaded image will be discarded, and our nicely transparent tiles will be opaque.

Once the tileset is loaded, select it from the **Tilesets** pane. You will see three tiles: blue, green, and red. Right-click (or *Ctrl* + click) on the blue tile and select **Tile Properties...**. Double-click on **<new property>** and name it `Goal`. Under **Value**, enter `Yes`. Then click on **OK** to store the property. This will identify the blue tile as a goal tile. Repeat the same process for the green tile, except name it `Health` with a value of `Yes`. Finally, the red tile should be set with the property `Blocked` with a value of `Yes`.

Now that we have our logic tiles defined, we need to build something with them. Create a new layer, named **triggers**. With the **triggers** layer selected, draw blue tiles on the positions of the goal markers, and draw green layers on our health cacti. Because the tiles have partial transparency, you can see the ground tile through the colored tile.

Our next logic layer we need is to define the walls and other impassable tiles. We create a new layer, named `walls`. (Make sure you are drawing on the correct layer; the layer currently active will be highlighting in the **Layers** pane.) Using the red tile, we draw over all walls and rocks in the tile map.

The same area of the map now looks like the following screenshot:

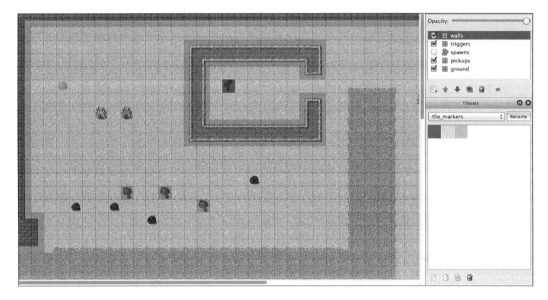

Spawn layer

We have only one more layer to complete the tile map. We now add an **Object Layer** to the map. Objects are features on the map that do not necessarily correspond to tiles. We will be using this layer to identify spawn points for both the hero and the enemies. Let's create an object layer, and name it `spawns`. With the spawn layer selected, you will see that different options in the toolbar are selected. Select the **Insert Object** button from the toolbar. The following screenshot shows how it looks:

Now click on the map to create an object near the opening in the walls on the left side of the map. It will display as a grey square. Now you can right-click (or *Ctrl* + click) on the box to get a menu. Select **Object Properties**. In the window, name this "playerSpawn". This will be the location where the hero will be created. You will notice that there are both x and y coordinates, as well as width and height. For our use, we will not be using the width and height. The x and y coordinates look a little odd. That is because these are tile coordinates. Tile coordinates are similar to the coordinates we are used to in cocos2d, except the (0, 0) coordinate corresponds to the top-left corner, not the bottom-left. When we use these, we will have to do some translation on these coordinates, but we will deal with that later.

Now, we need to make a few more objects on the tile map, preferably keeping most of them farther away from the hero's spawn point. For each of these, we will name them with incremental names `EnemySpawn1`, `EnemySpawn2`, and so on. For our game, we have chosen to have 11 enemy spawn points to add some variety. Once these are all created, let's save the map as `desert_map.tmx`.

Understanding TMX format

Now, we will go ahead and add our `.tmx` file and our two PNG files to our project. If you select the `.tmx` file in Xcode, you can read and edit it directly in the Xcode editor. Go ahead and look at the `desert_map.tmx`. It is a plain XML file, so it is fairly easy to understand most of the parameters. For now, look at the top of the file where the `<tileset>` tags are. You need to make sure there isn't a file path attached to the source value. The first few lines of the file should look like the following screenshot:

```
<?xml version="1.0" encoding="UTF-8"?>
<map version="1.0" orientation="orthogonal" width="50" height="50" tilewidth="32" tileheight="32">
 <tileset firstgid="1" name="tmw_desert_spacing" tilewidth="32" tileheight="32" spacing="1" margin="1">
  <image source="tmw_desert_spacing.png" trans="ff00ff" width="265" height="199"/>
 </tileset>
 <tileset firstgid="49" name="tile_markers" tilewidth="32" tileheight="32">
  <image source="tile_markers.png" width="96" height="32"/>
```

Here you can see that all of the parameters we put in Tiled for the map and the tilesets is all represented in easily readable and *changeable* text. This is important for creating the Retina version of this map.

Creating an HD map

As we said earlier, the usual direction is to create the HD version of everything first, and downscale it to the SD resolution. Because we started with a tile set that was in non-Retina resolution, we opted to build that version first, and then upscale everything.

The first thing we need to do is take both of our tile set PNG images and convert them into HD sized assets. We did this by using Photoshop, and resized them to 200 percent, and then saved them as -hd files. When doing the resizing (regardless of the tool), make sure that it is not doing any clever antialiasing or anything like that. By allowing Photoshop to use its **Resample Image** option, it will leave strange edges on all the tiles, where it feathers out the black separator lines into the tiles themselves. We just need a straight doubling of the pixels for this operation.

Now comes the easier part of making an HD map. Copy the `desert_map.tmx` as a new file, `desert_map-hd.tmx`. Add all three of these -hd files into Xcode as well, and edit the new TMX file. Since we have just doubled all of the tile sizes, we need to edit the sizes in the TMX file. In the `<map>` section, change the `tilewidth` and `tileheight` properties to `64`, since that is our HD tile size. Make the same changes to the parameters for both `<tileset>` sections. We also need to change the `spacing` and `margin` on the desert tileset to `2` and `2`. Finally, the width and height for both `<image>` sections need to be doubled from their former values.

As a final step, we need to change the image source values to reflect the –hd filenames. These should be `tmw_desert_spacing-hd.png` and `tile_markers-hd.png`.

There is one set of values that will not be correct – the object positions. Since these are not tile-based, they will look a little odd if you reload the new –hd tilemap into Tiled. You could compensate for this in code, but our preference is to reload the –hd tilemap into Tiled, and manually move these around. That is the approach we used for this game.

Implementing the tilemap

So far, we've spent considerable time without really building the project, so now let's turn our attention to our Xcode project. The first thing we need to do is load the tilemap into the layer. We will need to persist the tilemap, so first let's look at the header to see our variables.

Filename: `TDPlayfieldLayer.h` (partial)

```
CCTMXTiledMap *_tileMap;
CCTMXLayer *_ground;
CCTMXLayer *_triggers;
CCTMXLayer *_pickups;
CCTMXLayer *_walls;
CCTMXObjectGroup *spawns;

NSInteger tmw; // tilemap width
NSInteger tmh; // tilemap height
NSInteger tw; // tile width
NSInteger th; // tile height
```

Here you see that we keep the tilemap, as well as individual variables for each layer. We also introduce a few NSInteger variables to store the values of several important numbers, as a shorthand to avoid repeatedly writing a relatively long bit of code. Let's look at the relevant sections of the init method.

Filename: TDPlayfieldLayer.m (partial)

```
// Load the map
self.tileMap = [CCTMXTiledMap tiledMapWithTMXFile:
                    @"desert_map.tmx"];
self.ground = [_tileMap layerNamed:@"ground"];
self.triggers = [_tileMap layerNamed:@"triggers"];
self.pickups = [_tileMap layerNamed:@"pickups"];
self.walls = [_tileMap layerNamed:@"walls"];
self.triggers.visible = NO;
self.walls.visible = NO;

[self addChild:_tileMap z:-1];

// Load the spawn object layer
spawns = [_tileMap objectGroupNamed:@"spawns"];
NSAssert(spawns != nil, @"'spawns' missing");
```

That is all it takes to load the tilemap on a layer. You will notice we set the visible attributes for both the triggers and walls to NO. For debugging, you can easily set these to YES, and the map will look more like it does in Tiled, with the colored overlays on the trigger tiles. You will also notice we only add the _tileMap to self, and not the layers within the tilemap. This is because the TMX handling classes of cocos2d are built to assume the tilemap should be kept together and used together. Finally, we load the spawns object group a little differently, because object layers are stored a little differently in the file.

There is a second set of initializations that we do to make it easier to write the code later.

Filename: TDPlayfieldLayer.m

```
// Shorthand for tilemap sizes, with retina fix
tmw = _tileMap.mapSize.width;
tmh = _tileMap.mapSize.height;
tw = _tileMap.tileSize.width /
                CC_CONTENT_SCALE_FACTOR();
th = _tileMap.tileSize.height /
                CC_CONTENT_SCALE_FACTOR();
```

Here we are using the "shorthand" variables that we identified in the header file. This allows us to write shorter lines of code when referencing any of these values. Because the tiles are represented in pixel sizes only, we divide them by the CC_CONTENT_ SCALE_FACTOR() to ensure that we are dealing with the sizes in points, not pixels.

Adding our hero

Now that we have a world to live in, we need to add our hero. We have broken out our hero into a separate class, but first let's look at how we figure out where the hero will spawn. As you may recall, we have the location **playerSpawn** marked on the map. Now, we need to translate that location into game coordinates.

Filename: TDPlayfieldLayer.m

```
-(void) addHero {
    // Get the player spawn location
    NSMutableDictionary *playerSpawn =
                    [spawns objectNamed:@"playerSpawn"];
    NSAssert(playerSpawn != nil, @"playerSpawn missing");
    int x = [[playerSpawn valueForKey:@"x"] intValue];
    int y = [[playerSpawn valueForKey:@"y"] intValue];
    CGPoint heroPos = ccp(x / CC_CONTENT_SCALE_FACTOR(),
                        y / CC_CONTENT_SCALE_FACTOR());

    // Create the player
    hero = [TDHero heroAtPos:heroPos onLayer:self];
    [self addChild:hero];
}
```

Here you see that we create an NSMutableDictionary from the playerSpawn. The data is stored in this way inside the TMX map, because the format does allow us to add other properties to the objects (in our case, we care only about the coordinates). We extract the x and y coordinates for the playerSpawn object, but then we alter the coordinates by dividing them by the CC_CONTENT_SCALE_FACTOR(). Why? Remember that the TMX file format produced by Tiled is not a cocos2d-specific format, so everything is represented as pixels. We divide the coordinates by the CC_CONTENT_SCALE_FACTOR(), which will give us the correct location in points. We then call the constructor for our TDHero class, and add the hero to the layer. We also store a reference to the hero in the hero variable. Now let's see how the TDHero is constructed.

Filename: TDHero.h

```
@class TDPlayfieldLayer;

@interface TDHero : CCNode {
    TDPlayfieldLayer *parentLayer;
    CCSprite *sprite; // sprite for the hero
}

@property (nonatomic, retain) CCSprite *sprite;

+(id) heroAtPos:(CGPoint)pos onLayer:(TDPlayfieldLayer*)layer;

-(void) shoot;
-(void) rotateToTarget:(CGPoint)target;

@end
```

The hero keeps a reference to the TDPlayfieldLayer (using a forward declaration to avoid an import loop), and we keep a reference to the sprite. You will notice that we have TDHero as a subclass of CCNode, not CCSprite. We do this to keep the class more uniform with the TDEnemy class we will look at later. By having the CCSprite as a variable inside a CCNode subclass, it makes it easier to use a single class with different graphics. By keeping these two classes more uniform, it makes it easier to remember how to code the collision and movement classes. Now let's look at the implementation:

Filename: TDHero.m

```
+(id) heroAtPos:(CGPoint)pos onLayer:(TDPlayfieldLayer*)layer {
    return [[[self alloc] initForHeroAtPos:pos onLayer:layer]
                                              autorelease];
}

-(id) initForHeroAtPos:(CGPoint)pos onLayer:(TDPlayfieldLayer*)layer
{
    if((self = [super init])) {

        // Keep a reference to the layer
        parentLayer = layer;

        // Build the sprite
        self.sprite = [CCSprite
                    spriteWithSpriteFrameName:IMG_HERO];
        [sprite setPosition:pos];
```

```
        // Add the sprite to the layer
        [parentLayer addChild:sprite z:2];
    }
    return self;
}
```

Here we have a convenience constructor, and the `init` method. We keep a reference to the parent layer, build a sprite, set its opening position, and add the sprite to the parent layer. Yes, we already added the hero (of `TDHero` class) to the parent layer. That is a "handle" on the `CCNode` that we need to keep to avoid having it autorelease. But that does not add the sprite to the layer, so we add that separately. We want our hero to be able to rotate in the direction he is heading, so we will add a rotation method.

Filename: `TDHero.m`

```
-(void) rotateToTarget:(CGPoint)target {
    // Rotate toward player
    CGPoint diff = ccpSub(target,sprite.position);
    float angleRadians = atanf((float)diff.y /
                               (float)diff.x);
    float angleDegrees=CC_RADIANS_TO_DEGREES(angleRadians);
    float cocosAngle = -angleDegrees;
    if (diff.x < 0) {
        cocosAngle += 180;
    }
    sprite.rotation = cocosAngle;
}
```

This is a fairly standard rotation method that is often used in sample projects. It calculates the angle between the sprite and the target coordinate passed to it. The calculation results in radians, converts that to degrees, and sets the new rotation.

Our hero also needs to be able to shoot. Let's take a look at that:

Filename: `TDHero.m`

```
-(void) shoot {
    // Create a projectile at hero's position
    TDBullet *bullet = [TDBullet
                    bulletFactoryForLayer:parentLayer];
    bullet.position = self.sprite.position;
    bullet.rotation = self.sprite.rotation;
    bullet.isEnemy = NO;

    // Add bullets to parentLayer's array
```

```
    [parentLayer addBullet:bullet];

    // Play a sound effect
    [[SimpleAudioEngine sharedEngine] playEffect:SND_SHOOT];
}
```

Here we see that we will also have a `TDBullet` class as a factory for new bullets. We will take a closer look at bullets later in the chapter. For now, you see that we set the bullet to be at the same position and rotation as the hero, and we set an `isEnemy` flag, so we can make friendly-fire impossible. We send the bullet to the parent layer to be added, and we play a sound effect.

Focus on the hero

If we were to go forward with the code thus far, we have a slight problem. The hero is nowhere on the screen, as we see in the following screenshot:

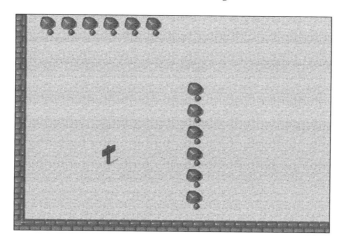

We need a way to focus the view on the hero, but at the same time we need to make sure that we never see any area outside the map. Ray Wenderlich posted a wonderfully compact method of doing this in one of his tutorials at `http://www.raywenderlich.com`.

Filename: `TDPlayfieldLayer.m`

```
- (void)setViewpointCenter:(CGPoint) position {
    // Method written Ray Wenderlich
    // Posted at www.raywenderlich.com
    int x = MAX(position.x, size.width / 2);
    int y = MAX(position.y, size.height / 2);
    x = MIN(x, (_tileMap.mapSize.width *
```

```
                    _tileMap.tileSize.width) - size.width / 2);
        y = MIN(y, (_tileMap.mapSize.height *
                    _tileMap.tileSize.height) - size.height/2);
        CGPoint actualPosition = ccp(x, y);
        CGPoint centerOfView = ccp(size.width/2,
                                   size.height/2);
        CGPoint viewPoint = ccpSub(centerOfView,
                                   actualPosition);
        self.position = viewPoint;
    }
```

The first x and y assignments get the MAX value of either middle of the screen, or the passed position. Then it takes that result and selects the MIN of that value or the right edge of the map minus half a screen. This paired calculation will give you the coordinates of the hero, unless he is near the edge of the screen, in which case it will give the coordinates of a point that is exactly half a screen away from the nearest edge. We then subtract the center of the screen size from the actual position on the map, and we end up with a screen coordinate perfect for the layer's position. You will notice that this actually works by repositioning the layer itself. Here we use it only for following the hero, but if you wanted to call the player's attention to some other feature of the map (show them the goal, for example) you can use this same method by passing it a different coordinate.

Controlling the hero with SneakyJoystick

Now, we need a way to control our hero. For our game, we will be using two different control methods, joystick and tilt. We will look at the joystick control first.

Our joystick control will use the SneakyJoystick class, available at https://github.com/sneakyness/SneakyInput. SneakyInput/SneakyJoystick. This is probably the most commonly used joystick class in the cocos2d community. It has a lot of features (such as skinning the joystick with better graphics), which we will not be using in this project, but which are definitely worth exploring in the projects you will create.

We create a new layer to handle the controls, TDControlLayer. In some projects, it doesn't make a big difference how you organize your objects on layers. When you are using a scrolling tilemap, however, separation of your layers is essential. If you don't put your controls on a separate layer, as soon as you scroll the tilemap, the controls will scroll off-screen. By keeping them as a separate layer (that is *not* a child of the tilemap's layer), the controls will be fixed in the screen positioning you want, regardless of any map scrolling.

Filename: TDControlLayer.m

```
-(void) addJoystick {
    SneakyJoystickSkinnedBase *leftJoy =
            [[[SneakyJoystickSkinnedBase alloc] init]
             autorelease];
    leftJoy.backgroundSprite = [ColoredCircleSprite
        circleWithColor:ccc4(255, 255, 0, 128) radius:32];
    leftJoy.thumbSprite = [ColoredCircleSprite
        circleWithColor:ccc4(0, 0, 255, 200) radius:16];
    leftJoy.joystick = [[[SneakyJoystick alloc]
        initWithRect:CGRectMake(0,0,64,64)] autorelease];
    leftJoystick = leftJoy.joystick;
    leftJoy.position = ccp(64,36);
    [self addChild:leftJoy z:30];
}
```

Most of this method is concerned with the building of the images used for the sprite. We are using a simple example with colored circles to represent the base of the joystick and the thumb. (The "thumb" is the movable part of the joystick, adopting the term from scrollbar controls). We build the joystick, and add it to the layer.

We also need a fire button in our game, so we will use the SneakyButton class for it.

Filename: TDControlLayer.m

```
-(void) addFireButton {
    SneakyButtonSkinnedBase *rightBut =
            [[[SneakyButtonSkinnedBase alloc] init]
             autorelease];
    rightBut.position = ccp(420,36);
    rightBut.defaultSprite = [ColoredCircleSprite
        circleWithColor:ccc4(255, 255, 255, 128) radius:32];
    rightBut.activatedSprite = [ColoredCircleSprite
        circleWithColor:ccc4(255, 255, 255, 255) radius:32];
    rightBut.pressSprite = [ColoredCircleSprite
        circleWithColor:ccc4(255, 0, 0, 255) radius:32];
    rightBut.button = [[[SneakyButton alloc]
        initWithRect:CGRectMake(0, 0, 64, 64)] autorelease];
    rightButton = rightBut.button;
    rightButton.isToggleable = YES;
    [self addChild:rightBut];
}
```

The setup of the `SneakyButton` is very similar to the `SneakyJoystick`, except instead of the base and thumb images, we set up the alternate images for the button press.

Now that we have built the controls, let's see how to use them. We schedule an `update` method on this layer, and the `update` handles parsing the controls.

Filename: `TDControlLayer.m`

```objc
- (void)update: (ccTime)delta {
    // Do nothing if the touches are off
    if ([pf preventTouches]) {
        return;
    }
    if ([pf isGameOver]) {
        [[CCDirector sharedDirector] replaceScene:
                            [TDMenuScene node]];
    }
    if (isTiltControl) {
        // Tilt code here
    } else {
        // If the stick isn't centered, then we're moving
        if (CGPointEqualToPoint(leftJoystick.stickPosition,
                        CGPointZero) == NO) {
            // Pass the call to the playfield
            [pf applyJoystick:leftJoystick
                        toNode:pf.hero.sprite
                    forTimeDelta:delta];
        }
    }
    // If the button is active, let the playfield know
    if (rightButton.active) {
        [pf setHeroShooting:YES];
    } else {
        [pf setHeroShooting:NO];
    }
}
```

This is all of the update method, except for the tilt control section, which we will get to in a few moments. We handle a couple of standard cases first (preventTouches and isGameOver), and then we check the joystick. If the stickPosition is equal to CGPointZero, it means the stick is centered, so we don't actually have any movement requested. If they are not equal, then we need to send the message to the hero to move. We do this by sending a call to the playfield layer (pf is a reference to it), and pass some parameters to it. (The method call is a fairly standard one when using SneakyJoystick. That is why the terminology in the method call is a little different from the other code.) We then check to see if the button has its active property set. If it does, then we need to shoot. We again pass that call to the playfield layer to set a Boolean variable, heroShooting. This class does not have any direct connections to the TDHero class. The call routing is done by way of the playfield layer, which acts as liaison between the two classes.

Tilt controls

The addition of tilt controls to our game is almost trivial. Since the tilt control will only be replacing the joystick, we will still need the button to be used, so it makes sense for these two control methods to be housed in the same class.

Filename: TDControlLayer.m

```
-(void) addTiltControl {
    // Set up the accelerometer
    self.isAccelerometerEnabled = YES;

    [[UIAccelerometer sharedAccelerometer]
                setUpdateInterval:1.0 / 60];
    [[UIAccelerometer sharedAccelerometer] setDelegate:self];
}


- (void)accelerometer:(UIAccelerometer *)accelerometer
didAccelerate:(UIAcceleration *)acceleration {
    // Accelerometer values based on portrait mode, so
    // we reverse them for landscape
    accelX = acceleration.y * 7;
    accelY = -acceleration.x * 7;
}
```

With these two simple methods, we have most of the code we need to make the tilt controls functional. In the `addTiltControl` method, we turn on the accelerometer and set its delegate to this class. That delegate uses a callback, which is the second method listed in the preceding code. At the frequency specified, the `accelerometer:didAccelerate:` method will be called. On each call, we store a modified version of the acceleration values in our `accelX` and `accelY` variables. Because our game is in landscape and the accelerometer reports only in portrait-based values, we reverse the `x` and `y` values. We multiply them by 7 to provide a larger change value. Testing found 7 to be a good multiplier value.

Finally, we have a small bit of code to add into our update method.

Filename: `TDControlLayer.m` (update method, under `Tilt Code here`):

```
// Tilt code here
CGPoint heroPos = [pf getHeroPos];
CGPoint newHeroPos = ccp(heroPos.x + accelX,
                         heroPos.y + accelY);

[pf rotateHeroToward:newHeroPos];
[pf setHeroPos:newHeroPos];
```

Here we could have easily taken the same approach as with the joystick and passed everything to the playfield layer, but we wanted to show an alternate approach with this control. There is no difference in the performance of having the code here or in the playfield layer (as all called methods are in `pf` anyway). The code itself calculates a new position for the hero by adding the `accelX` and `accelY` values to the coordinates. It then calls to rotate the hero, and then move the hero.

To wrap up the control section, let's look at the constructor and the `init` methods.

Filename: `TDControlLayer.m`

```
+(id) controlsWithPlayfieldLayer:(TDPlayfieldLayer*)
                  playfieldLayer withTilt:(BOOL)isTilt {
    return [[[self alloc]
                  initWithPlayfieldLayer:playfieldLayer
                  withTilt:isTilt] autorelease];
}


-(id) initWithPlayfieldLayer:(TDPlayfieldLayer*)playfieldLayer
                                withTilt:(BOOL)isTilt {
    if(self = [super init]) {
        pf = playfieldLayer;
        isTiltControl = isTilt;
```

```
    if (isTiltControl) {
        // Set up the tilt controls
        [self addTiltControl];
    } else {
        // Set up the joystick
        [self addJoystick];
    }

    // Add the fire button (all modes)
    [self addFireButton];

    [self scheduleUpdate];
    }
    return self;
}
```

We will be creating the control layer with two parameters: the playfield layer, and a Boolean value to indicate if we want tilt controls or not. Based on the `isTilt` value, we either create the joystick or we start with tilt. That's all it takes to implement both control mechanisms.

Interpreting the controls

Now we turn our attention to the `TDPlayfieldLayer` class to see how we fully interpret the control methods that were called in the control layer. We'll start with the joystick control:

Filename: `TDPlayfieldLayer.m`

```
- (void)applyJoystick:(SneakyJoystick*)joystick
           toNode:(CCSprite*)sprite
       forTimeDelta:(float)delta {

    // Scale up the joystick's reading to faster movement
    CGPoint scaledVelocity = ccpMult(joystick.velocity,
                                     200);

    // Apply the scaled velocity to the position
    float newPosX = hero.sprite.position.x +
                        scaledVelocity.x * delta;
    float newPosY = hero.sprite.position.y +
                        scaledVelocity.y * delta;
    CGPoint newPos = ccp(newPosX, newPosY);

    // Rotate the hero
```

```
        [hero rotateToTarget:newPos];

        // Set the new position
        [self setHeroPos:newPos];
    }
```

We start by creating a `scaledVelocity` variable, which is the data from the joystick times `200`, to give a larger value than the joystick's reading. We then apply this to the hero's position. You will notice we multiply the `scaledVelocity` by the delta time. We do this to allow for variable update time, so the movement is not jerky, if there is any lag. We then tell the hero to rotate toward the new position, and set the hero's position to the new value.

Now we will look at an abbreviated version of the `setHeroPos` method. We will revisit this later to add some more logic to it. For now, it is very simple.

Filename: `TDPlayfieldLayer.m`

```
    -(void) setHeroPos:(CGPoint)pos {
        // Set the new position
        hero.sprite.position = pos;

        // Center the view on the hero
        [self setViewpointCenter:pos];
    }
```

For now, the `setHeroPos` method simply sets the hero's position and then centers the view on the hero. Nothing fancy, but it gets the job done. At this point, we have used a couple of small pass-through methods that we should mention.

Filename: `TDPlayfieldLayer.m`

```
    -(CGPoint) getHeroPos {
        return hero.sprite.position;
    }

    -(void) rotateHeroToward:(CGPoint)target {
        [hero rotateToTarget:target];
    }
```

As we mentioned before, we want the playfield to be the central point of contact, so these two methods provide easy data pass-throughs that can be called from other classes. Both of these classes were used in the control layer, but they really do nothing special except reduce the number of classes that are directly connected to each other.

Building the HUD

We have a third layer that we need to build, the heads-up display (HUD) layer. This is a mostly trivial layer to implement, but it must be its own layer, for the same reasons we discussed with the controls. If this were on the main layer, the HUD would scroll off-screen whenever we moved away from the first view.

Filename: `TDHUDLayer.m`

```
-(void) addDisplay {
    // Add the fixed text of the HUD
    CCLabelTTF *kills = [CCLabelTTF
                    labelWithString:@"Kills:"
                    fontName:@"Verdana" fontSize:16];
    [kills setAnchorPoint:ccp(0,0.5)];
    [kills setPosition:ccp(10,305)];
    [kills setColor:ccRED];
    [self addChild:kills];

    CCLabelTTF *health = [CCLabelTTF
                    labelWithString:@"Health:"
                    fontName:@"Verdana" fontSize:16];
    [health setAnchorPoint:ccp(0,0.5)];
    [health setPosition:ccp(140,305)];
    [health setColor:ccGREEN];
    [self addChild:health];

    CCLabelTTF *goals = [CCLabelTTF
                    labelWithString:@"Goalposts Left:"
                    fontName:@"Verdana" fontSize:16];
    [goals setAnchorPoint:ccp(0,0.5)];
    [goals setPosition:ccp(300,305)];
    [goals setColor:ccBLUE];
    [self addChild:goals];

    // Add the kill counter
    lblKills = [CCLabelTTF labelWithString:@""
                    fontName:@"Verdana" fontSize:16];
    [lblKills setAnchorPoint:ccp(0,0.5)];
    [lblKills setPosition:ccp(60,305)];
    [lblKills setColor:ccRED];
    [self addChild:lblKills];

    // Add the health counter
    lblHeroHealth = [CCLabelTTF labelWithString:@""
```

```
                    fontName:@"Verdana" fontSize:16];
    [lblHeroHealth setAnchorPoint:ccp(0,0.5)];
    [lblHeroHealth setPosition:ccp(200,305)];
    [lblHeroHealth setColor:ccGREEN];
    [self addChild:lblHeroHealth];

    // Add the goal counter
    lblGoalsRemaining = [CCLabelTTF labelWithString:@""
                    fontName:@"Verdana" fontSize:16];
    [lblGoalsRemaining setAnchorPoint:ccp(0,0.5)];
    [lblGoalsRemaining setPosition:ccp(430,305)];
    [lblGoalsRemaining setColor:ccBLUE];
    [self addChild:lblGoalsRemaining];
}
```

By now this should be simple code to read. We create three labels that are the fixed names of the stats presented: kills, health, and goals. We then create three counter labels for the corresponding values. This handles the initial construction of the layer, but we need to be able to update the values easily, so we create three helper methods.

Filename: TDHUDLayer.m

```
-(void) changeHealthTo:(NSInteger)newHealth {
    NSString *newVal = [NSString stringWithFormat:@"%i %%",
                        newHealth];
    [lblHeroHealth setString:newVal];
}

-(void) changeGoalTo:(NSInteger)newGoal {
    NSString *newVal = [NSString stringWithFormat:@"%i",
                        newGoal];
    [lblGoalsRemaining setString:newVal];
}

-(void) changeKillsTo:(NSInteger)newKills {
    NSString *newVal = [NSString stringWithFormat:@"%i",
                        newKills];
    [lblKills setString:newVal];
}
```

Now we have three methods that allow us to easily change the values of the counter labels as needed. As you probably figured out, we will be calling these directly from the playfield layer. There is nothing fancy here, just code that works. You could always embellish this by adding some animation when the values change, or some other graphic flair. Since this code is self contained in its own layer, you can expand this without any changes to the playfield layer.

Scene construction

We now have three layers for our game, and some layers need to know about the others. Nothing can be a child of the playfield layer, due to the scrolling issue. This is exactly the type of situation that causes us to prefer the separation of scene and layer files, unlike the common template format (a scene method embedded in the CCLayer class). If we were to do that, in which class would you include the scene method, since there is really not one parent layer? (Some would argue that the HUD should be the master layer, with others as children of it. Technically, that works too. We're not fans of that structure, however). Our solution is in the construction of the TDPlayfieldScene class.

Filename: TDPlayfieldScene.m

```
@implementation TDPlayfieldScene

+(id) sceneWithTiltControls:(BOOL)isTilt {
    return [[[self alloc] initWithTiltControls:isTilt]
                                      autorelease];
}

-(id) initWithTiltControls:(BOOL)isTilt {
    if( (self=[super init])) {
        TDHUDLayer *hudLayer = [TDHUDLayer node];
        [self addChild:hudLayer z:5];

        TDPlayfieldLayer *pf = [TDPlayfieldLayer
                    layerWithHUDLayer:hudLayer];
        [self addChild: pf];

        TDControlLayer *controls = [TDControlLayer
                    controlsWithPlayfieldLayer:pf
                    withTilt:isTilt];
        [self addChild:controls z:10];

    }
    return self;
}

@end
```

This allows us to build all three layers in the correct order, with all being children of the scene. This way, none of the layers are children of each other. The playfield layer can be initialized with a reference to the HUD layer, and the controls can be initialized with a reference to the playfield layer. Everything works, and it is easily readable. This construction also makes it trivial to determine the hierarchy of the scenes and layers. The following screenshot shows what our game looks like with all layers included:

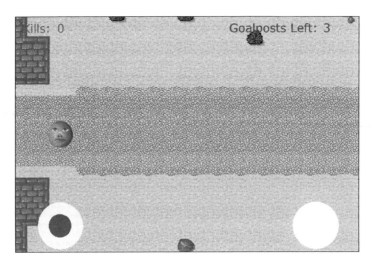

Tile helper methods

One of the challenges in using tile maps is that we have at least two different coordinate positions that can be used to refer to a position on the map: pixels on the tilemap, and the tile coordinates. The tile coordinates relate to each individual tile, so the top left tile is (0,0) and the bottom right is (49,49) for our 50 by 50 map. What we need are some helper methods to easily convert between the two.

Filename: `TDPlayfieldLayer.m`

```
-(CGPoint)tileCoordForPos:(CGPoint)pos {
    // Convert map posiiton to tile coordinate
    NSInteger x = pos.x / tw;
    NSInteger y = ((tmh * th) - pos.y) / th;

    return ccp(x,y);
}
```

Here we are finally making use of the shorthand variables we saw in the `init` method. As a refresher, the variables are as follows:

- `tmw` = tilemap width

- `tmh` = tilemap height

- `tw` = tile width

- `th` = tile height

So the x value is the position divided by the tile width. For the y value, the calculation is a little longer, because the origin point of the tile map is top left instead of bottom left. By multiplying the tilemap height times the tile height we have the total map height. From that we subtract the position, and then divide the result by the tile height. This gives us the reversed y positioning that we need. The final `CGPoint` from this method is the tile coordinate for the given position.

Filename: `TDPlayfieldLayer.m`

```
- (CGPoint)posForTileCoord:(CGPoint)tileCoord {
    // Convert the tile coordinate to map position
    NSInteger x = (tileCoord.x * tw) + tw / 2;
    NSInteger y = (tmh * th)-(tileCoord.y * th)-th / 2;

    return ccp(x, y);
}
```

This method reverses the same calculation that we just saw. One callout on this method is the last bit of each formula. The "core" of the formulas will result in the edge of the tile being converted. By adding half the tile width (or subtracting half of the tile height), the end result is the center of the tile, which is what we want.

Tile self-identification

We need some methods to perform what we refer to as self-identification. This is where we can "ask" each tile about any special properties.

Filename: `TDPlayfieldLayer.m`

```
- (BOOL)isValidTileCoord:(CGPoint)tileCoord {
    if (tileCoord.x < 0 || tileCoord.y < 0 ||
        tileCoord.x >= tmw ||
        tileCoord.y >= tmh) {
        return FALSE;
    } else {
        return TRUE;
    }
}
```

The first of these methods is the isValidTileCoord method, so we can check to see if a tile coordinate being passed is even on the map. A simple check on the lower bounds (zero) and the upper bounds (tilemap width, tilemap height) will allow us to return a Boolean value to identify if this is a valid tile.

Filename: TDPlayfieldLayer.m

```
-(BOOL)isWallAtTileCoord:(CGPoint)tileCoord {
    // If it is invalid, act like it is a wall
    if ([self isValidTileCoord:tileCoord] == NO) {
        return YES;
    }

    int gid = [self.walls tileGIDAt:tileCoord];
    NSDictionary *properties = [_tileMap
                                propertiesForGID:gid];

    return ([properties valueForKey:@"Blocked"] != nil);
}
```

This method uses the isValidTileCoord: method to determine if the tile is valid. If it is not, then we can treat it as though it is a wall and return YES. Otherwise, we get the tile's GID for the specified tile coordinate in the walls layer. (**GID** is a **Global Identifier** used by the tilemap.) We then poll the tilemap to get any properties related to that tile. We return the value for the key Blocked. If you recall when we built the map in Tiled, we gave the red tile a property of Blocked, with a value of Yes. Here is where we get the benefit of that tilemap. With this simple check, we can "ask" the map if there is a wall, and get a definitive answer. How easy is that?

We follow the same basic logic to identify both goal markers and health powerups.

Filename: TDPlayfieldLayer.m

```
-(BOOL)isGoalAtTileCoord:(CGPoint)tileCoord {
    int gid = [self.triggers tileGIDAt:tileCoord];
    NSDictionary *properties = [_tileMap
                                propertiesForGID:gid];

    return ([properties valueForKey:@"Goal"] != nil);
}

-(BOOL)isHealthAtTileCoord:(CGPoint)tileCoord {
    int gid = [self.triggers tileGIDAt:tileCoord];
    NSDictionary *properties = [_tileMap
                                propertiesForGID:gid];

    return ([properties valueForKey:@"Health"] != nil);
}
```

As you can see, the code is virtually identical between these methods. If you were so inclined, you could extrapolate a base method that could do both, but we prefer explicit method calls in this case, mostly because we only have two types of triggers.

Smarter hero walking

With the code that we have covered so far, our hero will walk around without any awareness of the special tiles that we have placed, so he will walk right through walls. We need to fix this. Now that we have added methods to make it fairly simple to determine where our special triggers are, we can revisit the setHeroPos method, which we started earlier. This is a complete replacement of the earlier method.

Filename: TDPlayfieldLayer.m

```
-(void) setHeroPos:(CGPoint)pos {
    // Get the tile coordinates
    CGPoint tileCoord = [self tileCoordForPos:pos];

    // Check if the new tile is blocked
    if ([self isWallAtTileCoord:tileCoord]) {
        // Return without allowing the move
        return;
    }

    // Check if the hero picked up health
    if ([self isHealthAtTileCoord:tileCoord]) {
        // Remove it from the map
        [_triggers removeTileAt:tileCoord];
        [_pickups removeTileAt:tileCoord];
        // Add health to the player
        [self heroGetsHealth];
    }

    // Check if the hero grabbed a goal
    if ([self isGoalAtTileCoord:tileCoord]) {
        // Remove it from the map
        [_triggers removeTileAt:tileCoord];
        [_pickups removeTileAt:tileCoord];
        // Add goal to the player
        [self heroGetsGoal];
    }

    // Set the new position
    hero.sprite.position = pos;

    // Center the view on the hero
    [self setViewpointCenter:pos];
}
```

We begin the method by converting the new hero position to a tile coordinate. We then check to see if this is actually a wall. If the desired coordinate is a blocked tile, then the method will return without moving the hero. This will effectively prevent the hero from walking on any of the blocked tiles. We then check for health powerups or goal markers, using our helper methods. If we have picked up a goal or health, we remove the corresponding tile from both the _triggers and the _ pickups layers. Removing it from the _pickups layer will take away the visible tile, and removing it from the _triggers layer will prevent us from triggering the same event the next time the player passes over this tile. In both cases, we call out to the appropriate handling method to take action on the item that was picked up. After this new code, we see the same hero positioning and viewpoint centering code we saw earlier. Let's look at the item pickup handler methods.

Filename: TDPlayfieldLayer.m

```
-(void) heroGetsHealth {
    heroHealth = heroHealth + 40;
    [hudLayer changeHealthTo:heroHealth];
}
```

We decided that the hero should have a 40 point boost to his health when he picks up one of the odd cactus things. We update the heroHealth variable, and update the HUD by calling out to the hudLayer for the changeHealthTo: method we saw earlier.

Filename: TDPlayfieldLayer.m

```
-(void) heroGetsGoal {
    heroGoalsRemaining--;
    [hudLayer changeGoalTo:heroGoalsRemaining];

    if (heroGoalsRemaining <= 0) {
        // hero wins
        isGameOver = YES;
        preventTouches = YES;
    }
}
```

For the goal, we adjust the heroGoalsRemaining variable and change the HUD in a similar fashion. However, since the goals are the point of the game, we check to see if all the goals have been reached (picked up). If so, we set the isGameOver and preventTouches to YES, which will end the game when the next update loop runs.

Time for bullets

All this running around and hitting walls is fine and good, but we need to be able to shoot, don't we? As you may recall from our discussion of the TDControlLayer class, you will recall that when the button is pressed we simply set the Boolean variable heroShooting to YES. We handle this value in the TDPlayfieldLayer update method.

Filename: TDPlayfieldLayer.m

```
-(void) update:(ccTime) dt {
    // If the shoot button is pressed
    if (heroShooting) {
        // We limit the hero's shoot speed to avoid
        // massive "bullet rain" effect
        if (currHeroShootSpeed > 0) {
            currHeroShootSpeed -= dt;
        } else {
            // Ready to shoot
            [hero shoot];
            currHeroShootSpeed = shootSpeed;
        }
    } else {
        // Get ready to shoot next press
        currHeroShootSpeed = 0;
    }

    // Move the enemies

    // Move the bullets

    // Check collisions

    // Is the game over?
    if (isGameOver) {
        [self gameOver];
    }
}
```

We have left a few blanks here to fill in later, but this is the structure of the entire `update` method. When the `heroShooting` variable is YES, we evaluate the `currHeroShootSpeed` variable. If it is greater than zero, we subtract the delta time from it. If it has reached zero, we call the hero's `shoot` method. We then reset the `currHeroShootSpeed` to the value of the `shootSpeed` variable. This is set in the `init` method, and is set to a value of `0.2` to avoid ridiculous machine-gunning of bullets. This means you can only shoot a maximum of once every 0.2 seconds. That's still fast enough, isn't it? If the hero is not shooting (that is, not pressing the shoot button), then we reset the `currHeroShootSpeed` variable to `0`. This allows the hero to shoot immediately when they press the button without having this "cooldown" timer delaying their shot.

TDBullet class

Now that we know how to shoot, we need to know what we're shooting.

Filename: `TDBullet.m`

```
+(id) bulletFactoryForLayer:(TDPlayfieldLayer*)layer {
    return [[[self alloc] initForLayer:layer
            withSpriteFrameName:IMG_BULLET] autorelease];
}

-(id) initForLayer:(TDPlayfieldLayer*)layer
        withSpriteFrameName:(NSString*)spriteFrameName {
    if((self = [super
                initWithSpriteFrameName:spriteFrameName])) {

        parentLayer = layer;

        totalMoveDist = 200;
        thisMoveDist = 10;

        isDead = NO;

    }
    return self;
}
```

Here we use the convenience method `bulletFactoryForLayer` to build the bullet. Because the `TDBullet` is a `CCSprite` subclass, we can use a call to `super` `initWithSpriteFrameName` to build the sprite. We keep a reference to the parent layer, and we set the `totalMoveDist` variable to be our limit of how far the bullet can travel before it expires. The variable `thisMoveDist` is used to determine how far on each update the bullet should travel. Most of the work of this class is done in the `update` method.

Filename: TDBullet.m

```
-(void) update:(ccTime)dt {

    if (isDead) {
        return;
    }
    // Calculate the movement
    CGFloat targetAngle =
            CC_DEGREES_TO_RADIANS(-self.rotation);
    CGPoint targetPoint = ccpMult(ccpForAngle(targetAngle),
                                  thisMoveDist);
    CGPoint finalTarget = ccpAdd(targetPoint, self.position);

    self.position = finalTarget;

    totalMoveDist = totalMoveDist - thisMoveDist;

    if (totalMoveDist <= 0) {
        [parentLayer removeBullet:self];
        return;
    }

    // Convert location to tile coords
    CGPoint tileCoord = [parentLayer tileCoordForPos:
                         self.position];

    // Check for walls.  Walls stop bullets.
    if ([parentLayer isWallAtTileCoord:tileCoord]) {
        [parentLayer removeBullet:self];
    }
}
```

We begin this method by checking to make sure this bullet is not dead. It is possible to call update on a bullet in the process of being discarded, so this will prevent us from trying to move an object as it is being dereferenced. We then go through a bit of code that takes the current rotation and calculates a target in that direction that is thisMoveDist away from the current position. We subtract this from the totalMoveDist value, so we can keep track of how far the bullet has left to move. If the totalMoveDist variable reaches zero, then we call to the parentLayer object to remove the bullet. If it is not zero, we convert the bullet's current position to a tile coordinate using the method in the parentLayer. We then check to see if the tile is a wall. If it is, the bullet is removed, because we do not want the bullets to go through the walls.

We also have two bullet-handling methods in the playfield layer.

Filename: `TDPlayfieldLayer.m`

```
-(void) addBullet:(TDBullet*)thisBullet {
    [self addChild:thisBullet z:5];
    [bulletArray addObject:thisBullet];
}

-(void) removeBullet:(TDBullet*)thisBullet {
    [thisBullet setIsDead:YES];
    [bulletArray removeObject:thisBullet];
    [thisBullet removeFromParentAndCleanup:YES];
}
```

If you recall from our review of the `TDHero` class, when the `shoot` method is called, it builds a bullet and then passes that bullet to the `addBullet` method of the layer stored in the `parentLayer` variable. Here you can see what that does. It adds it to the layer, and then adds the bullet to the `bulletArray` array. When we need to remove a bullet, we first set the bullet's `isDead` property to `YES`, and then remove the bullet from the array and the layer.

The final bit of the bullet movement code that we need is in the `update` method of the `TDPlayfieldLayer`. We need to add a couple of lines there:

Filename: `TDPlayfieldLayer.m` (update method, under `Move The Bullets`):

```
for (int i = 0; i < [bulletArray count]; i++) {
    [[bulletArray objectAtIndex:i] update:dt];
}
```

This is nicely compact code, just as we like it. Here we iterate through all the bullets in the `bulletArray`, and call each one's `update` method, with the current delta. We iterate using a traditional `for` loop instead of fast enumeration (that is `for (TDBullet *aBullet in bulletArray)`) because we may be calling for some bullets to die in this loop. Mutating the array while using fast enumeration will cause a crash. Don't believe us? Try it and you'll see for yourself.

Building the enemy

Now we have a world to run around in and bullets to shoot, but nobody to stop us from reaching our goals. We need to add some enemies to spice it up. As we go through the enemy handling code, keep in mind how we set up the hero. You will see a lot of similarities, and we could have compressed them into a single base class, but opted not to do so for clarity's sake.

Filename: TDEnemy.m

```objc
+(id) enemyAtPos:(CGPoint)pos onLayer:(TDPlayfieldLayer*)layer {
    return [[[self alloc] initForEnemyAtPos:pos onLayer:layer]
                                            autorelease];
}


-(id) initForEnemyAtPos:(CGPoint)pos
                  onLayer:(TDPlayfieldLayer*)layer  {
    if((self = [super init])) {
        // Keep a reference to the layer
        parentLayer = layer;

        // Build the sprite
        [self buildEnemySpriteAtPos:pos];

        // Add the sprite to the layer
        [parentLayer addChild:sprite z:2];

        // Set the max shooting speed
        maxShootSpeed = 3;
    }
    return self;
}
```

Here we have the constructors for the TDEnemy class. We keep a reference to the parentLayer, set the maxShootSpeed variable, and we call out to the buildEnemySpriteAtPos method.

Filename: TDEnemy.m

```objc
-(void) buildEnemySpriteAtPos:(CGPoint)pos {
    sprite = [CCSprite
              spriteWithSpriteFrameName:IMG_ENEMY];
    [sprite setPosition:pos];
}
```

Why did we break this method out separately, instead of embedding these two lines in the init method? We did this to make subclassing of the TDEnemy class easier. Because we have kept this separate, we can override this method without needing to override the init method in any subclasses of the TDEnemy. This allows us to not repeat the boilerplate init method for both enemy classes, when the only difference is the sprite used.

Filename: TDEnemy.m

```
-(void) rotateToTarget:(CGPoint)target {
    // Rotate toward player
    CGPoint diff = ccpSub(target,sprite.position);
    float angleRadians = atanf((float)diff.y / (float)diff.x);
    float angleDegrees = CC_RADIANS_TO_DEGREES(angleRadians);
    float cocosAngle = -angleDegrees;
    if (diff.x < 0) {
        cocosAngle += 180;
    }
    sprite.rotation = cocosAngle;
}
```

This rotation method works the same way that the rotation method in the hero class operates. It determines the angle toward the specified target, and rotates accordingly.

Filename: TDEnemy.m

```
-(void) moveToward:(CGPoint)target {
    // Rotate toward player
    [self rotateToTarget:target];

    // Move toward the player
    CGFloat targetAngle =
            CC_DEGREES_TO_RADIANS(-sprite.rotation);
    CGPoint targetPoint = ccpForAngle(targetAngle);
    CGPoint finalTarget = ccpAdd(targetPoint,
                                sprite.position);
    CGPoint tileCoord = [parentLayer
                        tileCoordForPos:finalTarget];

    if ([parentLayer isWallAtTileCoord:tileCoord]) {
        // Cannot move - hit a wall
        return;
    }

    // Set the new position
    sprite.position = finalTarget;
}
```

Here we are using some basic movement code. The enemy will determine the most direct path toward the hero, and try to move there. Just as we did with the hero and bullets, the enemies are unable to pass through walls. We don't have any special handling for the enemy to do something different when they hit a wall, so they will continue to try to move into a wall for as long as it is between the hero and the enemy. Not too smart, but this is supposed to be your basic enemy grunt. Not too bright.

Filename: TDEnemy.m

```
-(void) shoot {
    // Create a projectile at hero's position
    TDBullet *bullet = [TDBullet
                           bulletFactoryForLayer:parentLayer];
    bullet.position = self.sprite.position;
    bullet.rotation = self.sprite.rotation;
    bullet.isEnemy = YES;
    [bullet setColor:ccRED];

    // add bullets to parentLayer's array
    [parentLayer addBullet:bullet];

    // Play a sound effect
    [[SimpleAudioEngine sharedEngine] playEffect:SND_SHOOT];
}
```

This method is virtually identical to the hero's shoot method, with two exceptions. The first is that we set the isEnemy variable to YES, to identify that this is a bullet fired by an enemy unit. The second is that we set the bullet's color to red. The sprite we are using is blue, so this gives the enemy a "bad guys shoot red" effect. Everything else in this method is identical.

Filename: TDEnemy.m

```
-(void) update:(ccTime)dt {
    currShootSpeed = currShootSpeed - dt;

    // Take a step
    [self moveToward:[parentLayer getHeroPos]];

    if (ccpDistance(sprite.position,
                    [parentLayer getHeroPos]) < 250) {
        // Limit the shoot speed
```

```
    if (currShootSpeed <= 0) {
        // Ready to shoot
        [self shoot];
        currShootSpeed = maxShootSpeed;
    }
  }
}
```

In the enemy's `update` method, we move toward the hero's position on each update. We also check to see if the distance from the enemy to the hero is less than 250 points. If it is, then the enemy will try to shoot. Since he is already rotated toward the hero, he will always shoot directly at the hero.

Just as with the bullets, we need to make a small addition to the main layer's `update` method to make the enemies move.

Filename: `TDPlayfieldLayer.m` (update method, under `Move The Enemies`):

```
for (int i = 0; i < [enemyArray count]; i++) {
    [[enemyArray objectAtIndex:i] update:dt];
}
```

This is virtually identical to the movement code for the bullets. For each update, we instruct each enemy to move himself.

Adding the enemies

We now know how the enemy class is constructed, and how to make them move, so next we need to add them to the game itself.

Filename: `TDPlayfieldLayer.m`

```
-(void) addEnemyOfType:(EnemyType)enemyType {
    // Randomly pick a spawn point
    NSString *enemySpawnID = [NSString stringWithFormat:
                              @"EnemySpawn%i",
                              (arc4random() % 11) + 1];

    // Get the point
    NSMutableDictionary *enemySpawn = [spawns objectNamed:
                                       enemySpawnID];
    float x = [[enemySpawn valueForKey:@"x"] floatValue];
    float y = [[enemySpawn valueForKey:@"y"] floatValue];

    // Retina-ize the position (TMX files are in pixels)
```

```
    x /= CC_CONTENT_SCALE_FACTOR();
    y /= CC_CONTENT_SCALE_FACTOR();

    if (enemyType == kEnemyEasy) {
        // Create the enemy (will put itself on the layer)
        TDEnemy *enemy = [TDEnemy enemyAtPos:ccp(x,y)
                                      onLayer:self];

        // Add it to the array
        [enemyArray addObject:enemy];
    }
    else if (enemyType == kEnemyHard) {
        // Create the enemy (will put itself on the layer)
        TDEnemySmart *enemy = [TDEnemySmart
                               enemyAtPos:ccp(x,y)
                               onLayer:self];

        // Add it to the array
        [enemyArray addObject:enemy];
    }
}
```

If you recall when we built the tilemap, we designated objects on the map named EnemySpawn1, EnemySpawn2, and so on. Now we can finally use those spawn points. We don't like the idea of enemies always spawning at the same spot, so we randomly pick a number between 1 and 11 using arc4random(). We use this to build a string that corresponds to an object name on our spawns layer of the tilemap. We can't use these values directly, because of the points versus pixels issue, so we divide the x and y coordinates by the CC_CONTENT_SCALE_FACTOR() to get the correct positioning.

Here you see we have defined two types of enemy: kEnemyEasy and kEnemyHard. We use the same basic constructor for both, but the hard enemy will use the TDEnemySmart class instead (we'll get to that later).

Now, we need to be able to build enemies of both types in the game.

Filename: TDPlayfieldLayer.m

```
-(void) addEnemies {
    // Add some enemies
    for (int i = 0; i < 5; i++) {
        [self addEnemyOfType:kEnemyEasy];
    }
```

```
    for (int i = 0; i < 3; i++) {
        [self addEnemyOfType:kEnemyHard];
    }
}
```

We simply step through two `for` loops to add the specified number of enemies for each type. The numbers are arbitrarily chosen, and you can adjust them as you see fit to provide a hard enough challenge for you.

Collision handling

At this point we have everything we need, except for a way to make bullets hit the hero and enemies. What fun is shooting if you can't hit anything?

Filename: `TDPlayfieldLayer.m`

```
-(void) checkCollisions {
    NSMutableArray *bulletsToDelete =
                        [[NSMutableArray alloc] init];

    for (TDBullet *aBullet in bulletArray) {
        if (CGRectIntersectsRect(aBullet.boundingBox,
                            hero.sprite.boundingBox)
                        && aBullet.isEnemy) {
            // Hero got hit!
            [self heroGetsHit];
            [bulletsToDelete addObject:aBullet];
            [aBullet removeFromParentAndCleanup:YES];
            break;
        }
        // Iterate through enemies, see if they got hit
        for (TDEnemy *anEnemy in enemyArray) {
            if (CGRectIntersectsRect(aBullet.boundingBox,
                        anEnemy.sprite.boundingBox)
                    && aBullet.isEnemy == NO) {
                //Enemy got hit
                [self enemyGetsHit:anEnemy];
                [bulletsToDelete addObject:aBullet];
                [aBullet removeFromParentAndCleanup:YES];
                break;
            }
        }
    }
```

```
    // Remove the bullets
    for (int i = 0; i < [bulletsToDelete count]; i++) {
        [bulletArray removeObjectsInArray:bulletsToDelete];
    }

    [bulletsToDelete release];
}
```

As we have seen, all the bullets in the game are stored in a single array, bulletArray. We iterate through that array and first check to see if a bullet hit the hero. We use CGRectIntersectsRect to see if there is any overlap of the boundingBox objects of the bullet and the hero. We also check the bullet's isEnemy property to make sure it is an enemy bullet. (Remember, we don't want any friendly-fire!) If the bullet is touching the hero and an enemy fired it, we register the collision. We call the heroGetsHit method, add the bullet to the bulletsToDelete array, and remove the bullet from the layer. Why didn't we use the removeBullet method that we saw earlier? We can't use that because we would be removing the bullet from the array while iterating through it, which would cause a mutation (leading to a crash). Because we need to remove the bullets after the iteration is done, we use the bulletsToDelete array instead.

If the hero was not hit by a bullet, we then iterate through all enemies in the enemyArray. We do a similar check of each boundingBox and make sure it is not an enemy-fired bullet. If the enemy is hit, we call the enemyGetsHit method, and pass it a reference to the enemy that was hit.

Finally, we remove all bullets from the bulletsToDelete array (when the other loops are done) so we can remove them safely.

We trigger the collision check in the update method, as follows.

Filename: TDPlayfieldLayer.m (update method, under Check collisions):

```
    [self checkCollisions];
```

We check for collisions at the end of every update, so we can always be using the current state of the game field.

Everybody gets hit

Now, we will look at the methods that were called when the hero or an enemy gets hit by a bullet. First, we will look at the hero.

Filename: `TDPlayfieldLayer.m`

```
-(void) heroGetsHit {
    // Decrease the hero's health
    heroHealth = heroHealth - 20;
    [hudLayer changeHealthTo:heroHealth];

    // Play the effect
    [[SimpleAudioEngine sharedEngine] playEffect:SND_HERO];

    if (heroHealth <= 0) {
        // Hero died.
        isGameOver = YES;
        preventTouches = YES;
    }
}
```

Our hero is pretty tough, so a single bullet isn't enough to kill him. Instead, we subtract 20 from his health and update the HUD. If his health has reached zero, he is dead. We set the `isGameOver` variable to `YES` so it will be handled at the end of the update loop. This is why collisions are handled after the movement, and game over is checked for after the collision handler.

Filename: `TDPlayfieldLayer.m`

```
-(void) enemyGetsHit:(TDEnemy*) thisEnemy {
    // Get rid of the enemy
    [thisEnemy.sprite removeFromParentAndCleanup:YES];
    [enemyArray removeObject:thisEnemy];

    // Score the kill
    heroKills++;
    [hudLayer changeKillsTo:heroKills];

    // Play the effect
    [[SimpleAudioEngine sharedEngine] playEffect:SND_ENEMY];

    // Spawn a new enemy to replace this one
    [self addEnemyOfType:kEnemyEasy];
}
```

When an enemy gets hit, they die immediately. We could have given them a health level like the hero, but who wants really strong enemies? We remove the enemy from the layer and remove it from the enemyArray. Because we want to track our hero's kill count, we increment his kills and call to the hudLayer to update the display. We then play a death sound, and spawn a new enemy. As it is written, we will only spawn easy enemies when any enemy dies. This could be modified, if you prefer to do something like randomly picking a new enemy type. We decided that the hard enemies were the commanders, and you can't as easily replace a commander as a grunt.

Game over, man

We have seen where we set game over conditions, so let's look at the actual game over method. It's pretty basic, but it serves its purpose.

Filename: TDPlayfieldLayer.m

```
-(void) gameOver {
    [self unscheduleUpdate];

    NSString *msg = @"You win!";

    if (heroHealth <= 0) {
        msg = @"You died.";
    }

    [hudLayer showGameOver:msg];

    CCDelayTime *delay = [CCDelayTime actionWithDuration:3.0];
    CCCallBlock *allowExit = [CCCallBlock actionWithBlock:^{
        preventTouches = NO;
    }];

    [self runAction:[CCSequence actions: delay, allowExit,
                       nil]];
}
```

The first thing we do at game over is to unschedule the update so the enemies stop moving. As you may recall, when we have been setting the isGameOver variable, we have also been setting preventTouches to YES. That flag will stop any input from being accepted (as we saw in the update method of the TDControlLayer class), so here we just need to stop everything else from moving. If the hero is out of health, he died. Otherwise, they must have won, since the only two ways for the game to end are dying or collecting all of the goals. We call out the hudLayer to the showGameOver method, and then we set up a 3.0 second delay before the preventTouches is reset to NO. Once preventTouches is reset to NO from within the CCCallBlock action, then the TDControlLayer will accept the next touch to send the player back to the menu.

You might be asking why we put the game over message in the hudLayer class. This is for convenience, since we really don't want to display user messages on the same layer as the tilemap. We could have created another layer for just the game over message, but that seemed like extra code that wasn't really needed. So we put it in the hudLayer class.

Filename: TDHUDLayer.m

```
- (void) showGameOver:(NSString*)msg {

    CGSize size = [[CCDirector sharedDirector] winSize];

    CCLabelTTF *gameOver = [CCLabelTTF labelWithString:msg
                    fontName:@"Verdana" fontSize:30];
    [gameOver setColor:ccRED];
    [gameOver setPosition:ccp(size.width/2,
                            size.height/2)];
    [self addChild:gameOver z:50];
}
```

We display the message that was passed as the contents of a label, which we center on the screen. Obviously, this is pretty simple and barebones, but it serves its purpose. Feel free to dress it up and make it more sensational, if you so desire. For now, this is what you see when you die:

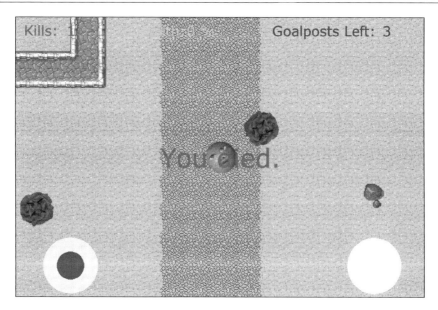

Smarter enemies

We have a fully functional game at this point, except for fleshing out the smarter enemies. After quite a bit of experimentation, we have found several things that don't work to improve the enemies, and a couple of things we can do to make them better. We tried using an enemy that used A* Pathfinding, which is considered the "gold standard" of pathfinding algorithms. However, this was not a great answer for the enemies, as they would stop and pause to recalculate a new route, which would often take a second or two, depending on how far away from the hero they were. If you had a couple of these enemies in the game at the same time, the entire system would freeze for a second or two. Not good.

After trying some different approaches (and different A* implementations), we have settled on a hybrid enemy pathfinding. Most of the time it works like a standard enemy. The difference is when it hits a wall, it changes to use A* Pathfinding to negotiate a route to the hero around the wall. As soon as it reaches that destination, it reverts to the standard movement code.

Code not covered here

We have decided that, far from being experts at `A* Pathfinding`, we will be using the `A*` code written by Johann Fradj, and published in a tutorial at `http://www.raywenderlich.com`. We have included it in this project with the permission of both Johann Fradj and Ray Wenderlich. (Thanks to you both!)

Instead of covering this code method by method, I will instead refer you to his tutorial, from which this code was taken:

`http://www.raywenderlich.com/4970/how-to-implement-a-pathfinding-with-cocos2d-tutorial`

He explains it better than we can, and it is a very good explanation. Instead of quoting his code in detail here, we will instead explain our modifications to his code, and our rationale for doing so. (We might miss some minor modifications, but we'll try to cover the major ones.)

The first major modification we made is to rename the class `ShortestPathStep` to `AStarNode`. This is because it is a shorter name, and it was originally being overlaid on an earlier code base. Really, it was mostly because we wanted a shorter name that felt like a better description to us.

Our entrance to the `A*` code is in the `moveTowardWithPathfinding` method in the `TDEnemySmart` class. We perform our `rotateToTarget` at the beginning of this class, so we are always pointed in the right direction.

The other major change we made to the code is to insert the Boolean variable `isUsingPathfinding` to control when the `A*` code would recursively call itself. Because we wanted to revert to simple pathfinding after an obstacle was passed, we turn off the `isUsingPathfinding` in each of the `if` statements in the `popStepAndAnimate` method.

We urge you to read Johann's wonderful tutorial (as well as a related *Introduction To A* Pathfinding* that is linked to from that tutorial) to learn more about how `A* Pathfinding` works, as well as consulting the source code bundle for this chapter to see how our `TDEnemySmart` class is constructed.

Summary

We have covered a lot of material that is familiar yet new here. We have leveraged quite a few community resources for this project. We built our tile map with Tiled. We used SneakyJoystick rather than build our own joystick and button classes. We have dipped our toe in the A* waters with the help of Johann Fradj. We kept our layers separated into functional units so we could keep our code cleaner and more performant. Not to mention we had the opportunity to ponder why an orange would be the mortal enemy of lettuce.

This game is very basic on purpose. Once you master the concepts we covered here, it is easy to leverage this project to power a much bigger (and more sensible, perhaps) game. One of the great things about creating a game with tilemaps is that there is a lot of directly reusable code from game to game. For instance, the isValidTile, isWall, and so on methods are easily adaptable to any tilemap-based project. Reusability of code is key to writing code faster.

As we have probably made clear, we are big fans of open source tools and projects, both to use for our own development, but also to learn from those with much more experience.

Now we need to take a deep breath before we take on the final project of this book: An endless runner.

9
Running and Running and Running...

In this chapter we will be exploring randomly generated landscapes, how to create a lot of different enemies with very little code, parallax scrolling, and using particle effects for extra visual flair. We've covered a lot of the smaller housekeeping details several times, so for this project we will be focusing on the new, interesting code and not re-covering old ground.

In this chapter we will cover:

- Randomizing terrain
- Endless scrolling parallax backgrounds
- Using your own sensors
- Animation made simple
- Particle effects

The game is...

This time around we will be designing a side scrolling endless runner. The endless runner game style has really taken off in the mobile gaming world, and it is a fun game style to implement using Cocos2d. Basic gameplay will be a simple two-touch control method: touches on the left half of the screen make the hero jump and touches on the right half of the screen will make the hero shoot. The game will scroll continuously, leaving no time for the player to stop and rest. As the game progresses, it will steadily increase the scrolling speed, so it gets harder the longer you play. For all of our graphics (except for the background images), we will be using the Planet-X graphics created by James Macanufo at `http://tintanker.com`, used here with the creator's permission. You can find his original images at `http://tintanker.com/makegameswithus`. If you enjoy the graphics, James deserves full credit for this fun and whimsical set.

Design review

When you are designing a side-scrolling endless runner, there are two primary design approaches. Some will use a physics engine like Box2D or Chipmunk to help control all of the object interactions. We will be taking the other approach by building our own lightweight physics engine for the game. All of our ground will use square tiles, so we can easily identify the surfaces our hero can walk on safely. We will build sensors on the top of all walkable surfaces, as well as building sensors underneath each of our walking characters (hero and enemies). The hero will be in a fixed x coordinate on the screen, and the world will scroll past the hero. We will have two types of enemies: flying and walking. Both will have similar behavior, but the walkers will have the sensors we mentioned to allow them to walk back and forth on their platforms. Enemies will not be allowed to walk off the platforms to their death. We will also implement a two level endless parallax background from scratch. Finally, we want some fun effects when enemies (or the hero) die. We will be using particle effects, built using Particle Designer. We will only measure the player's success in the game with one metric: distance travelled. That about covers the basics of the design, so let's take a peek at the finished game:

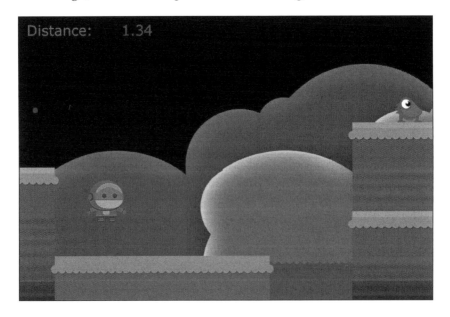

Building the ground

We will start by building the random ground tiles. For our game, we have three types of ground, with three ground images for each type, so we can build stacks with them. For organization, the image that has a gradient color (the bottom) will be identified as 1, the middle as 2, and the top (with the grassy surface) as 3. Let's take a look at the code to build the ground, in two parts.

Filename: `ERPlayfieldLayer.m` (addGround..., part 1)

```objc
-(void) addGroundTileswithEnemies:(BOOL)haveEnemies {
    // Randomize nearly everything about the ground
    NSInteger platformWidth = (arc4random() % 5) + 2;
    NSInteger platformHeight = (arc4random() % 4) + 1;
    NSInteger platformType = (arc4random() % 3) + 1;

    switch (platformHeight) {
        case 1:
            [platformStack addObject:[NSNumber
                                        numberWithInt:3]];
            break;
        case 2:
            [platformStack addObject:[NSNumber
                                        numberWithInt:1]];
            [platformStack addObject:[NSNumber
                                        numberWithInt:3]];
            break;
        case 3:
            [platformStack addObject:[NSNumber
                                        numberWithInt:1]];
            [platformStack addObject:[NSNumber
                                        numberWithInt:2]];
            [platformStack addObject:[NSNumber
                                        numberWithInt:3]];
            break;
        case 4:
            [platformStack addObject:[NSNumber
                                        numberWithInt:1]];
            [platformStack addObject:[NSNumber
                                        numberWithInt:3]];
            [platformStack addObject:[NSNumber
                                        numberWithInt:2]];
            [platformStack addObject:[NSNumber
                                        numberWithInt:3]];
            break;
    }
```

We start this method by randomizing the width, the height, and the type (graphic set) for the platform. The width and height are both expressed in terms of how many tiles we will use for this platform. You will notice that the width adds 2 to the result of the `arc4random()` call. This is because we want the platform to be a minimum of 2 tiles wide. Anything smaller is too challenging to land on, once we add enemies into the mix. We then move into a big `switch` statement, passing it the `platformHeight` variable. We have designed "stacks" for the different elevations to be more playable. The tile type 3 is the only type of walkable tile, so we need to make sure there is a walkable tile on top. This predefined stack approach guarantees we will have something that looks more pleasant and is playable. You will notice that the case 4 has two uses of tile type 3 (the walkable tile) in the stack. This will give that "stack" two separate platforms for the hero to walk on. We do this for variety, but also to make sure we don't have an impossible arrangement, if the terrain goes directly from an elevation 1 to an elevation 4. The lower surface gives the hero something else to land on.

Filename: `ERPlayfieldLayer.m` (addGround..., part 2)

```
for (int w = 0; w <= platformWidth; w++) {
    // Set the new X position for the tile
    maxTileX = maxTileX + tileSize;

    for (int i = 0; i < platformHeight; i++) {
        NSInteger currentTile = [[platformStack
            objectAtIndex:i] integerValue];

        NSString *tileNm = [NSString stringWithFormat:
            @"w%i_%i.png", platformType, currentTile];
        ERTile *tile = [ERTile
            spriteWithSpriteFrameName:tileNm];

        // Determine where to position the tile
        [tile setAnchorPoint:ccp(0.5,0)];
        float newY = i * tileSize;

        // Identify if we need a walkable surface
        if (currentTile == 3) {
            [tile setIsTop:YES];

            // Do we want enemies to spawn here?
            if (haveEnemies) {
                // Determine if we need an enemy here
```

```
                        if ((arc4random() % 13) < 1) {
                            // chance of an enemy walker
                            // Add it slightly above the ground
                            [self addWalkingEnemyAtPosition:
                             ccp(maxTileX, newY + tileSize)];
                        }
                    }
                } else {
                    [tile setIsTop:NO];
                }

                // Set the position (will also create sensor)
                [tile setPosition:ccp(maxTileX, newY)];

                [grndArray addObject:tile];
                [runnersheet addChild:tile z:currentTile];
            }
        }
    [platformStack removeAllObjects];
}
```

Now that we have a stack defined, we iterate through the number of tiles wide we
need. The maxTileX variable is populated with the x position we need for the current
stack of tiles. Once that is updated for the current stack, we enter another loop, based
on the platformHeight variable. We get the next tile from the platformStack array,
and build the sprite name in the tileNm variable. This is a case where the consistent
naming convention of the files really helps out. We then create a new ERTile
object. ERTile is a subclass of the CCSprite class, which we will look at in just a
few moments. We set the anchor point to center bottom so we can easily build the
tiles from the bottom of the screen, and we define the y value by multiplying times
the tileSize variable we define in our init method (50, the size in points of the
square tiles). We then check to see if the tile is type 3. Remember, tile 3 is a walkable
surface. If it is a walkable surface, we set the tile's isTop value to YES. (We also try to
generate an enemy on the walkable surface some percentage of the time.) Finally, we
set the position of the tile, add it to the grndArray array, and add the tile as a child
of the runnersheet (our CCSpriteBatchNode which houses all of our foreground
images). The last thing we do here is to remove all objects from the platformStack
array, so it will be ready for the next time we add ground.

ERTile class

We said that ERTile is a subclass of the CCSprite class, but for most purposes it acts like a normal sprite. Let's take a look at the implementation file to see why we need it.

Filename: ERTile.m

```
-(void) defineSensors {
    topSensor = CGRectMake(self.boundingBox.origin.x,
                           self.boundingBox.origin.y +
                           self.boundingBox.size.height - 10,
                           self.boundingBox.size.width,
                           5);
}


-(void) setPosition:(CGPoint)position {
    // Override set position so we can keep the sensors
    // together with sprite
    [super setPosition:position];

    if (isTop) {
        [self defineSensors];
    }
}
```

These two methods are the only methods included in the ERTile class. We define variables and properties for the topSensor and isTop, but that's it for this class. The main piece we need to understand is the sensor. The topSensor is a CGRect we define in relation to the bounding box of the tile. As you can see, this topSensor is the full width of the sprite and is 5 points high, a few points inside the top of the sprite. This is the level at which "ground" will be defined for this tile. To use this, we also override the setPosition method. When the setPosition method is called, it sends the same command to the super version of itself (that is, CCSprite class), and if the isTop value is YES, then it calls to the defineSensors method. We have to keep redefining it because the CGRect will otherwise stay exactly where you put it on screen, even if the sprite itself moves. By redefining it with every setPosition call, we guarantee it is exactly where we need it, relative to the tile.

There are other ways we could have accomplished this same effect, including invisible child sprites under the ERTile class. We have chosen this approach because a CGRect is a lot less resource intensive than defining another sprite for every tile (and character). For our purposes, this CGRect implementation is fast, reliable, and because we tie it into the overridden setPosition method, it is invisible to any other methods that manipulate the sprite.

Adding gap tiles

We don't want end-to-end ground, since we need the ability for our hero to fall to his death. We build these gap tiles in much the same fashion as the ground tiles, except the gap tiles are only one tile high.

Filename: `ERPlayfieldLayer.m`

```objc
-(void) addGapTiles {
    // Add spaces between tiles
    // Size of gap depends on current speed
    NSInteger gapRnd = arc4random() % 5;

    // Only create a gap some of the time
    if (gapRnd > 1) {
        // Largest gap allowed is 5 tiles
        NSInteger gapSize = MIN(5, scrollSpeed);

        // Determine which gap/water image to use
        NSInteger gapType = (arc4random() % 2) + 1;

        for (int w = 0; w < gapSize; w++) {
            // We make the water slightly narrower
            maxTileX = maxTileX + tileSize - 2;

            NSString *tileNm = [NSString
                stringWithFormat:@"gap%i.png", gapType];
            ERTile *tile = [ERTile
                spriteWithSpriteFrameName:tileNm];

            [tile setAnchorPoint:ccp(0.5,0)];

            // Put tile at bottom of screen
            [tile setPosition:ccp(maxTileX, 0)];

            // Gap tiles are not walkable
            [tile setIsTop:NO];

            [grndArray addObject:tile];
            [runnersheet addChild:tile z:-1];
        }
    }

    // 10 % chance of spawning a flying enemy
    if (arc4random() % 10 == 1) {
```

```
        float newY = (arc4random() % 40) + 250;
        [self addFlyingEnemyAtPosition:ccp(maxTileX, newY)];
    }
    // Always add more tiles after the gap
    [self addGroundTileswithEnemies:YES];
}
```

The structure of this method is pretty similar to the ground tile method. We start by using a randomizer to determine if we need a gap or not. We have a three in five chance that we will build a gap (if the gapRnd value is greater than 1). This lets us have some ground-to-ground passages for more variety. We control the width of the gaps a little differently. We take the MIN value of the scrollSpeed variable or 5, so when the game is scrolling slower, the gaps will also be smaller. But as the game ramps up in speed, we don't want any tile gaps larger than 5. The loop in this method is virtually identical to the one in the ground method, except these tiles are never walkable. We also randomize the creation of flying enemies over the gaps. The chance is lower than with walking enemies, and we randomize their starting elevation between y values of 250 and 289. Finally, whenever we build a gap, we immediately call the method to build the ground tiles. This ensures that we don't have to worry about which method to call later on. We simply call the addGapTiles method, and it takes care of both of these methods.

Scrolling the tiles

In our game, there is a lot that needs to be updated, so we have broken out our update method into individual methods for each type of update. Let's take a look at how we update the tiles.

Filename: ERPlayfieldLayer.m

```
-(void) updateTiles {
    //Update the ground position, if scrolling
    if (isScrolling) {
        for (CCSprite *aTile in grndArray) {
            [aTile setPosition:ccpAdd(aTile.position,
                                      ccp(-scrollSpeed,0))];
        }
        // Update HUD
        distanceTravelled = distanceTravelled +
                                    (scrollSpeed / 100);
        [hudLayer changeDistanceTo:distanceTravelled];

        // Speed up the scroll slowly
```

```
        scrollSpeed = scrollSpeed + 0.001;
    }

    // Reset the maxTileX value
    maxTileX = 0;

    // Check all tiles
    for (ERTile *aTile in grndArray) {
        // Check for tiles scrolled away
        if (aTile.position.x < -100) {
            [grndToDelete addObject:aTile];
            [aTile removeFromParentAndCleanup:YES];
        }

        // Check for the rightmost tiles
        if (aTile.position.x > maxTileX) {
            maxTileX = aTile.position.x;
        }
    }

    // Remove off-screen tiles
    [grndArray removeObjectsInArray:grndToDelete];
    [grndToDelete removeAllObjects];

    // Check if we need to add new tiles
    if (maxTileX < (size.width * 1.1)) {
        // Add a gap first
        [self addGapTiles];
    }
}
```

The first callout here is that we have a variable in our layer called isScrolling that controls whether or not the world is scrolling. It is a simple Boolean variable, used to start or stop the scrolling as we see fit. We also have a scrollSpeed variable, which controls the speed of the scroll. In our init method we start this at a value of 2.5f. In this method, we go through every tile in the grndArray array, and add the negative of the scrollSpeed value (to move everything left) to the current position of each tile. We then update our distance travelled, and call out to the HUD to update the display. (Note: we will not be discussing the HUD layer here. It is structurally the same as how we built the HUD in *Chapter 8, Shoot, Scroll, Shoot Again*, so flip back there for a refresher, if needed). We also increase the scroll speed a little bit each time this method is called, so the speed will slowly increase as the game progresses.

After we move everything, we need to do some tile maintenance. We look for any tiles whose x value is less than -100, and remove them. At the same time, we reset the maxTileX value to the x position of the rightmost tile we find. If that maxTileX value is less than 1.1 times the width of the screen, we call to the addGapTiles method to build some gaps and ground. That's all it takes to make a scrolling, randomly generated ground.

There is one slight issue, however. There will be visible seams between the tiles. Fortunately, this has a simple fix. In the cocos2d source files, there is a file called ccConfig.h. Open this file and find the line (line 85, in the 2.0 version) that looks like:

Filename: ccConfig.h

```
#define CC_FIX_ARTIFACTS_BY_STRECHING_TEXEL 0
```

Change the value of 0 to 1, and the seams disappear. How easy is that?

Parallax background

Before we move on to our hero, let's turn our attention to the other endless element of the game: the background. We want to have a two-layer parallax background that is endlessly scrolling. A parallax background is simply one that has multiple layers that scroll at different rates, to simulate the way that distant terrain looks like it is moving slower than closer terrain. We simulate this by throttling the scrolling speed of each layer of the background to a relative speed. Let's look at our background class and see how it works.

Filename: ERBackground.h

```
-(id) init {
    if(self = [super init]) {
        size = [[CCDirector sharedDirector] winSize];

        bg1 = [CCSprite spriteWithFile:@"bg_mtns.png"];
        [bg1 setAnchorPoint:ccp(0,0)];
        [bg1 setPosition:ccp(0, 0)];
        [self addChild:bg1];

        bg2 = [CCSprite spriteWithFile:@"bg_mtns.png"];
        [bg2 setAnchorPoint:ccp(0,0)];
        [bg2 setPosition:ccp(1001, 0)];
        [self addChild:bg2];

        [bg2 setFlipX:YES];
    }
    return self;
}
```

The ERBackground class is a subclass of the CCLayer class. Here we simply add two sprites to the layer using the bg_mtns.png image. You will notice we aren't using a sprite sheet here. Since it is a single image, there would be minimal performance gains using a sprite sheet here. We position one at (0,0) and the other at (1001,0). The image itself is 1000 points wide, so this will put them one after the other. We flip the second sprite to add some variety to the landscape, even though we are using the same image twice.

Filename: ERBackground.m

```
-(void) useDarkBG {
    // Tint for darker mountains
    [bg1 setColor:ccc3(150,150,150)];
    [bg2 setColor:ccc3(150,150,150)];
}
```

We will be using the same image for both of the parallax layers, so we want to make one seem farther away. The useDarkBG method call will darken the image by about half when this method is called. Now we need to be able to move the background and make it endless.

Filename: ERBackground.m

```
-(void) update:(ccTime)dt {
    // Move the mountains by their scroll speed
    [bg1 setPosition:ccpAdd(bg1.position,
                            ccp(-bgScrollSpeed,0))];
    [bg2 setPosition:ccpAdd(bg2.position,
                            ccp(-bgScrollSpeed,0))];

    // If bg1 is completely off-screen, move after bg2
    if (bg1.position.x < (-1000 - initialOffset.x)) {
        [bg1 setPosition:ccpAdd(bg2.position,
                        ccp(1000 + initialOffset.x,0))];
    }

    // If bg2 is completely off-screen, move after bg1
    if (bg2.position.x < (-1000 - initialOffset.x)) {
        [bg2 setPosition:ccpAdd(bg1.position,
                        ccp(1000 + initialOffset.x,0))];
    }
}
```

When the update method is called, we move both images to the left by their designated bgScrollSpeed value. Then each background is checked to see if it is off-screen by 1000 points. If it is, then that sprite is repositioned to the right side of the other sprite. This means that every time one sprite is completely off-screen to the left, it is moved to the far right, so it will scroll through again. We obviously have a few parameters that need to be set from outside this class. Let's see how we set this up.

Filename: ERPlayfieldLayer.m (inside init)

```
// Build the scrolling background layers
background1 = [[ERBackground alloc] init];
[background1 setAnchorPoint:ccp(0,0)];
[background1 setPosition:ccp(0,0)];
[background1 useDarkBG];
[background1 setBgScrollSpeed:0.025];
[self addChild:background1 z:-2];

background2 = [[ERBackground alloc] init];
[background2 setAnchorPoint:ccp(0,0)];
[background2 setPosition:ccp(200,0)];
[background2 setInitialOffset:ccp(200,0)];
[background2 setBgScrollSpeed:0.1];
[self addChild:background2 z:-3];
```

Here you see that the background1 object calls the useDarkBG method, and sets a bgScrollSpeed value of 0.025, which is nice and slow. These are the mountains in the distance. The other layer, background2, sets its initial offset to be 200 to the right (and sets the corresponding position), so the mountains do not start exactly on top of each other. It also uses a faster scrolling rate of 0.1. That is all it takes to establish the mountains. The one piece that is left to complete the parallax is how to call the update method. We do not set any schedules in the ERBackground class. Instead, we call this update method manually from the playfield's update method:

Filename: ERPlayfieldLayer.m

```
-(void) update:(ccTime)dt {

    // Move the background layers
    [background1 update:dt];
    [background2 update:dt];
```

On each iteration of the playfield's update method, it calls out the background layers, and they take care of themselves with nothing else needed.

Our hero

Now we can turn our attention to our hero, the little spaceman. Let's start by looking through the ERHero class.

Filename: ERHero.m

```
+(id)spriteWithSpriteFrameName:(NSString *)spriteFrameName {
    return [[[self alloc] initWithSpriteFrameName:
            spriteFrameName] autorelease];
}


-(id) initWithSpriteFrameName:(NSString *)spriteFrameName {
    if(self = [super initWithSpriteFrameName:spriteFrameName]) {
        _state = kHeroFalling;

        // Let the hero take 5 hits before death
        heroHealth = 5;

    }
    return self;
}
```

The ERHero class is a subclass of CCSprite class. Because we need a custom init method for the sprite, we have overridden the spriteWithSpriteFrameName class method and the corresponding init method. As the _state variable might lead you to guess, the hero will be operating as a simple state machine. Let's see what states are valid:

Filename: ERDefinitions.m

```
typedef enum {
    kHeroRunning = 1,
    kHeroJumping,
    kHeroInAir,
    kHeroFalling
} HeroState;
```

Now we can look at how the states are changed for our hero.

Filename: ERHero.m

```
-(void) stateChangeTo:(HeroState)newState {
    // Make sure we are actually changing state
    if (newState == _state) {
        return;
    }
    // Stop old actions
    [self stopAllActions];
```

```
    // Reset the color if we were flashing
    if (isFlashing) {
        CCTintTo *normal = [CCTintTo actionWithDuration:
                            0.05 red:255 green:255 blue:255];
        CCCallBlock *done = [CCCallBlock actionWithBlock:^{
            isFlashing = NO;
        }];
        [self runAction:[CCSequence actions:normal,
                        done, nil]];
    }

    // Determine what to do now
    switch (newState) {
        case kHeroRunning:
            [self playRunAnim];
            break;
        case kHeroJumping:
            [self playJumpAnim];
            break;
        case kHeroFalling:
            [self playLandAnim];
            break;
        case kHeroInAir:
            // Leave the last frame
            break;
    }
    _state = newState;

    [self defineSensors];
}
```

We start by checking to make sure we are not trying to reassign to the same state. If we are, we exit. We then stop all actions, because most of the actions are related to animations, so we want to stop the prior ones before running the new animation. The isFlashing check relates to when the hero gets hit (he flashes red for a brief moment). We put this check in here to see if the hero was flashing when the state is changed. If he is flashing, then we force the hero back to normal color. We do this because the stopAllActions method will also stop all actions, including the "tint color" actions. The end result is that without this clause, the hero would get stuck with a red tint if his state changed when he got hit.

The core of the stateChangeTo method is the switch statement at the bottom. It evaluates the state and calls the appropriate animation method. Finally, it defines the sensors, to make sure we have current sensors in place.

Filename: `ERHero.m`

```
-(void) defineSensors {

    footSensor = CGRectMake(self.boundingBox.origin.x+20,
                            self.boundingBox.origin.y,
                            self.boundingBox.size.width-40,
                            1);
    fallSensor = CGRectMake(self.boundingBox.origin.x+20,
                            self.boundingBox.origin.y-3,
                            self.boundingBox.size.width-40,
                            2);
}

-(void) setPosition:(CGPoint)position {
    // Override set position so we can keep the sensors
    // together with sprite
    [super setPosition:position];

    [self defineSensors];
}
```

Here we see the same type of `defineSensors` method we saw in the `ERTile`
class. The difference for the hero is that he has two sensors: one on his feet, and one
below his feet. The `footSensor` variable will be used to identify state changes, and
the `fallSensor` variable will be used to determine if the hero should be falling.
We also use the same `setPosition` override method, for exactly the same reason:
to keep the sensors in place during movement. Let's see how the game looks with
the sensors visible:

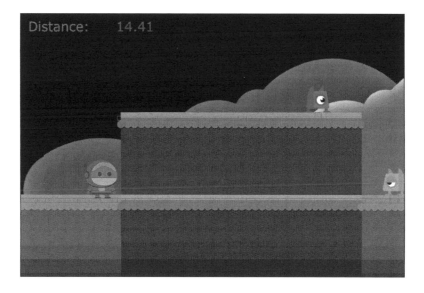

Animation loading

We have talked about playing animations, but we haven't actually created any yet. We will be using a helper method to load our animations.

Filename: ERPlayfieldLayer.m

```
-(void)buildCacheAnimation:(NSString*) AnimName
         forFrameNameRoot:(NSString*) root
            withExtension:(NSString*) ext
               frameCount:(NSInteger) count
                withDelay:(float)delay {
    // This method goes through all the steps to load an
    // animation to the CCSpriteFrameCache
    NSMutableArray *frames = [NSMutableArray array];

    // Load the frames
    for(int i = 1; i <= count; i++) {
        CCSpriteFrame *newFrame = [[CCSpriteFrameCache
                sharedSpriteFrameCache] spriteFrameByName:
                [NSString stringWithFormat:@"%@%i%@",
                root, i, ext]];
        [frames addObject:newFrame];
    }
    // Build the animation
      CCAnimation *newAnim  =[CCAnimation
                          animationWithSpriteFrames:frames
                          delay:delay];
    // Store it in the cache
    [[CCAnimationCache sharedAnimationCache]
            addAnimation:newAnim name:AnimName];
}

-(CCAnimate*) getAnim:(NSString*)animNm {
    // Helper to avoid typing this long line repeaedly
    return [CCAnimate actionWithAnimation:
            [[CCAnimationCache sharedAnimationCache]
            animationByName:animNm]];
}
```

Here we see our two helper methods. The first takes quite a few parameters to build the animation. We pass it the name we want the animation stored as, the root of the filename, the extensions of the filename, the number of frames for the animation, and the time delay between frames. This assumes that any animations loaded will have an incremental number in their filenames. It then goes through the process of loading each frame and adding it to the frames array. Finally, it builds the animation and stores it in the CCAnimationCache under the AnimName string specified. Once it is loaded, you can simply request the animation by name from the cache.

The code needed to load an animation from the cache is a fairly long line of code, so we have also built a helper method to assist with retrieving the frames, getAnim. It returns a CCAnimate object to the caller. If we were not using this helper method, we would have to repeat the same line of code found inside that method every time we wanted an animation. Combined, these two methods save us from writing a lot of repetitive code. Now let's get back to our hero.

Filename: ERHero.m

```
-(void) loadAnimations {
    [pf buildCacheAnimation:@"HeroRun"
          forFrameNameRoot:@"hero_run"
             withExtension:@".png"
                frameCount:4 withDelay:0.1];
    [pf buildCacheAnimation:@"HeroJump"
          forFrameNameRoot:@"hero_jump"
             withExtension:@".png"
                frameCount:3 withDelay:0.1];
    [pf buildCacheAnimation:@"HeroLand"
          forFrameNameRoot:@"hero_land"
             withExtension:@".png"
                frameCount:3 withDelay:0.1];
}
```

This method is all we need to load the hero's animations. We call this method from the playfield after we have created the hero, because we need to reference the playfield in order to call the helper method (which we assign to the variable pf).

Filename: ERHero.m

```
-(void) playRunAnim {
    CCAnimate *idle = [pf getAnim:@"HeroRun"];
    CCRepeatForever *repeat = [CCRepeatForever
                          actionWithAction:idle];
    [self runAction:repeat];
}
```

Here we see the fruits of our animation coding labor. When the state changes to kHeroRunning, this method is called. We use our helper method to get the animation, and set it up to repeat forever. This will keep him running until the state changes.

Filename: ERHero.m

```
-(void) playLandAnim {
    CCAnimate *land = [pf getAnim:@"HeroLand"];
    [self runAction:land];
}
```

The landing animation is similar, except we only play it once.

Filename: ERHero.m

```
-(void) playJumpAnim {
    CCAnimate *jump = [pf getAnim:@"HeroJump"];
    CCCallBlock *change = [CCCallBlock actionWithBlock:^{
        [self stateChangeTo:kHeroInAir];
    }];
    CCSequence *doIt = [CCSequence actions:jump, change, nil];

    [self runAction:doIt];

    // Play the sound effect
    [[SimpleAudioEngine sharedEngine]
                        playEffect:SND_HEROJUMP];
}
```

The jumping animation is the most complex of the three. We play the animation once, and then state change the kHeroInAir, and play a jumping sound. The state kHeroInAir is used for the time the hero is airborne, but no special animation is playing. The sprite will remain as the last frame of the previous animation.

That covers everything in the hero class except for methods related to shooting and getting hit. We will come back to those when we discuss bullets and collisions later.

Updating the hero

As we saw earlier with the tile updates, we have also broken out the updates for the hero into a separate method in the playfield layer. Let's take a look at that method.

Filename: ERHero.m

```
-(void) updateHero:(ccTime)dt {
   CGPoint newPos = hero.position;

   BOOL isFalling = YES;

   // The hero is going up
   if (hero.state == kHeroJumping ||
                  hero.state == kHeroInAir) {
      jumpTimer = jumpTimer - dt;

      if (jumpTimer <= 0) {
         // Jump ending, descend
         [hero stateChangeTo:kHeroFalling];
      } else {
         // Apply a force up for the hero
         newPos = ccpAdd(hero.position, ccp(0,3));
      }
   }

   // If hero is falling, apply our gravity
   if (hero.state == kHeroFalling) {
      newPos = ccpAdd(hero.position, ccp(0,-3));
   }

   // Check if the hero is touching the ground
   for (ERTile *aTile in grndArray) {
      if (CGRectIntersectsRect(hero.footSensor,
                               aTile.topSensor)) {
         // push hero up 1 point if his feet hit the ground
         newPos = ccpAdd(hero.position, ccp(0,1));
         [hero stateChangeTo:kHeroRunning];
      }

      // See if the fall sensor detects anything below
      if (CGRectIntersectsRect(hero.fallSensor,
                               aTile.topSensor)) {
         // Not falling
         isFalling = NO;
      }
   }
```

```
    // Check if hero should fall
    if (isFalling && hero.state == kHeroRunning) {
        [hero stateChangeTo:kHeroFalling];
    }

    // Move the hero
    [hero setPosition:newPos];

    // Check if hero has fallen off screen
    if (hero.position.y < -40) {
        [self gameOver];
    }
}
```

In this method we parse through all the different states that we may need to trigger or react to. If the hero is jumping, we decrease the `jumpTimer` variable by the current delta value. The `jumpTimer` variable controls how long the hero can be in the air in a single jump. When the timer reaches zero, the hero's state changes to `kHeroIsFalling`. If the timer is still greater than zero, we increase the hero's y position by 3 points. (As you may recall, the hero is always at the same x position, so we only have to concern ourselves with the y axis). If the hero is falling, then we apply our gravity by decreasing his y position by 3 points.

We then begin to make use of our sensors. We check to see if the hero's `footSensor` is touching any tile's `topSensor`. If it is, we push the hero up by 1 point, and change his state to `kHeroRunning`. We also check each tile to see if there is any contact between the hero's `fallSensor` and the tile's `topSensor`. If there is contact with any tile's sensor, then the `isFalling` local Boolean variable is set to NO. If there is no contact with any tile sensors, then the `isFalling` variable will still have the original YES we assigned to it, so we know the hero should be falling. We then check to see if the hero is currently running and if the `isFalling` variable is YES, then we change his state to `kHeroFalling`. After all of that, we actually set the new position to the hero. The last check is to see if the hero has fallen off the screen. If he has, we call the `gameOver` method.

Touch controls

Now that we have a hero to control, we need to look at the control methods.

Filename: `ERPlayfieldLayer.m`

```
- (BOOL) ccTouchBegan:(UITouch *)touch withEvent:(UIEvent *)event {
    if (preventTouches) {
        return YES;
```

```
    }

    if (isGameOver) {
        [[CCDirector sharedDirector] replaceScene:[ERMenuScene
                                                        scene]];
        return YES;
    }

    CGPoint loc = [touch locationInView:[touch view]];
    CGPoint convLoc = [[CCDirector sharedDirector]
                        convertToGL:loc];

    if (convLoc.x < size.width/2) {
        // Jump if left side of screen
        if (hero.state == kHeroRunning) {
            // Jump from the ground
            [hero stateChangeTo:kHeroJumping];
            // Reset the jump timer
            jumpTimer = maxJumpTimer;
            // Allow hero to double-jump
            allowDoubleJump = YES;
        } else if (allowDoubleJump) {
            // Allow a second jump in the air
            [hero stateChangeTo:kHeroJumping];
            // Reset the jump timer
            jumpTimer = maxJumpTimer;
            // Prevent a third jump
            allowDoubleJump = NO;
        } else {
            return NO;
        }
    } else {
        // Shoot if right side of screen
        [hero shoot];
    }
    return YES;
}
```

After checking whether touches should be prevented or whether game over conditions have been met, we compare the locations of the touch to the left or right half of the screen. If the touch is on the left and the hero is currently running, we change state to kHeroJumping. We set the jumpTimer variable to the value of the maxJumpTimer variable (defined in the init method as 0.85), and we also set the allowDoubleJump variable to YES. This state change will trigger the correct movement behavior (moving up) in the updateHero method we just saw. We set the allowDoubleJump variable to give the player a little extra help. As you can see, the allowDoubleJump variable is only evaluated if the hero is not currently in the kHeroRunning state. Most of the code is the same as the first clause of the if statement, except we reset the allowDoubleJump to NO. Combined, this will allow the player to double-jump in mid-air, but it will prevent air-jumping a third time. (If you allow unlimited jumps from mid-air, the hero can actually fly forever!)

The final else clause will catch any touches on the right-hand side of the screen, and send the message to the hero to shoot.

Filename: ERPlayfieldLayer.m

```
-(void) ccTouchEnded:(UITouch *)touch withEvent:(UIEvent *)event {
    if (isGameOver) {
        return;
    }

    CGPoint loc = [touch locationInView:[touch view]];
    CGPoint convLoc = [[CCDirector sharedDirector]
                        convertToGL:loc];

    // Release the jump
    if (convLoc.x < size.width/2) {
        // Jump if left side of screen
        [hero stateChangeTo:kHeroFalling];
    }
}
```

We wrap up the touch handler by looking at the ccTouchEnded method. Here we must first check to make sure we are not in a game over condition. Without this check, if the hero died while a touch was still occurring, the game would crash as soon as the finger was lifted (since the hero sprite would be dead and gone).

Most of this is concerned with jumping, as you could probably assume. If the touch was on the left-hand side (jumping side), then we change the state to kHeroFalling, so gravity can take over.

Shooting bullets

Now we turn our attention to the bullets and allowing our hero to shoot. Let's look at the simple ERBullet class.

Filename: ERBullet.h

```
@interface ERBullet : CCSprite {
    BOOL isShootingRight;
    BOOL isHeroBullet;
}

@property (nonatomic, assign) BOOL isShootingRight;
@property (nonatomic, assign) BOOL isHeroBullet;

@end
ERBullet.m:
@implementation ERBullet

@synthesize isShootingRight;
@synthesize isHeroBullet;

@end
```

Our ERBullet class is nothing more than a subclass of the CCSprite class with a couple of extra Boolean variables to track. The isShootingRight Boolean variable helps us keep track of direction of travel for the bullet. Since we are only designing the game to allow flat trajectories for the bullets, we really just need to know if it is going left or right. We also use the isHeroBullet variable so we can keep track of whose bullet it is, for collision detection purposes. We will not allow "friendly fire", so enemies won't kill other enemies in this game. Now we can look at what the hero does when instructed to shoot.

Filename: ERHero.m

```
-(void) shoot {
    // Create a bullet at hero's position
    ERBullet *bullet = [ERBullet
                spriteWithSpriteFrameName:IMG_BULLET];
    [bullet setColor:ccBLUE];
    [bullet setIsShootingRight:YES];
    [bullet setIsHeroBullet:YES];
    [bullet setPosition:self.position];

    // Tell the playfield to add the bullet
```

```
        [pf addBullet:bullet];

        // Play the sound effect
        [[SimpleAudioEngine sharedEngine]
                    playEffect:SND_HEROSHOOT];
    }
```

We create a new bullet at the hero's position, give it a nice blue color, and set our two Boolean variables to YES. The hero is only travelling to the right, so that's the only direction his bullets will travel. We then call out to the playfield to the addBullet method. We wrap it up by playing a nice shooting sound. Let's turn to that addBullet method next.

Filename: ERPlayfieldLayer.m

```
    -(void) addBullet:(ERBullet*) thisBullet {
        [runnersheet addChild:thisBullet z:3];

        [bulletArray addObject:thisBullet];
    }
```

Not much here, either. We add the bullet to the batch node, and we add the bullet to the bulletArray array. So why did we do this here, and not in the hero's shoot method? For one, we will be using this same method when adding enemy bullets. The other reason is that we don't want to have the bulletArray array accessible outside of the playfield layer itself, so it is much easier to use this method to insert the bullet into that array.

As you might imagine, there is also a separate update method for the bullets. Let's go there now.

Filename: ERPlayfieldLayer.m

```
    -(void) updateBullets {
        for (ERBullet *bullet in bulletArray) {
            if (bullet.isShootingRight) {
                // Move the bullet right
                bullet.position = ccpAdd(bullet.position,
                                    ccp(10,0));

                // Remove bullets that are off the screen
                if (bullet.position.x > size.width) {
                    [bulletsToDelete addObject:bullet];
                    [bullet removeFromParentAndCleanup:YES];
                }
            } else {
```

```
        // Move the bullet left
        bullet.position = ccpAdd(bullet.position,
                               ccp(-10,0));

        // Remove bullets that are off the screen
        if (bullet.position.x < 0) {
            [bulletsToDelete addObject:bullet];
            [bullet removeFromParentAndCleanup:YES];
        }
    }
}

    // Remove deleted bullets from the array
    [bulletArray removeObjectsInArray:bulletsToDelete];
    [bulletsToDelete removeAllObjects];
}
```

This method style should be familiar by now. We iterate through all the bullets in the `bulletArray` array, and move each bullet either left or right, depending on the value of `isShootingRight` variable. If the bullet goes off-screen, it is added to the `bulletsToDelete` array, which is then used after the loop to remove the bullets from the `bulletArray`. Of course, at this point the bullets won't interact with anything, but we need to have some enemies to shoot at before we deal with collisions.

Enemies everywhere

We want to have enemies in our game. A lot of enemies. We need to have flying enemies as well as walking enemies. With the wonderful Planet-X graphics we are using, the designer created six types of creatures in six colors. We are using all but one type of creature (the swimming creature didn't fit this game), so we have 12 flying enemy types and 18 walking enemy types. In our game there is no difference in the behavior of the creatures, but it does give more of a visual flair to the game to have this much variety. Because we will be randomly creating enemies throughout the game, we don't want to be reloading the animations into the cache every time a new creature is spawned, so we build all of the enemy animations when the playfield is loaded.

Filename: `ERPlayfieldLayer.m`

```
-(void) loadEnemyAnimations {
    // Build all walking enemy animations
    for (int i = 1; i <= 18; i++) {
        // Build the names for the image and animation
        NSString *root = [NSString stringWithFormat:
```

```
                         @"walk%i_", i];
        NSString *anim = [NSString stringWithFormat:
                         @"%@move", root];

        // Build the animation into the cache
        [self buildCacheAnimation:anim
                forFrameNameRoot:root
                    withExtension:@".png"
                      frameCount:4 withDelay:0.1];
    }

    // Build all flying enemy animations
    for (int i = 1; i <= 12; i++) {
        // Build the names for the image and animation
        NSString *root = [NSString stringWithFormat:
                         @"fly%i_", i];
        NSString *anim = [NSString stringWithFormat:
                         @"%@move", root];

        // Build the animation into the cache
        [self buildCacheAnimation:anim
                forFrameNameRoot:root
                    withExtension:@".png"
                      frameCount:4 withDelay:0.1];
    }
}
```

Because we have kept our naming convention consistent (that is, walk1_1.png, walk1_2.png, and so on) we can easily construct our names in a loop. We first load the walking enemies in a loop, and we assemble two strings to help us. The root parameter is the first part of the file name before the incremental frame numbers. The anim variable will add the word "move" to the end of the root name, to load the animation under that name. So the fifth walker's animation will be named walk5_move. We then call the same helper method we used for the hero to load the animation frames for all of the walkers. The second half of the method repeats the same process, except it loads the flying creatures' animations.

Now we can start to look at the EREnemy class, which will look very familiar.

Filename: EREnemy.m

```
- (void) defineSensors {
    fallSensor = CGRectMake(self.boundingBox.origin.x+20,
                            self.boundingBox.origin.y-10,
```

```
                             self.boundingBox.size.width-40,
                             10);
    }
    -(void) setPosition:(CGPoint)position {
        // Override set position so we can keep the sensors
        // together with sprite
        [super setPosition:position];

        [self defineSensors];
    }
```

We define a `fallSensor` variable for the enemy, using the same structure as we did for the hero. We also override the `setPosition` method for this class to refresh the `fallSensor` every time it is repositioned.

Filename: `EREnemy.m`

```
    -(void) shoot {
        // Create a bullet at enemy's position
        ERBullet *bullet = [ERBullet
                                spriteWithSpriteFrameName:IMG_BULLET];
        [bullet setColor:ccRED];
        [bullet setIsShootingRight:self.isMovingRight];
        [bullet setPosition:self.position];
        [bullet setIsHeroBullet:NO];

        // Tell the playfield to add the bullet
        [pf addBullet:bullet];

        // Play the sound effect
        [[SimpleAudioEngine sharedEngine]
                                playEffect:SND_ENEMYSHOOT];
    }
```

The enemy's `shoot` method is very similar to the hero's `shoot` method. Obviously, the `isHeroBullet` Boolean variable is set to `NO` here. Also, the `isShootingRight` variable sets itself to one of the new variables that is contained in the `EREnemy` class.

Filename: `EREnemy.h`

```
    BOOL isMovingRight;
    BOOL isFlying;
    ccTime shootTimer;
```

These variables help us keep better track of the enemies. The `isFlying` and `isMovingRight` Boolean variables are self-explanatory. The `shootTimer` for the enemies is kept in this class, where the hero's is kept as part of the playfield layer itself. Now that we have seen all of the `EREnemy` class (except for getting hit), we can look at how we create the enemies in the game.

Filename: `ERPlayfieldLayer.m`

```
-(void) addWalkingEnemyAtPosition:(CGPoint)pos {
    // Randomly select a walking enemy
    NSInteger enemyNo = (arc4random() % 18) + 1;

    // Build the name of the enemy
    NSString *enemyNm = [NSString stringWithFormat:@"walk%i",
                        enemyNo];

    // Build the initial sprite frame name
    NSString *enemyFrame = [NSString
                        stringWithFormat:@"%@_1.png", enemyNm];
    EREnemy *enemy = [EREnemy
                        spriteWithSpriteFrameName:enemyFrame];
    [enemy setPosition:ccpAdd(pos,
                        ccp(0, enemy.contentSize.height/2))];
    [enemy setIsMovingRight:NO];
    [enemy setFlipX:NO];
    [enemy setIsFlying:NO];
    [enemy setPf:self];

    // Add this enemy to the layer and the array
    [runnersheet addChild:enemy z:5];
    [enemyArray addObject:enemy];

    // Set the enemy in motion
    NSString *moveAnim = [NSString
                        stringWithFormat:@"%@_move", enemyNm];
    CCAnimate *idle = [self getAnim:moveAnim];
    CCRepeatForever *repeat = [CCRepeatForever
                        actionWithAction:idle];
    [enemy runAction:repeat];
}
```

As we did when we created the ground tiles, we randomize the selection of the enemyNo, and use that to build the correct initial frame name for the new EREnemy object. When we set the position, we add the requested position (pos) to half of the content size of the enemy itself. We do this because the enemy has a default center anchorPoint, and the position passed is the top of the tile we want the enemy to be standing on. So by adding half of the height, we position the enemy perfectly standing on the tile below. (We don't want to change the anchorPoint, because then we would have to do this type of adjustment for all bullets fired by the enemies.) All enemies will start by facing to the left, and since these are walking enemies, they will have isFlying set to NO. After adding the enemy to the batch node and to the enemyArray array, we get the animation we loaded for this particular enemy, and set it to repeat forever. That's all we need to create the walking enemies.

Filename: ERPlayfieldLayer.m

```objc
-(void) addFlyingEnemyAtPosition:(CGPoint)pos {
    // Randomly select a walking enemy
    NSInteger enemyNo = (arc4random() % 12) + 1;

    // Build the name of the enemy
    NSString *enemyNm = [NSString stringWithFormat:@"fly%i",
                         enemyNo];

    // Build the initial sprite frame name
    NSString *enemyFrame = [NSString
                           stringWithFormat:@"%@_1.png", enemyNm];
    EREnemy *enemy = [EREnemy
                     spriteWithSpriteFrameName:enemyFrame];
    [enemy setPosition:pos];
    [enemy setIsMovingRight:NO];
    [enemy setFlipX:NO];
    [enemy setIsFlying:YES];
    [enemy setPf:self];

    // Add this enemy to the layer and the array
    [runnersheet addChild:enemy z:5];
    [enemyArray addObject:enemy];

    // Set the enemy in motion
    NSString *moveAnim = [NSString
                         stringWithFormat:@"%@_move", enemyNm];
    CCAnimate *idle = [self getAnim:moveAnim];
    CCRepeatForever *repeat = [CCRepeatForever
                              actionWithAction:idle];
    [enemy runAction:repeat];
}
```

As we look at how we add flying enemies, you will notice this is the same basic code structure as the walking enemy. The only real differences are that the names of the sprite frames begin with `fly` instead of `walk`, and we don't have to change the starting position for the flying enemies, because they will not interact with the ground at all. Now we can move to the enemy `update` method.

Filename: ERPlayfieldLayer.m

```
-(void) updateEnemies:(ccTime)dt {
    // Only update the enemies while scrolling
    if (isScrolling == NO) {
        return;
    }

    // Loop through all enemies
    for (EREnemy *anEnemy in enemyArray) {
        BOOL noGround = YES;

        // Check movement direction
        if (anEnemy.isMovingRight) {
            // Moving against the scroll
            [anEnemy setPosition:ccpAdd(anEnemy.position,
                        ccp(-scrollSpeed + 2,0))];
        } else {
            // Moving with the scroll
            [anEnemy setPosition:ccpAdd(anEnemy.position,
                        ccp(-scrollSpeed - 2,0))];
        }

        // Updates for walking enemies only
        if (anEnemy.isFlying == NO) {
            // Check if the enemy is touching the ground
            for (ERTile *aTile in grndArray) {
                // See if the sensor detects anything below
                if (CGRectIntersectsRect(anEnemy.fallSensor,
                            aTile.topSensor)) {
                    // Ground is under foot
                    noGround = NO;
                }
            }

            // If there is no ground underfoot, turn around
            if (noGround) {
                if (anEnemy.isMovingRight) {
```

```
            [anEnemy setIsMovingRight:NO];
            [anEnemy setFlipX:NO];
        } else {
            [anEnemy setIsMovingRight:YES];
            [anEnemy setFlipX:YES];
        }
    }
}

// Enemy can shoot, with time delay
if (anEnemy.shootTimer <= 0) {
    [anEnemy shoot];
    anEnemy.shootTimer = 2.0;
} else {
    anEnemy.shootTimer = anEnemy.shootTimer - dt;
}

// Check for enemies off screen
if (anEnemy.position.x < -50) {
    // If off-screen to the left, add to delete
    [enemiesToDelete addObject:anEnemy];
    [anEnemy removeFromParentAndCleanup:YES];
}
}

// Remove deleted enemies from the array
[enemyArray removeObjectsInArray:enemiesToDelete];
[enemiesToDelete removeAllObjects];
}
```

We begin the updateEnemies method by making sure the playfield is scrolling. If
not we exit, because we don't want the enemies to move. Then we iterate through
all the enemies in the enemyArray and move them left or right, according to how
their isMovingRight Boolean variable is set. The middle section of the update is
concerned only with walking enemies. For each walking enemy, we iterate through
all tiles to see if their fallSensor is touching any tiles. This is exactly the same as
what we did for the hero with the isFalling Boolean variable the updateHero
method. If there is no ground, instead of making in the enemy fall, we flip the
graphic to face the opposite direction, and change the isMovingRight Boolean
to the opposite value. If an enemy reaches the edge of a ledge, this will make it
turn around.

We then have a simple `shootTimer` loop for the enemies. Each enemy will shoot every 2 seconds. Because we have non-intelligent enemies (they move back and forth, but never pursue the player), it makes sense to have this form of blind shooting for the enemies.

Finally, we check to see if any enemies are off-screen to the left, and remove them in the usual fashion. Now our enemies can move and everybody can shoot, we need some collision detection.

Collision handling

We need to be able to check for three different types of collisions. We need to be able to have bullets hit the enemies. We need the hero to get hit. We also need to react when the hero runs into an enemy. Let's look at the method for this, which is in two parts.

Filename: `ERPlayfieldLayer.m` (`checkCollisions`, part 1)

```
-(void) checkCollisions {
    BOOL isHeroHit = NO;

    for (ERBullet *bullet in bulletArray) {
        // Enemy bullets
        if (bullet.isHeroBullet == NO) {
            if (CGRectIntersectsRect(hero.boundingBox,
                                bullet.boundingBox)) {
                // Hero got hit
                [bulletsToDelete addObject:bullet];
                [bullet removeFromParentAndCleanup:YES];
                isHeroHit = YES;
                break;
            }
        } else {
            // Hero bullets

            // Check all enemies to see if they got hit
            for (EREnemy *anEnemy in enemyArray) {
                if (CGRectIntersectsRect(anEnemy.boundingBox,
                                    bullet.boundingBox)) {
                    [bulletsToDelete addObject:bullet];
                    [bullet removeFromParentAndCleanup:YES];
                    [enemiesToDelete addObject:anEnemy];
                    [anEnemy gotShot];
                    break;
                }
            }
        }
    }
}
```

We start by iterating through all bullets in the array. If the bullet is an enemy bullet (isHeroBullet == NO), then we check the boundingBox of the bullet with the boundingBox of the hero. If they intersect, we add the bullet to the bulletsToDelete array, remove the bullet, and set the isHeroHit Boolean to YES. We use a Boolean variable for the hero hit here because we will be doing another hero collision check within this method. Since the hero's death causes the hero to be removed, the game would crash if the hero was shot and ran into an enemy at the same time.

If the bullet is a "hero bullet", we iterate through all enemies to determine if the bullet is intersecting with an enemy boundingBox. If it is, we add the bullet to the bulletsToDelete array, remove the bullet, add the enemy to the enemiesToDelete array, and send the message to the enemy that it got shot.

Filename: ERPlayfieldLayer.m (checkCollisions, part 2)

```
    // Check for enemy and hero collisions
    for (EREnemy *anEnemy in enemyArray) {
        if (CGRectIntersectsRect(anEnemy.boundingBox,
                        hero.boundingBox)) {
            // Trigger the enemy's hit
            [enemiesToDelete addObject:anEnemy];
            [anEnemy gotShot];
            // Trigger the hero's hit
            isHeroHit = YES;
            break;
        }
    }

    // We process this here because there could be
    // multiple collisions with the hero
    if (isHeroHit) {
        [hero gotShot];
    }

    // Remove deleted bullets from the array
    [bulletArray removeObjectsInArray:bulletsToDelete];
    [bulletsToDelete removeAllObjects];

    // Remove deleted enemies from the array
    [enemyArray removeObjectsInArray:enemiesToDelete];
    [enemiesToDelete removeAllObjects];
}
```

In the second half of this method, we start by iterating through all the enemies. For each enemy, we check to see if the enemy's boundingBox intersects with the hero's boundingBox. If they intersect, we register a collision for both hero and enemy in the same manner as we did with the bullets.

After we have resolved the collisions, we check the isHeroHit variable to see if he got shot. If he got shot, we send the gotShot message to the hero. As the final bit of cleanup, we handle the bulletsToDelete and enemiesToDelete arrays the same as usual: we use them to remove the deleted objects from the bulletArray and EnemyArray, and then use the removeAllObjects method to empty the deletion arrays.

Getting shot with particles

The last unresolved bits of code that we need to look at are the gotShot routines for both the enemy and the hero. The enemies die after a single hit, so their method is a simpler place to start.

Filename: EREnemy.m

```
-(void) gotShot {
    CCParticleSystemQuad *emitter = [CCParticleSystemQuad
                    particleWithFile:@"enemydie.plist"];
    [emitter setPosition:self.position];
    [pf addChild:emitter z:50];

    [self removeFromParentAndCleanup:YES];

    // Play the sound effect
    [[SimpleAudioEngine sharedEngine]
                    playEffect:SND_ENEMYDEAD];
}
```

When an enemy gets shot, the first thing we do is to create a particle system. Particles can be coded in one of two ways. The first would be to manually set all of the parameters regarding the particle system by hand, and test and retest until you achieve the desired effect. The alternate approach (one that is more widely used) is to use a commercially available tool, Particle Designer, available at http://particledesigner.71squared.com. Particle Designer allows you to see the results of changing every parameter in real time, so you can experiment until you achieve the desired result. Once you have what you want, you can save it as a .plist file, and use it as we have done here. We created a CCParticleSystemQuad object using the plist file, set the position, and added it to the layer. That's all we needed to do for this one-shot particle. (If you want to know how much manual coding we are avoiding by using Particle Designer, open the enemydie.plist file in Xcode and see all the values stored in it.)

After we trigger the particle, we simply remove the enemy from its parent and play a nice death sound. Let's see the aftermath when an enemy is shot:

Death of hero

The hero getting hit adds a little complexity, because the hero can take five hits before he dies. If he doesn't die, we want him to flash red briefly.

Filename: ERHero.m

```
-(void) gotShot {
    // Subtract one from hero health
    heroHealth--;

    // Determine if the hero is dead
    if (heroHealth <= 0) {
        // Spawn a death particle
        CCParticleSystemQuad *emitter = [CCParticleSystemQuad
                        particleWithFile:@"ExplodingRing.plist"];
        [emitter setPosition:self.position];
        [pf addChild:emitter z:50];

        // We don't clean up to avoid block failure
        [self removeFromParentAndCleanup:NO];

        // Play the sound effect for death
        [[SimpleAudioEngine sharedEngine]
```

```
                    playEffect:SND_HERODEATH];

        // Trigger game over
        [pf gameOver];
    } else if (isFlashing == NO) {
        // Flash the hero red briefly
        isFlashing = YES;
        CCTintTo *red = [CCTintTo actionWithDuration:0.05
                                   red:255 green:0 blue:0];
        CCTintTo *normal = [CCTintTo actionWithDuration:0.05
                                   red:255 green:255 blue:255];
        CCCallBlock *done = [CCCallBlock actionWithBlock:^{
            isFlashing = NO;
        }];
        [self runAction:[CCSequence actions: red, normal,
                                 done, nil]];

        // Play the got hit sound effect
        [[SimpleAudioEngine sharedEngine]
                        playEffect:SND_HEROHIT];

    }
}
```

We first reduce the hero's health by one. Then we check if the hero should be dead or not. If his health is zero, we spawn a new particle system centered on the hero, remove the hero, play a death sound, and then call the gameOver method. It should be noted that the ExplodingRing.plist file we use here is actually a particle that ships with Cocos2d, and is used as part of the Particle test.

If the hero is not dead, then we check the value of the hero's isFlashing variable. If he isn't currently flashing, we build a small action sequence that will tint the hero red for a duration of 0.05, then tint it back to normal (all max values return the sprite color to its original color). Then we play a sound effect, and call it done.

Summary

We have put a lot of interesting pieces together in this game. We have dynamic terrain, randomized enemies, shooting, jumping, endless backgrounds, and (hopefully) some fun while building and playing it. You will notice that there are a few less interesting bits we have not covered in depth. Please, consult the code bundle to explore the other pieces of the game, like the "Dramatic Entrance" when the hero starts the game by being dropped off by a space ship. There is also some helpful debugging code we used for the sensors (commented out) in the bottom of the `ERPlayfieldLayer.m` file. By enabling that code, you can see the sensor boxes drawn while the game is playing.

It is our sincere hope that these projects have instructed, entertained, and perhaps even inspired you in your own pursuits. Each of the games, designed with a "bare bones" approach, gives plenty of room for exploration and expansion. If you create something wonderful as a result of having been inspired by these projects, please let us know! We look forward to hearing from you.

Index

Thank you for buying
Creating Games with cocos2d for iPhone 2

About Packt Publishing

Packt, pronounced 'packed', published its first book "*Mastering phpMyAdmin for Effective MySQL Management*" in April 2004 and subsequently continued to specialize in publishing highly focused books on specific technologies and solutions.

Our books and publications share the experiences of your fellow IT professionals in adapting and customizing today's systems, applications, and frameworks. Our solution based books give you the knowledge and power to customize the software and technologies you're using to get the job done. Packt books are more specific and less general than the IT books you have seen in the past. Our unique business model allows us to bring you more focused information, giving you more of what you need to know, and less of what you don't.

Packt is a modern, yet unique publishing company, which focuses on producing quality, cutting-edge books for communities of developers, administrators, and newbies alike. For more information, please visit our website: www.packtpub.com.

About Packt Open Source

In 2010, Packt launched two new brands, Packt Open Source and Packt Enterprise, in order to continue its focus on specialization. This book is part of the Packt Open Source brand, home to books published on software built around Open Source licences, and offering information to anybody from advanced developers to budding web designers. The Open Source brand also runs Packt's Open Source Royalty Scheme, by which Packt gives a royalty to each Open Source project about whose software a book is sold.

Writing for Packt

We welcome all inquiries from people who are interested in authoring. Book proposals should be sent to author@packtpub.com. If your book idea is still at an early stage and you would like to discuss it first before writing a formal book proposal, contact us; one of our commissioning editors will get in touch with you.

We're not just looking for published authors; if you have strong technical skills but no writing experience, our experienced editors can help you develop a writing career, or simply get some additional reward for your expertise.

Flash iOS Apps Cookbook

ISBN: 978-1-84969-138-3   Paperback: 420 pages

100 practical recipes for developing iOS apps with Flash Professional and Adobe AIR

1. Build your own apps, port existing projects, and learn the best practices for targeting iOS devices using Flash

2. How to compile a native iOS app directly from Flash and deploy it to the iPhone, iPad or iPod touch

3. Full of practical recipes and step-by-step instructions for developing iOS apps with Flash Professional

Cocos2d for iPhone 0.99 Beginner's Guide

ISBN: 978-1-84951-316-6   Paperback: 368 pages

Make mind-blowing 2D games for iPhone with this fast, flexible, and easy-to-use framework!

1. A cool guide to learning cocos2d with iPhone to get you into the iPhone game industry quickly

2. Learn all the aspects of cocos2d while building three different games

3. Add a lot of trendy features such as particles and tilemaps to your games to captivate your players

Please check **www.PacktPub.com** for information on our titles

Cocos2d for iPhone 1 Game Development Cookbook

ISBN: 978-1-84951-400-2   Paperback: 446 pages

Over 90 recipes for iOS 2D game development using cocos2D

1. Discover advanced Cocos2d, OpenGL ES, and iOS techniques spanning all areas of the game development process

2. Learn how to create top-down isometric games, side-scrolling platformers, and games with realistic lighting

3. Full of fun and engaging recipes with modular libraries that can be plugged into your project

iOS Development using MonoTouch Cookbook

ISBN: 978-1-84969-146-8   Paperback: 384 pages

109 simple but incredibly effective recipes for developing and deploying applications for iOS using C# and .NET

1. Detailed examples covering every aspect of iOS development using MonoTouch and C#/.NET

2. Create fully working MonoTouch projects using step-by-step instructions..

4. Recipes for creating iOS applications meeting Apple's guidelines.

Please check **www.PacktPub.com** for information on our titles